THE BEST EVER BOOK OF
CROSSWORDS

THE BEST EVER BOOK OF
CROSSWORDS

ARCTURUS

ARCTURUS

This edition published in 2015 by Arcturus Publishing Limited
26/27 Bickels Yard, 151–153 Bermondsey Street,
London SE1 3HA

ISBN: 978-1-78404-766-5
AD004818US

Printed in China

CONTENTS

INTRODUCTION

Good things come in small packages – diamond rings, cell phones, and the little puzzles in this book.

The crosswords you're about to solve are 11x13 squares in size, which is smaller than the standard 13x13 or 15x15 puzzles you normally see in your local newspaper. They're designed for you to knock out in one sitting – why, you might even see fit to take care of two or three of them before you get up from your chair! How's that for a sense of accomplishment?

But these puzzles are still every bit as full of good stuff as their larger cousins. They also have all the fun wordplay, clues and answers you've come to expect from a top-quality crossword. Answers, as ever, are at the back of the book.

Note that the puzzles start off containing a hint when the answer has more than one word, like the clue "Casual greeting: 2 wds." for the answer HI THERE. The remaining puzzles, however, do not have the "2 wds."-style hints, so keep an eye out for those tricky answers later on.

The game's afoot – so grab a pen or pencil and jump right in! The puzzles are small but the book is large, so you've got many hours of solving fun ahead.

Levi Davis

1

Across

1 Lacking imagination
8 Concorde, e.g.
11 Bubbler
12 Kickoff tool, in football
13 Levelheaded: 3 wds.
15 Cuts back on calories
16 Diminish, as a nuisance
17 "Allure" shelfmate
18 Paris's Arc de Triomphe de l'___
19 High-speed hookup, for short
20 Handle props, say
21 About
22 Arose
24 Nobelist Hammarskjöld
27 Nutty mushrooms
28 Frankie Avalon's "___ Dinah"
29 Accord
30 Move, as a plant
31 It may give you ten minutes more: 2 wds.
33 Thrice, in prescriptions
34 Asmara is its capital
35 Dorm room, sometimes
36 All in the family

Down

1 Like suit shoulders, perhaps
2 Adds more lubricant
3 "1984" author
4 "À votre ___!"
5 Firm parts: abbr.
6 Perfect score, as it were
7 Making
8 Country singer George ___
9 Agree out of court
10 A little laughter: var., hyph.
14 "I'm on ___" ("Saturday Night Live" song): 2 wds.
18 2, 4, 6, 8, and so forth
20 Good looker?
21 Ratio words: 2 wds.
22 Italian poem
23 Monastery, maybe
24 Leave
25 Renée of "The Big Parade"
26 Blow up: 2 wds.
27 Essentials
28 Atlanta-based airline
30 Commuter line
32 "___ on my bed my limbs I lay": Coleridge

Across

1 Vampire killers
7 Actress Derek and singer Diddley
10 Harness ring
11 1980 NFL MVP Brian
12 Live oak
13 Click "undo," e.g.
14 "Darn it!"
15 Find a new chair for
17 Receiver Collinsworth or Carter
18 Painter Andrea del ___
19 "Shoot!"
20 Big name in Egyptian kings
21 "Touched by an Angel" co-star
23 Back up
26 ___ Club
30 Live on a minimum salary
31 Suffix with saliva
32 Some N.C.O.s
34 Change the wallpaper, say
35 Noble, in Essen
36 Kitchen gadget
38 Food sticker
39 Nutrition author Davis
40 Carrier to Copenhagen
41 Mix anew, as greens

Down

1 Unpleasant smell
2 Staying power?
3 ___ Monkeys ("I Bet You Look Good on the Dancefloor" band)
4 Santa alias: 2 wds.
5 Dusk, to Donne
6 Antares, for one
7 Those who wait
8 Morphine, e.g.
9 Scraps: hyph.
11 Abby Cadabby's show: 2 wds.
16 Those girls, to Juanita
20 The "R" in AARP
22 Punta del ___, Uruguay
23 Accountant's count
24 Bowls facilities
25 Lures
27 Danny of "Do the Right Thing"
28 Poses (for)
29 Sleeping sounds
33 Bandy words
37 Dutch city

Across

1 Ann ___, Mich.
6 Dimin.'s musical opposite
11 The king of France: 2 wds.
12 Hipbones
13 When penitents come back from lunch?: 2 wds.
14 Singer Lenya
15 ___ choy
16 Mauna ___, Hawaii
18 North Carolina city: abbr.
19 "___ we alone?"
20 Bible study sch.
21 "___-brainer": 2 wds.
22 "White" peaks in N.H.
24 Vision: prefix
26 Beyond the pale?
28 Canker ___
31 Bleating mothers
33 Store's goods, for short
34 Solid rock center?: 2 wds.
36 Beaujolais, e.g.
38 Manhattan addition
39 Bering, e.g.: abbr.
40 "Act your ___!"
41 "Read Across America" org.
42 Bore
44 "Delphine" author Madame de ___
46 "…___ man with seven wives…": 3 wds.
47 "___ of Endearment"
48 Element that's tested for in people's basements
49 Approval: hyph.

Down

1 "Sweet Home ___"
2 Comebacks
3 Crushed by grief: hyph.
4 Suffix with ball
5 Cambodian cabbage?
6 Aids in joining: hyph.
7 "Now We Are Six" character
8 Weird
9 "Paradise Lost" character
10 Half of the band Gnarls Barkley
17 Antipoverty agcy.
23 Homophone of "so"
25 Cruise of "Mission: Impossible III"
27 Carson City native, e.g.
29 Holds high
30 Phrase in a dictionary: 2 wds.
32 E-mail ID, in short
34 Buzzing
35 Leaf opening
37 Bird houses
43 Eisenhower's command, for short
45 Brew "for two"

4

Across

1 Throat ailment, commonly
6 Crete's tallest summit: 2 wds.
11 Philadelphia suburb on the Main Line
12 "Belling the Cat" author
13 "Garfield: ___ of Two Kitties": 2 wds.
14 Big African animal, for short
15 Fancy duds: 2 wds.
17 Complete taxing work?
18 Bunched in with
21 Organ parts
25 Built in a plant: abbr.
26 Scooby-___ (cartoon dog)
27 Frozen french fries brand: hyph.
31 Auto parts giant
32 "Metamorphosis" protagonist
34 "Lonely Boy" singer: 2 wds.
39 Acrylic fiber
40 "___ Time": Hemingway stories: 2 wds.
41 "Lovergirl" singer ___ Marie
42 Mary Poppins, e.g.
43 Jim ___, NHL goalie and 1996 Vezina winner
44 "Good grief!"

Down

1 Fitness centers
2 Russian pop duo
3 Dappled sorrel, chestnut, or bay
4 Said "ne'er," e.g.
5 Dish with seasoned rice
6 Monument material
7 Tittered: hyph.
8 Deity with cow's horns
9 "Stop that!"
10 G.I.'s address
16 Chihuahua bark
18 "Yo te ___"
19 Producer: abbr.
20 Chemical ending
22 "Bleak House" girl
23 Cut (off), as branches
24 "___ man walks into a bar…": 2 wds.
28 "The Day ___" (Longfellow): 2 wds.
29 "A Tale of Two Cities" character
30 Soul, to Solange
31 "Get off my case": 2 wds.
33 Lowlife
34 A, in geometry
35 Marlin or Cardinal, e.g.
36 Chaplin, nee O'Neill
37 Bergman in "Casablanca"
38 Prohibitionists
39 Like some stocks, for short

5

Across

1 "Master"
6 "State" or "national" starter
11 "Waterworld" girl
12 Low, moist area
13 Picnickers run races in them: 2 wds.
15 Carrier to Stockholm
16 "The Waste Land" monogram
17 New Year, in Hanoi
18 "Fighting" football team
20 Dorm room staple
23 Belle & Sebastian's "For the Price of ___ of Tea": 2 wds.
26 Indivisible unit
27 Autostrada sights
28 "___ Love Her": 2 wds.
29 ___ Safer (journalist who co-founded "60 Minutes")
30 #1 Oak Ridge Boys hit
32 Author LeShan
34 Chemical suffix
35 "Can ___ least sit down?": 2 wds.
38 "I Love Lucy" actress: 2 wds.
41 One way to saute: 2 wds.
42 Georgia of "The Mary Tyler Moore Show"
43 Large-eyed lemur
44 Della of "Touched by an Angel"

Down

1 Fall mos.
2 Celebes ox
3 Candies that burn the mouth
4 Dockworker's org.
5 Had a skirmish with
6 Japanese immigrant
7 Ice Cube, Dre, et al., once
8 Like military maneuvers
9 Peter's costar in "A Shot in the Dark"
10 Medical advice, often
14 Christiania, now
18 Train track bar: hyph.
19 Monetary unit of Nigeria
20 Diminutive, in Glasgow
21 2,000 lb.
22 Undertaking
24 Adaptable truck, for short
25 "Gangnam Style" rapper
27 Without end
29 State where the Mississippi R. originates
31 Lab bottles
32 "… there is no ___ angel but Love": Shakespeare
33 Bedrock pet
35 "Bus Stop" playwright
36 Poker "bullets"
37 Distant: prefix
39 "Rocky ___"
40 "Wheel of Fortune" purchase: 2 wds.

6

Across

1 Believed
5 Native Israeli Jews
11 "Typee" follower
12 "How to Steal a Million" star Peter
13 Stuff to put on your sandwich if you find strips or bits too crunchy?: 2 wds.
15 Pointed arch
16 Suffix for abnormalities
17 ___ Root, Nobelist for Peace: 1912
20 Asterisk, to a phone dialer
23 Christiaan Huygens famously observed it
27 Best seller
28 Former name of the cable network Versus (hidden in COOLNESS)
29 King, in Portugal
30 Spiral-shaped pasta
32 French clergyman
33 Flavorful
35 "Doesn't look good": 2 wds.
38 Mulligan, maybe
42 Came to one's senses: 3 wds.
45 What we breathe: 2 wds.
46 "Don't rock the ___!"
47 Doria of Genoa
48 Madrid maiden: abbr.

Down

1 "King of the road"
2 Slate, for example
3 Sets of points, in geometry
4 Redecorate: 2 wds.
5 Absorb, with "up"
6 ___ Z (you name it): 2 wds.
7 Exit: 2 wds.
8 Engine parts
9 "Hard ___!" (captain's cry)
10 Philly team
14 "Regnava ___ silenzio" (aria from "Lucia di Lammermoor")
18 Long Island airport
19 "Star Wars" name
20 Nasdaq unit: abbr.
21 Familia member
22 A.B.A. member: abbr.
24 City, in slang
25 Civil War fighter, for short
26 Never, in German
28 "Cat ___ Hot Tin Roof": 2 wds.
31 Babylonian goddess
32 Improvises: hyph.
34 "Lost" setting: abbr.
35 Court grp.
36 Los Angeles mayor, 2001-2005
37 Didn't have enough
39 "Young Frankenstein" assistant
40 ___ room
41 "I'd Rather Go Blind" singer ___ James
43 Hotfoot it, old-style
44 "The ___ of Good Feelings"

7

Across

1 Mix, as a salad
5 "Potemkin" setting
11 An organic compound
12 Grosser
13 "Oh, ___!"
14 Conceive
15 Spotted
17 Bauxite, e.g.
18 "Alice doesn't live here ___"
23 "___ we forget"
25 Take out ___ in the paper (publicize): 2 wds.
26 Burden of the conscience-stricken
28 Brothers' name in children's literature
29 Mexican men, colloquially
30 Ethel Merman, for one
31 Stamp or Trent D'Arby
33 Backseat driver, e.g.
36 Kitchen aid
38 Deli dangler, maybe
42 Cajun cooking vegetable
43 Come to
44 Engravers' equipment
45 Malaysian island, capital George Town
46 "All's Well That ___ Well"

Down

1 Pace, in classical music
2 Being broadcast, as a radio show: 2 wds.
3 Wine waiter
4 High-five, e.g.
5 "Murder on the ___ Express"
6 Papa
7 Ship's dir., perhaps
8 Calypso kin
9 "Quiet on the ___!"

10 "___ we having fun yet?"
16 Bringing up the rear
19 K follower
20 Thin variety of paper: hyph.
21 Animal of the constellation Aries
22 Teacher's deg.
24 "… or ___!"
26 Figure out
27 "It's no ___!"
28 Delight
30 Performing in a theater
32 Presiding deity
34 Broadcast
35 Cup
37 Central point
38 Drain, as energy
39 Cow, maybe
40 Linked-computers acronym
41 "America's Most Wanted" letters

Across

1 Classic TV equine: 2 wds.
5 U.S. Capitol's vicinity: 2 wds.
11 "True Colors" actress Merrill
12 Like Bart, among the Simpson siblings
13 Bank
14 Hear
15 Opposite WNW
16 Element ending
17 Brit. award
18 Canadian wildcats
21 "Citizen Kane" actor Everett
23 Alternatives to plasma TVs
27 Next year's juniors, for short
28 Italian goodbyes
29 "___ facto"
30 Bit of wit: 2 wds.
31 Accommodate
33 Diplomat: abbr.
36 "Man of a Thousand Faces" Chaney
37 "Peer Gynt" character
40 Anne ___ Lindbergh
42 Admits, with "up"
43 "___ later": 2 wds.
44 Brother of Abel
45 Cloverleaf component: hyph.
46 Ballyhoo

Down

1 Catalog things: abbr.
2 Inlets
3 Wraps up
4 Actor Daniel ___ Kim
5 Extra special
6 Prevailing weather
7 "Inc." spots?
8 Abbr. after many a general's name
9 Go-aheads
10 "___ cost to you!": 2 wds.
16 Motel and B&B, e.g.
19 "Hurray!"
20 "___ Blade" (Thornton drama)
21 Fed. support benefit
22 Chop (off)
24 Left: 2 wds.
25 Scooby-___ (dog detective)
26 Fast plane, for short
28 Invent, as a new word
30 Enlarge, like a photo: 2 wds.
32 Come to fruition
33 Schoolyard comeback: 2 wds.
34 Big name in faucets
35 ___ Rabbit ("Uncle Remus" character)
38 Barber's motion
39 Feudal worker
41 Hand-woven rug
42 "Oh my!" in Edinburgh

9

Across

1 Alternatives to Paper Mates
5 Looks for
11 Wings
12 Surgeon's tool
13 Boomers' kids
14 GI's stint peeling potatoes, for example: 2 wds.
15 Domestic: 2 wds.
17 "___ at the Races": 2 wds.
18 Blabs
22 "De profundis," for one
23 1990 NBA Finals MVP ___ Thomas
24 Group of schools in one area, for short (hidden in JAMES DEAN)
25 A doz. doz.
26 Graceful fliers
29 Buddhist saint
31 Refuges
32 Washington baseball team, for short
33 Arm benders
35 "Relax, and that's an order!": 2 wds.
38 Not just one
41 Emerges victorious in, as a game: 2 wds.
42 Halo, e.g.
43 Chinese philosopher of long ago: hyph.
44 AAA recommendations

Down

1 Lunch holder, maybe
2 French Guiana's Royale, e.g.
3 Soft drink company known for ginger ale: 2 wds.
4 Marvin Gaye classic "___ Healing"
5 ____-Seltzer
6 Yellowstone sight
7 Guitarist Segovia
8 "E.R." venue
9 ___ Offensive
10 Babe's home
16 Poe's "The Narrative of Arthur Gordon ___"
17 Beasts of burden
19 Last bugle call of the day: 2 wds.
20 "___ Theme" ("Doctor Zhivago" song)
21 ___ put (Olympics event)
22 "Fur is Dead" gp.
27 Div. including the Braves and Marlins: 2 wds.
28 Enjoys a Cruz?
29 "Wheel of Fortune" buy: 2 wds.
30 One place for seafood: 2 wds.
34 "La Belle et la ___"
35 Carpentry tool
36 Carrere of "Wayne's World"
37 "Achtung Baby" co-producer Brian
39 Due follower
40 "My dog ___ fleas"

Across

1 Foreign assembly
6 "Candid Camera" request
11 Old Oldsmobile
12 Dog-___
13 Like some ideal credit cards: 2 wds.
15 ___ bath
16 Like some stocks, initially
17 Skeleton part, in Padua
19 Former Serbian capital
22 Conciliatory
25 Biblical verb
26 Native American group: 2 wds.
28 "Absolutely!"
29 "You ___ bother!"
30 "Awesome!": abbr.
31 E.M. Forster's "A Room With a ___"
32 Room in the house on "The Brady Bunch"
33 City where the Taj Mahal is
37 "Rebel Without a Cause" actress: 2 wds.
41 Do the numbers again
42 Corkwood
43 Gall
44 To the most extreme degree: 2 wds.

Down

1 "Do the Right Thing" pizzeria
2 "The Time Machine" aristocrats
3 Eye needed in a "Macbeth" recipe
4 McCain is one
5 2,000 pounds
6 Handle: 2 wds.
7 "Newsweek" writer Peyser
8 E.U. member, shortly
9 "___ Girls"
10 Aug. hours in Akron
14 Arturo ___, Italian orchestra conductor
18 1951 Scrooge player Alastair
19 Character to "avoid," in 1989 Domino's Pizza ads
20 Library cataloging datum, briefly
21 "Don't change it"
22 Month after Nisan
23 "___ Lama Ding Dong" (1961 hit)
24 Barely managed, with "out"
25 Recoiled: 2 wds.
27 Shirt with artwork, maybe
31 South African grassland
32 Big name in root beer
34 Pebble Beach pastime
35 Santa ___, Calif.
36 Hebrew month
37 Govt. agency whose official early history is entitled "Controlling the Atom"
38 ___ Arann (Irish carrier)
39 Plato's "T"
40 "Chicago" lyricist

Across

1 "___ forgive those who ...": 2 wds.

5 Raspy

11 Battle of Normandy locale

12 Fathers, slangily: 2 wds.

13 Bill of fare

14 Moses parted it: 2 wds.

15 Put off

17 Congo river

18 "Tell me if you're coming" initials

22 Actress Patsy of "Absolute Beginners"

24 Attack, with "into"

25 "First Blood" director Kotcheff

26 Law, in Lyon

27 Everest's is 29,028 ft.

29 Faze

32 Ancient stringed instrument

33 Prefix meaning "both"

34 Sensible

38 Easy to control

41 "___ I say more?"

42 ___ back (downsized)

43 Class for foreigners, for short

44 Mark Twain's Tom

45 Phisher's acquisitions, for short

Down

1 #1 spot

2 Mailing courtesies: abbr.

3 Sank: 2 wds.

4 Accustoms

5 Stinger

6 Cassini of fashion

7 Venomous snakes

8 Apt. ad figure

9 "Comprende?"

10 "Bambi" character

16 "Aladdin" character

19 Bite

20 Early fiddle

21 Ballet bend

22 TV music vendor: hyph. 2 wds.

23 Slick, like some fish

28 To be sure

29 Not fit for kids, as a movie: 2 wds.

30 "What ___ saying?": 2 wds.

31 Butchers' offerings: hyph. 2 wds.

35 On the safe side, at sea

36 "___ Flux" (Charlize Theron film)

37 Cholesterol varieties, initially

38 Sheet music markings

39 Mozart's "L'___ del Cairo"

40 As the crow cries

12

Across

1 "The Conning Tower" columnist, for short (hidden in HALF PAGE)
4 ___ cry
7 Mental figures, familiarly
10 Break out
11 "___ pales in Heaven the morning star": Lowell
12 Batman and Robin, e.g.
13 That, in Chile
14 A.T.M. maker
15 Attention, metaphorically
16 "Roll With Me, Henry" singer James
18 Glazed fabric
20 Actress Téa
22 Saps
25 Badminton court dividers
29 ___ Peninsula (part of Egypt)
30 Enter, as data: 2 wds.
31 "Res ___ loquitur"
32 Pledge
33 "Lovergirl" singer ___ Marie
35 "Slums of Beverly Hills" director Jenkins
38 ___-mutton: hyph.
42 ___ Mae Brown (Whoopi Goldberg's "Ghost" role)
43 Former White House inits.
45 Thor Heyerdahl craft
46 "___ want a hula hoop…" (Chipmunks): 2 wds.
47 ___ in "Oscar"
48 "The shakes", initially
49 Fourposter, e.g.
50 Gene material, briefly
51 Letters in a help wanted ad

Down

1 Beat it
2 After
3 "He loves," in Latin
4 Bog
5 Ursus ___ (brown bear)
6 Aired a second time
7 Footnote word
8 Paris's ___ d'Orsay
9 Aching
17 Former capital of Kazakhstan: hyph.
19 Animal, vegetable or ___?
21 Center opening
22 "___: Miami" (CBS hit)
23 "Hooray!" preceder, when repeated
24 German pronoun
26 "Concentration" pronoun
27 ___ for tat
28 Bend in timber
30 Former Hungarian ruler
32 Deck figure
34 "I don't understand," to computers
35 ___ of the Unknowns
36 "Song of the South" song syllables
37 Domestic
39 "Das Lied von der ___"
40 Cat, in Catalonia
41 Beauvais's department
44 "Enemy of the State" org.

Across

1 Clamors
5 "Heroes" villain
10 "… a dagger which ___"
(Macbeth): 2 wds.
11 Line feeder, of a sort
12 Narrow, thin strip
13 Baseball act: hyph.
14 Activity for black belts
16 Applications
17 Jerry Mathers TV role
19 "Call Me Maybe" singer
Carly ___ Jepsen
21 Water polo teams, e.g.
25 "___ we there yet?"
26 Wedding day phrase: 2 wds.
27 "Mamma ___!"
28 Bug
30 Berne's river
31 Most repellent
33 Halftime lead, e.g.
36 Outcasts
39 African language
41 "The Valley of Horses" author
42 Beams
43 Supercomputer inventor
44 "Strong Enough to Bend"
singer Tucker
45 Name in "Nine Stories"

Down

1 Old-school data storage
2 "La ___ Bonita" (Madonna song)
3 It won't get you drunk: 2 wds.
4 Bristles
5 "Come ___?" (Italian greeting)
6 Kind of smoothie
7 "Gentlemen Prefer Blondes" author
8 Bad fit?
9 Soaks, as flax
11 "Bloom County" character: 2 wds.
15 Gauguin's Pacific island
18 Lofty verse
19 Cold and wet
20 "All Things Considered" reporter Shapiro
22 Dilettantes
23 24 horas
24 Mediterranean isl.
29 In a fair way
32 "The final frontier"
33 At first, once
34 Former Russian parliament
35 Acquire
37 Enlarge, as a hole
38 Real last name of Roy Rogers
40 Bona ___ (goddess also called Fauna)

14

Across

1 "Ick!"

6 Coffee drink that simply means "milk" in Italian

11 Ford, to Chevrolet

12 Big name in printers

13 RM-81, rocket stage

14 Holy ___

15 Lousiana State Fair site

17 Early Ping-Pong score: hyph.

18 1977 best-selling Steely Dan album

19 8 x 10, often

23 "All in the Family" spinoff

26 Exams for aspiring D.A.s

27 Bind

29 Bookmarked address, briefly

30 As you like it: 2 wds.

33 Not the sharpest knife in the drawer

36 Computer acronym

37 "Goodbye, ___ Jean" (opening line of "Candle in the Wind")

38 "Cafe Terrace at Night" setting

39 Synthetic fabric

40 "Woman with ___" soap opera: 2 wds.

41 Down at the heels

Down

1 Mardi ___

2 Boxer's punch: 2 wds.

3 Modernize

4 Less ludicrous

5 Drudge

6 Joke: hyph.

7 Fit

8 "A Life for the ___"

9 "Hop ___!": 2 wds.

10 Make bigger, as a photo: abbr.

16 Brain scan, initially

18 ___ , amas, amat

20 Dessert wine

21 Ran

22 Maker of Touche Éclat, initially

24 Airs

25 Self-centered person

28 Ike's command, initially

31 Karenina and Paquin

32 Beach

33 Amt. you don't expect to pay

34 "Daily Bruin" publisher, initially

35 Tyne of "Judging Amy"

36 "___ approved" (motel sign)

15

Across

1 Supermodel Lanzoni

6 "Whatcha ___?"

10 Rochelle ___, romance novelist

11 Laid up: 2 wds.

13 Odd group that included Jermaine and Marlon: 2 wds.

15 Diminutive suffix, in Italian

16 Computer file suffix

17 Grand Coulee, for one

18 Tough girls

20 Japanese capital, once

21 Turn ___ profit: 2 wds.

22 Grand ___ (Caribbean island)

24 Composed

26 Borrowed: 2 wds.

29 Surveyor's nail

33 Law, in Dieppe

34 Detail

36 "May ___ excused?": 2 wds.

37 Type of newsgroup, initially

38 Back muscle, briefly

39 "___ was a merry old soul": 3 wds.

42 Arrive, as darkness: 2 wds.

43 Camels' pit stops

44 CD track, often

45 Exertion

Down

1 Beef or chicken dish

2 Rehab program: 2 wds.

3 Look good on

4 Aggravate

5 Bone: prefix

6 Patronizes, as a restaurant: 2 wds.

7 Canadian public filmmaking organization letters

8 Footnote word

9 Battle Born state

12 Incubus, for one

14 Pain-blocking drug

19 Northrop ___ Spirit (stealth bomber): 2 wds.

23 Polite reply from a ranch hand: 2 wds.

25 Bringing up

26 Hodgepodges

27 Court figures

28 Deceived: 2 wds.

30 Hairy

31 Common shrub

32 Abhor

35 Pop-up breakfast fare

40 Aunts, e.g.

41 Aviary sound

Across

1 "Pipe down!"
5 Minor
11 "Bamboo curtain" locale
12 "You are not!" retort: 3 wds.
13 Steely: 3 wds.
15 Biting
16 Followed
21 Easy mark
24 Badger
25 Home of Zeno
26 F.B.I. operative: hyph.
27 Dreamy fruit of Greek myth
29 ___ in the bud: 2 wds.
30 Sporty Italian cars
32 Race climax: 2 wds.
36 Best Actor of 1990: 2 wds.
40 Ancient meeting places
41 Latin 101 verb
42 Bargain-basement: hyph.
43 "Out of the Cellar" heavy metal band

Down

1 "Funny!": hyph.
2 Car-racing org.
3 "Your majesty"
4 Extinct duck-billed beast
5 Andalusian assents: 2 wds.
6 Surgeon's tool
7 "___ Believer": 2 wds.
8 Volkswagen hatchback
9 Neth.
10 Fros' mates
14 "Dear" advice-giver
17 Record holder
18 Theda Bara, e.g.
19 "Freejack"'s Morales
20 1978 WSMVP, Bucky
21 Ill-gotten gains
22 ___ vera
23 Four: prefix
28 Author Rushdie
29 Not yet final, at law
31 Emitted radiating lines
33 ___ Linda, Calif.
34 Art sch. class
35 "Ahem" relative
36 Tokyo carrier, initially
37 "I" problem?
38 "Tic-tac-toe, three in a ___"
39 "___ Sleep Comes Down to Soothe the Weary Eyes" (Dunbar poem)

Across

1 Woman in a "Paint Your Wagon" song
6 Docs for cats, maybe
10 Scarpered: 2 wds.
12 "Pumping ___"
13 Cassowary or moa, e.g.
14 Greek war goddess
15 Followed orders
17 "T" size: abbr.
19 66, e.g.: abbr.
20 "Lo's Diary" author ___ Pera
23 Ann Sheridan, ___ Girl
25 Checked things
27 Humidor item
28 NYC diplomat: 2 wds.
29 Second-grade sequence, initially
30 Paris measurement, a bit
   more than a yard
31 Alphabet chain
32 Engine speed, for short
34 Dungeons & Dragons
   game co., initially
35 "For unto us a child is born" source
37 Sonata, e.g.
40 Part of a percussion section
43 Actor Eric
44 Princess Fiona in "Shrek", e.g.
45 Rhinelander's "real"
46 Fashionable wheat

Down

1 "To ___ is human …"
2 "___ note to follow so…": 2 wds.
3 By and large: 3 wds.
4 French silk
5 Beyond closing time: hyph.
6 Competed
7 "Ol' Rockin' ___" (bin-mate of the
   1957 album "Ford Favorites")
8 Diminutive, as a dog
9 ___-Cat (winter vehicle used in "The Shining")
11 Experienced
16 Author known for using lowercase letters in his
   poems: 3 wds.
17 Nearby
18 Automaton
20 Release after the sequel: 2 wds.
21 Anatomical canals
22 According to: 2 wds.
24 Voting "yes"
26 "The loneliest number"
33 El ___, Tex.
35 "The City ___ War" (Cobra Starship song): 2 wds.
36 "Modern Maturity" org.
37 Award bestowed by Queen Eliz.
38 ___-Man (1980s video game)
39 Durham sch.
41 Immigrant's class, briefly
42 Grounded jet, briefly

Across

1 Traveling the streets of New York City, perhaps: 3 wds.
7 Make quick turns
11 "1984" author
12 Gen. Robt. ___: 2 wds.
13 Muhammad Ali's old name: 2 wds.
15 Opposite of "sans"
16 "___ Poetica"
17 Vacation destination: 2 wds.
21 "Atlas Shrugged" author Rand
22 Clues in
25 Snide comment: 2 wds.
28 Music system
29 "Didn't I tell you?"
30 Deteriorate: 3 wds.
33 Bygone daily MTV series, informally
35 World created by Jim Henson for the movie "The Dark Crystal"
36 Prime cause, slangily: 2 hyph. wds.
41 Ending to avoid?
42 Made a surprise attack
43 Stink, and then some
44 Mocking, evil looks

Down

1 Games grp.
2 "We Do Our Part" org.
3 Jimmy Stewart syllables
4 French equivalent of the Oscar
5 "It's ___!" (cry from Dr. Frankenstein)
6 "Saturday Night Live" duo consisting of Dan Aykroyd and John Belushi (with "The"): 2 wds.
7 White House monogram of the 1970s
8 Nervous: 3 wds.
9 Get warm, in a way
10 2002 Grammy winner Alicia or what she plays on her piano

14 Twenty, to Lincoln
17 Bursae
18 Myanmar money
19 Weave
20 Backboard attachment
23 At liberty
24 Timetable, briefly
26 "___ dat"
27 1983 Streisand film
31 ___ the Jebusite (Biblical figure who sold his threshing floor to David)
32 ___ Hawkins dance
33 Way up?: hyph.
34 "Shallow Hal" actor Kirby
37 100 qintars
38 "Fables in Slang" author
39 Celtic Neptune
40 The Mormons' letters

Across

1 Big name in infomercials

6 Boy with a bow

11 "What ___!": 2 wds.

12 End of ___: 2 wds.

13 ___ Park, N.J.

14 Stingy person

15 Foolish: hyph.

17 "Belling the Cat" fabulist

18 Ballet movement

20 Capital of South Dakota

25 Brings home, as bacon

27 African antelope

28 Utters "hello": 2 wds.

30 Mrs.'s counterparts, in Mexico

31 "Frasier" dog

33 Expect: 2 wds.

38 San ___, Calif.

39 Bête ___

40 ___ donna

41 "___ we all!"

42 "Dig?"

43 Counsels

Down

1 Arthur C. Clarke's "Rendezvous with ___"

2 Expressed surprise

3 Like some diets

4 Galway gals

5 Oklahoma natives

6 From head to toe: hyph.

7 Apartment, to a realtor

8 "Lion dog," briefly

9 Angry

10 ___ es Salaam

16 "___ Goes the Weasel"

18 Anatomical foot

19 ___ an der Thaya, Austrian town

21 "Hamlet" setting

22 Lofty

23 Biochemistry abbr.

24 Masthead contents, briefly

26 Nanny, for one: 2 wds.

29 "Esto perpetua" is its motto: abbr.

32 Middle eastern currency unit

33 Empty, like a cupboard

34 Working away: 2 wds.

35 Do followers: 2 wds.

36 Alencon's department

37 Soaks, as flax

38 Fuel economy letters

20

Across

1 Thai currency
5 Bangladesh's capital, old-style
10 All in ___ work: 2 wds.
12 Against a thing, legally: 2 wds.
13 Company with a lizard as its mascot
14 Kyle ___, time traveler in "The Terminator"
15 Equivalent of "lite": hyph.
17 Everest and Fuji, e.g.
18 Fatal disease of cattle, initially
20 "Get ___!": 2 wds.
22 Chantilly's department
24 Pendergrass and Riley
27 Gravestone, perhaps
29 San ___, Calif.
30 Blue-ribbon
32 Contraction before "It'll be fun!"
33 Be temporarily: 2 wds.
35 "___ Time transfigured me": Yeats
36 "Rock-hard" muscles
38 Prussian cavalryman
40 Princess in Woolf's "Orlando"
42 Santa's reindeer, e.g.
45 Country singer Travis
46 "Nuts" cartoonist Wilson
47 Carrying a lot of extra baggage, so to speak
48 Big top, e.g.

Down

1 Work at a grocery store, sometimes
2 Drink suffix
3 Emperor of Ethiopia 1930–74: 2 wds.
4 Longtime Magic 8 Ball maker
5 Dragged through the mud
6 "Wheel of Fortune" request: 2 wds.
7 Green drink: 3 wds.
8 "It is" to Pierre
9 "My Cup Runneth Over" singer
11 Chesterfield, e.g.
16 ___-rock (music genre)
18 Bruce, with "The"
19 Construction location
21 Money guarantor, initially
23 A.C. or D.C., e.g.
25 "Son of Frankenstein" shepherd
26 Loudness measure
28 Get going
31 Island where Brando lived: abbr.
34 Plod along
36 About: 2 wds.
37 Biting remark
39 "There's more than one way to skin ___": 2 wds.
41 Shaker ___, O.
43 Suffix with Caesar
44 "Inside the NBA" network, initially

21

Across

1 Show shock, in a way
5 Potbellied, plus
10 "Hawaii Five-O" episode-ending word
12 Casting choices?
13 Black TV cartoon animal: 3 wds.
15 Beanie Babies, e.g.
16 Fair hirer's abbr.
17 Labor group, initially
18 Computer add-on?
19 Application datum letters
20 Banquet
21 Orch. section
23 Heebie-jeebies
25 Doesn't dash off
27 Continues: 2 wds.
30 Some execs
34 "The Subject Was Roses" director Grosbard
35 Carrere of "Wayne's World"
37 "Give ___ break!": 2 wds.
38 Do the math, maybe
39 Spike TV, formerly
40 "___ Heldenleben": R. Strauss
41 Smallest state: 2 wds.
44 Peer pressure applier, perhaps
45 Network, e.g.
46 Actor Keach
47 Arp's art

Down

1 Campaigners' bloopers
2 Blue Jays' and Rays' group: 2 wds.
3 Fuse two pieces of metal
4 ___ Beta Kappa
5 Candy bar of caramel, peanuts and fudge: 2 wds.
6 Drone, e.g.
7 Cut out
8 Close tightly: 2 wds.
9 Prevents, legally
11 x, y, and z in math
14 Italian orchestra conductor
22 Lottery-running org., once
24 Perry Mason creator's initials
26 Unstable
27 Palace figures
28 Behind the times: 2 wds.
29 Oprah's character in "The Princess and the Frog"
31 1998 Masters and British Open winner Mark
32 Like marble
33 Gidget portrayer Dee
36 Apparent extremity of a ring of Saturn
42 12th of 12: abbr.
43 Ceiling

Across

1 Deep sleeps
7 Arcing shots
11 Brother and husband of Isis
12 "Alice's Restaurant" singer Guthrie
13 Goal-oriented activity
14 Breakfast, lunch or dinner
15 "The Joy of Signing" subj.
16 Poets' feet
17 Yield, as a dividend
19 Former "SNL" cast-member Horatio
21 "Rugrats" dad
22 Formal, casually
26 That girl in "That Girl"
27 "There but for the grace of God ___": 2 wds.
28 "___-ching!"
29 Beat-keeping movement: hyph.
31 "Hee ___"
32 Until (that time): 2 wds.
34 Barn bird
35 Contents of Pandora's box
38 The Magic, on scoreboards
40 Italian artist Guido
41 Clippers
44 Ballet move
45 "Marnie" star Tippi
46 Coastal raptors
47 Augments: 2 wds.

Down

1 Palindromic plea
2 Bear, in Bolivia
3 Paltry
4 "Lord of the Rings" baddies
5 Cambodian cash
6 Belarus, once, initially
7 Class for expecting mothers
8 Self-styled "Family City U.S.A."
9 Give away
10 Arias, usually
16 Calvary inscription
17 10th- or 11th-graders' exam letters
18 2 for Helium, e.g.: abbr. 2 wds.
20 Take a kid, legally
23 Academic types
24 "Heartbreak House" writer
25 Ketch relative
27 Breaks
30 Dutch bulbs
33 ___ and aahed
35 "House of Frankenstein" director ___ C. Kenton
36 Dogleg
37 Words with uproar or instant: 2 wds.
39 Foxx of "Sanford and Son"
41 "___ boom"
42 Abbr. after a name
43 ___ Balls (snack cakes)

23

Across

1. Addition figure
4. Amigo
7. Aladdin's hat
10. Jersey and shorts, say, briefly
11. George Sand's "Elle et ___"
12. A1A, I65, or 66, e.g.
13. Board member: abbr.
14. Prefix with meter
15. Bygone money
16. Court case standout: 2 wds.
19. Not, to a Scot
20. ___ Offensive
21. Disconnected
23. Turkish generals
26. "Get ___!"
27. Genesis vessel, in Genoa
28. Large-eyed lemur
30. Plains tribe
31. "Murder, ___"
32. Clinch, with "up"
33. Son of reggae star Bob, who sang "Tomorrow People": 2 wds.
38. "Do ___ Diddy Diddy" (1964 hit)
39. Delay
40. "___ pig's eye!": 2 wds.
41. Beechbone in "The Lord of the Rings," e.g.
42. Alkaline liquid
43. "Flying" Field role
44. Magazine no.
45. "A Midsummer Night's Dream" character
46. Three D followers!

Down

1. Beer, casually
2. Apartment, to a renter
3. Cop's postarrest recitation: 2 wds.
4. Made furrows
5. "Luxury Has Progressed" car company
6. Ray of "GoodFellas"
7. It's 15 feet from the hoop, in basketball: 3 wds.
8. List enders, briefly
9. God holding a thunderbolt
17. Banister
18. Veto, for example
21. Dot-commer's address, for short
22. "New" prefix
24. Game-one starter, usually
25. Carrier to Copenhagen
29. Six-headed monster with twelve feet from the "Odyssey"
30. Just Plains folks?
33. Two, in Germany
34. Fleming and Ziering
35. "The Say Hey Kid"
36. Plenty, informally
37. Half a Chinese circle

24

Across

1 Courage, informally
5 Attack verbally: 2 wds.
11 "Harry Potter" actress Watson
12 F equivalent: 2 wds.
13 Bookbinding leather
14 Deal maker
15 "Here's the answer!": 3 wds.
17 Changed to fit in
22 ___ fly
26 Agricultural warehouse
27 Not length
28 Basket fiber
29 "…a kid'll eat the middle of an ___ first"
30 Frees
31 Garden of Eden tempter
33 Deodorant type
38 Capella's constellation
42 Anise-flavored liqueur
43 Is behind
44 Avgolemono pasta
45 French president's residence
46 Attention-getters

Down

1 One of the Spice Girls
2 "Er, yeah": 2 wds.
3 Revenue collector: hyph.
4 Not loco
5 Choose
6 Court org. 1920–75: 2 wds.
7 Measure of conductance
8 "N'est ce ___?"
9 Hematite, for one
10 Broadcasting inits. since 1970
16 Clothes in a basket, say
18 "Check this out!"
19 Evergreen shrub
20 "Heroes" heroine Bishop
21 Accomplishes
22 "Terrible" phase
23 Be the father, in the Bible
24 "Jekyll & Hyde" actress Linda
25 Car roof feature: hyph.
28 Foreword: abbr.
30 Anxiety
32 "The ___ Has Landed"
34 "Amazing!"
35 "Absolutely!"
36 "Crazy Train" singer
37 Toilets, to a Brit.
38 "Thanks, but I already ___"
39 It often starts with "http"
40 2004 nominee
41 "___ for Innocent" (novel featuring private investigator Kinsey Millhone): 2 wds.

Across

1 Burning briquet, eventually
4 Invoice abbr.
7 Wray of "King Kong"
10 1944 initials
11 502, in Nero's day
12 A pint, maybe
13 "What's ___?"
14 Can. province
15 Financial regulators, initially
16 Failing grades
17 Burma's first P.M.
18 "Huh?" sounds
19 Org. with a "100 Years…" series
20 Bahaism, for one: abbr.
21 1968 battle period
22 ___ Spin (classic toy)
24 Walk nonchalantly
26 Center of a roast
28 Bogged down: 3 wds.
30 Bearded creatures
33 "Children of the Albatross" author
34 ___ tai
36 "Tarzan" extra
37 Chang's Siamese twin
38 Lizard, old-style
39 Tiger's "launch pad"
40 Six, to Italians
41 A little sun
42 ___ and outs
43 "My boy"
44 ___ Z: 2 wds.
45 Harem chamber
46 Alphabet trio
47 Fighting Tigers' home, for short
48 Australian state whose capital is Sydney, initially

Down

1 Lover of Dido, in myth
2 Tennis rival of Monica
3 Nonchalant greeting: 3 wds.
4 "She had ___ Presbyterian mind…", Steinbeck: 2 wds.
5 Famed pool player: 2 wds.
6 Like some heads
7 Long-running CBS news show: 3 wds.
8 Tennis great Gibson
9 Frothy
23 "___ any drop to drink": Coleridge
25 Part of a line, in geometry: abbr.
27 I, for one
28 Actually existing: 2 wds.
29 ___ spades (black playing card): 2 wds.
31 Flips
32 "Two for the ___," Gibson play
35 "What was ___ wanted?": 2 wds.

Across

1 Garfield's predecessor
6 Baltic natives
11 What bargain-hunters seek: 2 wds.
12 Buddhist saint
13 "You don't need to remind me": 2 wds.
14 2003 Mazda roadster
15 Home of the Nationals until 2007, initials
16 Built
18 A deer, a female deer
19 "___ Freischütz" (Weber opera)
20 Mr., abroad
21 University where "Animal House" was filmed
23 Jug handle, in archeology
24 Nonpro?
25 Padre's brother
26 Afflicts
28 Against
31 Fat measure, initially
32 Traffic duo?
33 Agent, briefly
34 Earnest requests
36 Wall Street operation, for short
37 Accessories for vampires
38 TV actress Georgia
40 Coeur d'___, ID
41 1986 Indianapolis 500 winner
42 Emerald, essentially
43 Quick squabble: hyph.

Down

1 Beehive, say
2 Plead: 2 wds.
3 Joe DiMaggio's nickname: 2 wds.
4 Inits. in 1970–80s rock
5 Applied a patch: 2 wds.
6 More weak, like excuses
7 "Spamalot" cowriter Idle
8 "Incorrect!": 3 wds.
9 Homers, in baseball slang
10 Bowls venues
17 "___ and Stimpy"
22 Get-___ (starts)
23 Department of eastern France
25 Folks thowing a Frisbee
26 1981 Genesis album
27 Pierce, in a way
28 Calgary Stampeders' grp.
29 Echo
30 Artemis's twin
32 Artistic frame
35 "___, meeny, miney, moe…"
39 Scot's "not"

27

Across

1 1924 Edna Ferber novel: 2 wds.
6 Ending for convert or combust
10 2005 "Survivor" locale
11 "Alas, to no ___ …"
12 Bikini, e.g.
13 Beat (out)
14 ___ point
15 "Aladdin" prince
17 Chemical suffix
18 Canyon or ranch ending
19 High school class
20 Bull's-eye: abbr.
21 Form 1040 IDs
23 Broadcast receivers
25 Fifth Greek letter
27 Countrified
29 Library ID
32 Latin examples, briefly
33 Racehorse, slangily
35 Capote, to friends
36 The "o" in Cheerios
37 ___ in the ointment
38 Ending for excels or exter
39 Ex-Yankee pitcher Hideki
41 Olympic symbol
43 Maj.'s superior: 2 wds.
44 At the right time: 2 wds.
45 Zaire's Mobuto Sese ___
46 Lots and plots

Down

1 Card suit
2 Horse operas
3 Explode in anger: 3 wds.
4 Different or potent ending
5 Soviet prison system
6 1961 Literature Nobelist Andric
7 Innate behavior: 2 wds.
8 Hoodwinked: 2 wds.
9 Church or town leaders
11 Elephant, e.g.
16 Beautiful sounding, as poetry
22 Harbor city: abbr.
24 "And how!": 2 wds.
26 Iniquitous
27 Lubes anew
28 "Casablanca" crook
30 Irish accent
31 Checkers of vital signs
34 Greek sandwiches
40 Ghostly greeting
42 Cecil Campbell, a.k.a. ___ Kamoze

28

Across

1 Argentine grassland
7 A.C.L.U. concerns: abbr.
10 And more: 2 wds.
11 Decree
12 Memorial Day event
13 Put trust in, with 'on'
14 Life, for one
16 Amo, amas, ___
19 Battery size letters
20 Dutch bloom
22 Small boat
26 CVI x XXV
27 Aleppo's land
28 "Venice of the Orient"
29 Days ___: 2 wds.
30 22.5 degrees, initially
32 Some dishes on rooftops, initially
33 Disease caused by a thiamine deficiency
37 Baguette or challah
38 Files, like a complaint
42 "Come Back, Little Sheba" playwright
43 Contacts quickly, perhaps: hyph.
44 Big Ten Conference sch.
45 Illuminated naturally

Down

1 ___ rally (high school event)
2 ___ crossroads: 2 wds.
3 Fold, spindle or mutilate
4 Picnic utensil: 2 wds.
5 Senate page, e.g.
6 City near Florence
7 Nada, across the Pyrenees
8 Nursery need, informally
9 Eye affliction
11 2003 Jamie Lee Curtis and Lindsay Lohan movie: 2 wds.
15 "Jerusalem Delivered" poet
16 Prefix with sphere or meter
17 Many-petaled flowers: abbr.
18 "Betsy's Wedding" star
21 Backup procedure: 2 wds.
23 ___-Z: classic Camaro model
24 Adidas alternative
25 Ephemeral manias
31 Caught congers
33 High-pitched electronic sound
34 A long, long time
35 Alternative to Mario Batali
36 Downey of "Touched by an Angel"
39 "Buck Rogers" actor Gerard
40 "___ Stone"
41 Mach 1 breaker, initially

Across

1 Hockey equipment
6 Holiest city for Muslims
11 Fourth month
12 So everyone can hear
13 Spot away from sunlight
14 ___ and fauna
15 ___-tac-toe
16 Greek letter
18 Big holder of beer
19 Game hunted in Alaska
20 Additionally
21 Wrath
22 Fun in the snow
24 Put a value on
26 Place to play: 2 wds.
28 Coral ___, Fla.
30 Person in charge at work
33 Actress Thompson
34 Volleyball barrier
36 Cashew or almond
37 Bobby of hockey fame
38 Attempt
39 Place for a pedicure
40 Army officer, casually
42 Pan or Frampton
44 Take the wheel
45 Out in the open
46 Screams
47 Natives of Belgrade

Down

1 Glue alternatives
2 Against the odds, as a struggle
3 Restaurant chain famous for rocking chairs: 2 wds.
4 Child
5 Caught some Z's
6 Mobster
7 Letter after kay
8 Blue Muppet: 2 wds.
9 Healers
10 Old sayings
17 More raspy, as a voice
23 "Runaway" singer Shannon
25 Cry and cry
27 Middles
28 Like some magazine pages
29 Fill with bubbles
31 Awesome
32 Begins
35 Mistakes like thsi
41 Shaving cream type
43 Night before

Across

1 Football throw
5 Clothing company with a famous catalog: 2 wds.
10 Eight, in Ecuador
11 Act properly
12 Spoken
13 Part of USA
14 Label again, as a computer file: 2 wds.
16 Lawman Eliot ___
17 American, to a Mexican
19 "Nonsense!"
21 Neither this ___ that
22 Kowtow
25 Historical time
26 Group that does entertainment for soldiers
27 Card game with its own colorful deck
28 "Stop telling me this!" while texting
29 Greek letter
30 Mountain ___
31 "Memoirs of a ___"
33 Reverberating sound
36 Got the benefits of, as planting crops
39 Alternative to a shirt
41 Mr., in Munich
42 Donkeys
43 Largest of the continents
44 Fires off, like an e-mail
45 Meal eaten with spoon

Down

1 Below average
2 Land measurement
3 "The Paris of the Orient"
4 Word before power or plexus
5 Actress Aniston, to friends
6 California city
7 Give five stars to, say
8 Christmas and New Year's
9 Takes down the aisle
11 "The Paris of South America": 2 wds.
15 Part of an hour
18 Complain in a petty way
19 Gamble
20 Give weaponry to
22 "The Paris of Eastern Europe"
23 "First of all..."
24 "Amazing!"
31 Squash or cucumber
32 Laughter sounds
33 Goes back, like the tide
34 Part of a crossword
35 Rhinoceros feature
37 One of the Great Lakes
38 Chess result, sometimes
40 "We're sinking!"

31

Across

1 Wine bottle plugs
6 Indiana basketball player
11 Music form with arias
12 Prior to, in dialect
13 Tribal healer: 2 wds.
15 Comes to a halt
16 Most recent
17 Wish you hadn't
18 "The Fresh Prince of ___-Air"
19 Golf peg
20 Ankle trouble
22 Superpower that disbanded in 1991
23 Tennis great Federer
25 Old-school data storage
28 Jousting weapons
32 Devilish type
33 "The ___ and the Pendulum"
34 Little crawler
35 Cinnamon and cardamom
37 Actor MacLachlan
38 William Goldman bestseller made into a Dustin Hoffman movie: 2 wds.
40 Similar
41 Respond
42 "See ya!"
43 Elaine's last name, on "Seinfeld"

Down

1 Up-and-___ (future big shots)
2 Become emotionally available: 2 wds.
3 More embarrassed, maybe
4 Singer Kristofferson
5 ___ fly (baseball play)
6 Group of experts
7 Several: 2 wds.
8 Astronomical wonders
9 Deletes
10 Person who gives a monthly check to a landlord
14 How this crossword was written: 2 wds.
18 Words about your life
21 "Raiders of the Lost ___"
22 Big coffee holder
24 Have brunch, say
25 Depressing
26 Chevrolet named for an African animal
27 Ghost
29 Grand ___ (Caribbean island)
30 Intertwine
31 Heart implants
33 One of the "Brady Bunch" boys
36 "Let them eat ___" (Marie Antoinette)
37 Leg joint
39 Heavenly body

32

Across

1 Rank below major: abbr.
5 Police officers
9 Neighbor of Michigan and Kentucky
10 Event with cowboys and clowns
11 Thomas, Horace or Aimee
12 Bets
13 Delivers a question
14 Be in possession of
15 Name for a dog, in cartoons
17 Slightly open
21 Wadded (up)
23 Superhero costume piece
24 Card game that's the Spanish word for "one"
25 Largest city in the USA
27 Jennings of "Jeopardy!" fame
28 Black gem
30 Least covered
32 When repeated twice, a "Seinfeld" catchphrase
33 Stone mined in Australia
34 No vote
36 Diner sandwiches
39 Madagascar, Jamaica or Sicily
42 Sound from an unhappy crowd
43 Run-down
44 Actress Redgrave
45 What a waiter hands you
46 Hip, like humor

Down

1 Medical condition often used as a plot twist in soap operas
2 "Eureka!" shouts
3 "Dark Side of the Moon" band: 2 wds.
4 One of two in the mouth, often removed
5 Brandy from France
6 Words of praise
7 Apiece
8 "Help!"
10 Uncooked
12 "Cheers" role for Harrelson: 2 wds.
16 Room in the house on "The Brady Bunch"
18 Child actor who played Anakin Skywalker: 2 wds.
19 Mimics
20 Money for the landlord
21 Floater on the sea
22 Designer Sui or tennis player Kournikova
26 Hat
29 Place described by Coleridge, or a 1980 Olivia Newton-John movie
31 ___-rouser (instigator)
35 Whatever number of
37 Handle food with a metal server
38 Company that made the Discman
39 Ending for real or surreal
40 "Understand?"
41 Deighton who wrote "The IPCRESS File"

33

Across

1 Largest island in the Caribbean
5 Beloved TV collie
11 Masterwork
12 Clothing
13 5-across and others
14 Not invincible
15 Jazz group
17 Buddy
18 Simon of Duran Duran
22 Woodwind instrument
24 Get ready for a test
25 Charged particle
26 Drink that's also a card game
27 Locates
30 "___ at the Bat"
32 Up to this point: 2 wds.
33 "That guy?"
34 Lots of leeway: 2 wds.
38 Working together
41 Situation
42 Signed up for
43 Small bills
44 One of the Seven Dwarfs
45 No, in Russia

Down

1 Word after Morse or zip
2 Stratford-___-Avon (Shakespeare's hometown)
3 Rabbit who said "What's up, doc?": 2 wds.
4 State to be true
5 Baby sheep
6 Ring-shaped coral islands
7 "Sesame ___" (kids' show)
8 Take a chair
9 Tax shelter of a sort
10 Fish that can be "electric"
16 One of the Three Stooges
19 Bully in the Encyclopedia Brown series: 2 wds.
20 Garfield's sidekick
21 Largest city in the U.S., on envelopes: 2 wds.
22 World Cup organization
23 ___ Lane (Clark Kent's co-worker)
28 Put in the dictionary
29 Meryl of "The Iron Lady"
30 Rebel Guevara
31 Summertime cooler, for short: 2 wds.
35 Whirlpool
36 "Understood": 2 wds.
37 Home in a tree
38 Auto racer Foyt and actress Cook
39 "omg thats 2 funny"
40 Tall tale

Across

1 Where snow peas live
5 Salt's buddy
11 Swedish superstore
12 Get to the party
13 Gusto
14 Talked (on and on and on...)
15 English RR car: 2 wds.
17 "Look where I'm pointing!"
18 Make a design, as on a coin
21 "Shoot!"
25 Myrna of movies
26 Prefix meaning "life"
27 Enemies
29 Russia's capital
32 Newton or Asimov
34 English RR car: 2 wds.
39 Hit the big time: 2 wds.
40 Conservative, in Cambridge
41 Show to be true
42 Oak or elm
43 Balance on the edge
44 42-acrosses used to
   make archery bows

Down

1 Dock
2 Tulsa's state: abbr.
3 Head of a college
4 Serenaded: 2 wds.
5 Team whose mascot is the
   San Diego Chicken
6 Computer's "I don't understand
   what you want"
7 Showed to be true
8 Long (for)
9 "The First Time ___ I Saw Your Face"
10 U.S. flag color

16 "Huh?" sounds
18 One of Santa's little helpers
19 "Hello!" to a cow
20 "See ya"
22 Alphabet openers
23 Brazilian city, briefly
24 This very moment
28 Quiet
29 Strong chess player
30 Paddle lookalike
31 "Star Trek" engineer
33 Clear soda
34 Say great things (about)
35 Dog in "Garfield" strips
36 Time gone by
37 Boat workers
38 Blinking pair
39 Shook hands with

35

Across

1 Attorney's field
4 In favor of
7 Wedding day words: 2 wds.
8 Devour
9 Used to be
12 The ideal man: 2 wds.
14 Mined matter
15 Italian city with a leaning tower
16 Advil alternative
18 "___ knew that!": 2 wds.
20 Jobs
21 Dictionary entry, for short
22 Washington's largest city
25 Becomes less emotionally guarded: 2 wds.
27 Long-winded tirades
29 Ending for classic or colonial
32 Crow sounds
33 Gauche
35 2,000 pounds: 2 wds.
38 Near-random guess
39 Mauna ___ (Hawaiian volcano)
40 Argument
42 The, in Germany
43 Yoko who sang "Every Man Has a Woman Who Loves Him"
44 Hi-___ (like some graphics)
45 Man's name that means "king" in Latin
46 Superlative ending

Down

1 Walked with difficulty
2 Where disks go, on some computers
3 Having suffered a little: 3 wds.
4 Simple coat hook
5 Chicago mayor ___ Emanuel
6 Bus driver on "The Simpsons"
9 Big prize at the Razzies: 2 wds.
10 "The Little Mermaid" mermaid
11 "That makes no ___!"
13 Fleming or Somerhalder
17 Pink outfit for a ballerina
19 "Interesting...": 2 wds.
23 Finish
24 Abbr. in many job listings
26 Irritant
27 Take to task
28 Native American boat
30 Pair seen in winter
31 Words after "I'll do" or "Please give them": 2 wds.
34 Dangerous snake
36 Stench
37 Number that's another number upside-down
41 Chicago White ___

Across

1 Greek letter
4 24-hour bank feature
7 Drain, as energy
10 Rule for society
11 Not he
12 Make a mistake
13 "Now it all makes sense!"
14 Breakfast disc
16 Hornet's cousin
18 Spot for a soak
19 Spider "houses"
21 Total guess
25 Korea in the 1950s, e.g.: 2 wds.
28 Prez played to an Oscar by Daniel
29 "What I think is..."
30 "Then Came ___"
31 Jennings of "Jeopardy!"
32 Fish propeller (3)
33 Main and Elm
35 Hip
37 Italy's capital, to its residents
38 Mono-
40 Discontinued car brand
43 ___ sale
47 "Don't let your food get cold!"
48 "Many moons ___ ..."
49 Hardly the life of the party
50 Stay out in the sun too long
51 "Never heard of him"
52 Past tense of 47-across
53 ___-Mex

Down

1 What a cat scratches with
2 "Hilarious!"
3 "My mistake": 3 wds.
4 Scary snake
5 "Our figures seem to be incorrect": 3 wds.
6 Waiter's offering
7 Baltic or Mediterranean
8 "Raiders of the Lost ___"
9 Not post-
15 "60 Minutes" network
17 Candy with a collectible dispenser
20 Elementary school students, half the time
22 Turn in a car, sometimes: 3 wds.
23 Aid in criminal activity
24 Uncle ___ (rice brand)
25 The lady of the house
26 In the thick of
27 Currency in Spain and Cyprus
34 Genre for The Shins
36 "Delish!"
39 Space shuttle org.
41 Challenge
42 Underworld river, or a 1970s-80s band
43 Uncooked
44 "Gross!"
45 Cow shout
46 Palindromic body part

37

Across

1 They're hard or soft, in Mexican restaurants
6 Item on a wrist
11 ___ time (it's spent by yourself)
12 Hello, to Hawaiians
13 Christmas season vehicle: 2 wds.
15 Finale
16 Weapon in "The Shining"
17 Made-up story
18 Gets going
20 Way of doing things
23 Lark
26 John Paul II and Benedict XVI
27 "It's ___ long time!": 2 wds.
28 Surrounding glow
29 Movie bad guy ___ Krueger
30 Brunch item
32 Man's nickname made of three consecutive letters of the alphabet
34 Perfect score, often
35 Outdoor sports store
38 Where dishes get done: 2 wds.
41 Phrase of clarification: 2 wds.
42 WWII hero Murphy
43 "Vote for ___" ("Napoleon Dynamite" catchphrase)
44 Requirements

Down

1 Scotch ___ (adhesive)
2 Thicke, Turing or Tudyk
3 Umbilical ___
4 Brad Paisley's "Waitin' ___ Woman": 2 wds.
5 Drugs up
6 Communion disc
7 Every bit
8 Where hoes and rakes are kept: 2 wds.
9 Popular tea
10 Despise
14 Big test
18 Old-school power source for trains
19 Send out a message of 140 characters or less
20 Health resort
21 "What did ___ say?"
22 Grew quickly
24 State between Ill. and O.
25 April follower
27 CIA head John
29 Get outta town
31 Prefix with centric
32 Decide to miss class
33 Noon or midnight
35 Roller coaster, e.g.
36 Oklahoma city that's also a woman's name
37 Eisenhower and Turner
39 Saturn or Subaru
40 Take to court

Across

1 Not cloudy
6 Piece of parsley
11 Hugh Lawrie show
12 Complain endlessly
13 Number of piano keys
15 Gobbled up
16 Actor Stephen of "V for Vendetta"
17 Mansion owner of fame, for short
18 Bic product
19 East, to Germans
20 Prefix meaning "three"
21 Cookie with a "Double Stuf" variety
23 Cups, saucers, etc.: 2 wds.
25 Manipulators
27 Person who writes music for a movie
30 Item on a stage
34 Peace: Lat.
35 Recipe instruction
37 Make a mistake
38 "___ luck?"
39 Eastern philosophical concept
40 High card
41 "Sweet dreams!"
44 Prepare to propose, perhaps
45 Inborn feature
46 Get the idea
47 Like beach towels, after a while

Down

1 Not top-of-the-line
2 Hang around
3 Oregon city
4 Kind of tree
5 Old-school
6 Fall wear
7 Greek letter
8 Some turns
9 "Where are you?" response: 2 wds.
10 Shape up: 2 wds.
14 Beatles classic
22 Your and my
24 Venomous viper
26 Pacific Northwest city
27 Defeats easily, in slang
28 Dog
29 Chemical element you're using right now
31 Carter defeater
32 Flower used in traditional medicine
33 Attractive
36 Taboos
42 "For ___ a jolly good..."
43 Common tax shelter

Across

1 Actress Naomi
6 Arrive at: 2 wds.
11 Pointer on a sign
12 Ohio city
13 Washington, Wyoming or West Virginia
14 Stands at a slant
15 Body part that also means "cool"
16 Quarterback Manning
18 Alternative to cake
19 Spooky claim
20 Chum
21 Cat, dog or parakeet
22 Long part of a flower
24 Underground system for waste management
26 Battering ___
28 Dinghy mover
29 Become part of again, as a Facebook group
32 "Saturday Night Live" piece
35 Yoko often in crosswords
36 Amount of hair gel
38 Compass dir.
39 Part of NCAA
40 "See ya later!"
41 Greek letter represented by H
42 Beatles drummer
44 Records
46 ___ and dangerous
47 Not here
48 President Roosevelt
49 Knitting needs

Down

1 Hoses down
2 Picasso or Grandma Moses
3 Show spun off of "M*A*S*H": 3 wds.
4 Little kid
5 Use a broom
6 Italian who said the Earth went around the Sun
7 ___ out a win
8 Old-school folder: 2 wds.
9 More upscale
10 Beginnings
17 "Leaving ___ Vegas"
23 Chinese chairman
25 Used to be
27 The human torso
29 Warn (someone), as a lion might: 2 wds.
30 Whole
31 Congressional "no" vote
33 Unpaid worker, often
34 Makes fun of
37 White of "The Golden Girls"
43 H.S. alternative
45 "Now it makes sense!"

Across

1 Pleased
5 Novelist Norman
11 Helper
12 Esteem highly
13 Gusto
14 House for two families
15 Navy boss
17 Gloria of pop
22 Ruckus
26 Mother ___ (big metals find)
27 With 28-across, game where you try to kill pigs
28 See 27-across
29 Otis's movie partner
30 Most sage
31 Put one foot in front of the other
33 Eroded: 2 wds.
38 Root vegetable
42 Sweet-talk
43 Take flight
44 Relax, as restrictions
45 Smithers on "The Simpsons," e.g.
46 "Next..."

Down

1 ___ Strip (area bordering Egypt and Israel)
2 Made up a story
3 Smith or Sandler
4 Sandwich shop
5 With 30-down, irate: 3 wds.
6 Grownup
7 Devilish type
8 Wee
9 Prior to, in poetry
10 Man's name that means "king" in Latin
16 Count (on)
18 Manning and Whitney
19 "Look out for my golf ball!"
20 Does some arithmetic
21 Home made of twigs
22 Christmas season purchases
23 Attending to the task at hand: 2 wds.
24 Stare
25 Hold (up)
28 ___ one's time (wait for the right moment)
30 See 5-down: 2 wds.
32 Rotini or rigatoni
34 Rapper on "Law & Order: SVU"
35 Ark captain
36 Zap
37 Beasts under a yoke
38 Romano or Charles
39 Many a DC road
40 Prefix with respect or associate
41 "___ the Walrus": 2 wds.

41

Across

1 Circus structures
6 Architectural style named for a royal family
11 Last words on the job, maybe: 2 wds.
12 Show one's feelings
13 Say bad words
14 Georgia city that rhymes with a breakfast food
15 Professor's aides, for short
16 "The Tell-Tale Heart" author's initials
18 Little kid
19 Munched on
20 Sandwich often made on Wonder Bread, briefly
21 "Bravo!"
22 Hand over
24 Shouted like a lion
26 Friendly
28 "My word!": 2 wds.
30 Throws in there
33 Neither fish ___ fowl
34 Attorney's field
36 Not post-
37 Bird that can't fly
38 Poehler of "Parks and Recreation"
39 Lane for a full car
40 Weighed down (with)
42 Not beneath
44 ___ on (encouraged)
45 Spud
46 Super-smart people
47 Not these

Down

1 Breath mint brand
2 State to be the same
3 Wasn't in a forgiving mood: 3 wds.
4 Opposite of 'taint
5 Hard to climb, like a hill
6 Brief office gig: 2 wds.
7 Thurman of "Gattaca"
8 Evidence that's been tampered with: 2 wds.
9 Peter of "Lawrence of Arabia"
10 Didn't buy
17 Mr. Lincoln
23 Depressing and introspective, like music
25 Pie ___ mode
27 Cuba, Tahiti and Sri Lanka
28 What a hopper uses: 2 wds.
29 Tribute
31 Huge numbers
32 Harsh
35 Earp at the O.K. Corral
41 "I saw a mouse!"
43 Scrooge's word

Across

1 Monies owed
6 Reid and Lipinski
11 Nebraska city
12 Scent
13 Acknowledged
14 Shish ___
15 "A Nightmare on ___ Street"
16 Leave amazed
18 Ending for rational or lion
19 Vardalos of "My Big Fat Greek Wedding"
20 "___ bad!"
21 Neither here ___ there
22 Plenty
24 Agreed-upon facts
26 Off in the distance
28 "___ Stone"
29 April rain
32 Other
35 One of two on the head
36 Soaking
38 Soap brand
39 The E in NYE
40 "Much ___ About Nothing"
41 Mischievous type
42 Word after time or money
44 San Antonio building
46 Put ___ to (stop): 2 wds.
47 18-wheelers
48 Goods
49 Sip

Down

1 Museum guide
2 Estevez of "The Breakfast Club"
3 1995 Val Kilmer movie: 2 wds.
4 Definite article
5 1978 Peace Nobelist Anwar ___
6 Sign on a tray of samples: 2 wds.
7 "Who ___ you?"
8 "Mrs. Doubtfire" actor: 2 wds.
9 Online bookstore
10 Scary swords
17 Pan used in Beijing
23 Tool with teeth
25 "Bravo!"
27 Money for finding lost pets
29 Go up and down
30 Cuba's capital
31 Wine color
33 Peak
34 Smoke out
37 Breakfast bread that may get burnt
43 Compass dir.
45 Grassland

43

Across

1 Hack

5 Rushing sound

11 Italy's currency, before the euro

12 "There was no choice for me!": 3 wds.

13 Not many: 2 wds.

14 All-___ (late study sessions, casually)

15 Settler

17 Walters of TV news

22 Where two peas go: 3 wds.

26 Kitchen appliance

27 Jay Leno rival: 2 wds.

29 Winds up

30 Birthday cake item

31 Obliterate

33 Not questions

38 Edge

42 "___ to the Chief"

43 Be that as it may: 2 wds.

44 Capital of Norway

45 Quickness to anger

46 Mishmash

Down

1 Applaud

2 LP player

3 Cookie with florets on it

4 Weakest piece, in chess

5 "Nothing Compares 2 U" singer: 2 wds.

6 Machine's sound

7 Horse's morsel

8 "___ to Billie Joe"

9 Narrow waterway: abbr.

10 Christmas sounds

16 Black, in poetry

18 Delivered, as a baby

19 Enthusiastic

20 Movie holder

21 "___ of Green Gables"

22 Decorated, as a cake

23 ___ of the above

24 "No ifs, ___ ..."

25 History

28 Hudson and Chesapeake

32 Bring up

34 "___ next?"

35 "___ of Eden"

36 Anger, with "up"

37 At a snail's pace

38 Came into contact with

39 Monopoly property, often: abbr.

40 Band from Athens, Ga.

41 Economics stat

44

Across

1 Taverns
5 Do an impersonation
10 "Everything's fine!": 2 wds.
11 Last letters in Greece
13 It's put on pasta: 2 wds.
15 Time of the past
16 Wedding day agreement: 2 wds.
17 Devoured
18 Goes off on a tirade
20 Take one's responsibilities seriously: 2 wds.
22 Not quick
23 Bother repeatedly
24 Eat away
26 Meryl of "Julie & Julia"
29 Feeling ill
33 Follower of eta
34 Coffee flavor
35 Ending for north, south, east or west
36 Cassette successors
38 Charged particle
39 Picnickers run races in them: 2 wds.
42 "Way down upon the ___ River..."
43 Bug that bugs cats
44 Has fun in the wintertime
45 Knight and Danson

Down

1 Dangerous dogs
2 Not knowing right from wrong
3 Ray of "Everybody Loves Raymond"
4 Musical genre from Jamaica
5 General feeling
6 Words said with steam coming out of your ears: 3 wds.
7 "Give ___ break!": 2 wds.
8 Lizard some keep as a pet
9 Prickly plant in Arizona
12 Accesses slowly
14 "___ the season..."
19 Use 140 characters or fewer
21 "You ___ Beautiful": 2 wds.
23 Move on one leg
25 Responded to a stimulus
26 Puts one foot in front of the other
27 Tosses
28 Car from Avis or Hertz
30 Roof growth in winter
31 Performed poorly when it counted, in sports
32 State whose largest city is Wichita
34 Submissions to an editor: abbr.
37 Performs
40 Chemistry suffix
41 Toward the back of the boat

Across

1 Wise bird
4 Absorbed, as a cost
7 Chair part
10 "___ won't be afraid" ("Stand by Me" line): 2 wds.
11 Toni Morrison novel "___ Baby"
12 "___ got it!"
13 "Seinfeld" role: 2 wds.
16 Another "Seinfeld" role
17 Dermatologist's hole
18 Helmsley of hotels
20 Away and in trouble
23 Everyday
27 Jeans name
29 Gawk
30 Old counter
32 Graze
33 "Come in!"
35 Play "Wheel of Fortune"
38 Hawaiian welcomes
42 Snide comment: 2 wds.
44 "Tarzan" extra
45 And so on
46 Confederate general
47 Battering device
48 "C'___ la vie!"
49 "___ & Order"

Down

1 "___ bitten, twice shy"
2 Cashmere, e.g.
3 Mona ___ (famous painting)
4 Make up (for)
5 Assume, as a role: 2 wds.
6 Go astray
7 Fancy wheels
8 For always
9 "Pretty Woman" star Richard
14 Old-fashioned woman's name
15 Besides: 2 wds.
19 Discouraging words
20 Pie ___ mode: 2 wds.
21 Spider's home
22 Eggs
24 Wild West?
25 "___ we alone?"
26 Was on the road to victory
28 Closest star to Earth, with "the"
31 Begins
34 Bumper sticker word
35 Wound reminder
36 ___ John's (pizza chain)
37 Thingy
39 Campus building
40 Part of town
41 Throw off, as poll results
43 "___-haw!"

46

Across

1 "Dancing Queen" band from Sweden
5 Spa treatment
11 Easy victory
12 Makes into law
13 Addition, subtraction and such
14 "I see it the same way!"
15 Guinea pig
17 Say it never happened
18 Some turns on the road
22 Showed over again
23 Set aside (for)
24 Not working today
25 Put ___ fight: 2 wds.
26 Songs for one person
29 Tennessee football player
31 The Sphinx's country
32 1998 movie with Jennifer Lopez and Woody Allen's voices
33 Get there
35 One of a kind
38 "Alice's Restaurant" singer Guthrie
41 Argues against
42 "Yeah, sure!": 2 wds.
43 Least convincing, like an excuse
44 No, to Russians

Down

1 What a shoulder holds
2 Constricting snake
3 Caterpillar of the future
4 Goddess for whom Greece's capital is named
5 Accomplishment
6 Actress Bassett
7 Library desk
8 Cold cubes
9 Devoured
10 Drug also called "acid"
16 Dictionary entry: abbr.
17 Clear up, as a cold windshield
19 What a 3-down may do: 2 wds.
20 November birthstone
21 Laurel or Mikita
22 Valentine's Day flower
27 Not translucent
28 Walks sassily
29 ___ chi (Chinese exercise)
30 Fruitlessly: 2 wds.
34 Relax
35 Web address, for short
36 Teacher's union
37 Computer company
39 "I Hope You Dance" singer ___ Ann Womack
40 Mel of baseball fame

Across

1 "Star ___"
5 Hairdos
10 Help, as a criminal
11 "L.A. Law" lawyer
12 City south of Hilton Head, SC: 2 wds.
14 Ziti, e.g.
15 Shampoo target
18 ___ oil
22 "Who ___?"
23 Kidney-related
24 Fix, in a way
25 Aged
26 Bouquet
29 Willing to believe anything
31 "Haystacks" painter
32 Less inept
33 Late hotelier Helmsley
35 Caribbean city: 2 wds.
40 Come to mind
41 ___-friendly
42 Goes for the gold?
43 Not crazy

Down

1 Functioned as
2 Lawyer's org.
3 Gun, as the engine
4 Piece of metal shot into paper
5 Fires
6 Henry Clay, for one
7 Breathe
8 Fruit often dried
9 Caribbean, e.g.
13 Drops off
15 "Beat it!"
16 Egypt's capital
17 Gas in air
19 One way to saute: 2 wds.
20 Opening part
21 Village leader
27 Lawyer ___ Belli
28 "Relax, and that's an order!": 2 wds.
29 "Peter Pan" dog
30 Old calculator
34 Some rolls of the dice
35 "Green Eggs and ___"
36 "Exodus" role
37 America
38 Big ___ (London attraction)
39 "We ___ the World"

48

Across

1 Butcher shop cuts
6 Flat, simple boats
11 Country whose capital is New Delhi
12 Hello, in Honolulu
13 Obeys an eight-sided traffic sign
14 "___ Christmas!"
15 Outlaw
16 Tree gunk
18 Refrigerator insignias
19 Make a choice
20 Driver's licenses and such
21 Devour
22 "You're getting on my ___!"
24 Palindromic German man's name
25 Ending for musket or mountain
26 Paris's country: abbr.
27 Chess or checkers
29 Hamster's cousin
32 New York or Tennessee, on a Monopoly board: abbr.
33 Football kicking tool
34 Yoko ___
35 Band that broke up in 2011
36 Every last bit
37 Alien's spaceship
38 Where e-mail lands
40 The devil
42 Elvis Presley hit "Blue ___ Shoes"
43 Girl who falls down a rabbit hole en route to Wonderland
44 Groups of cows
45 Little song

Down

1 Portugal's capital
2 Caught by a videocamera: 2 wds.
3 "The details are hazy on that...": 3 wds.
4 Quick shot of brandy
5 More likely to talk back
6 Ways onto (or off) the highway
7 Beer variety
8 "No problem at all": 3 wds.
9 Fighting words
10 Tells: 2 wds.
17 TV show interruptions
23 Letter that's a symbol of victory
24 Hockey great Bobby
26 Be down in the dumps: 2 wds.
27 Showy
28 Full version of 32-across
29 Hairstyling goop
30 "Actually...": 2 wds.
31 "___ Toons" (cartoon series)
33 April 15th payments
39 Like 1, 3 or 13
41 Boxer in "The Rumble in the Jungle"

49

Across

1 Catholic service
5 Common exercise
11 Soon, to a poet
12 Heir's concern
13 Data
14 President, say
15 After expenses
16 Lion's share
17 Movie actors with no lines
19 ___ butter
23 Sit in on, as a class
25 Actress Gardner
26 Aspect
28 TV host with a role in "The Color Purple"
30 Narcissist's problem
31 Took part in a democracy
33 ___ Virginia
35 Writing utensil
38 "Beware the ___ of March"
40 Man's name that reverses to another man's name
41 Swindler: 2 wds.
44 Promising words
45 Gentle wind
46 Department store section
47 Grow irate: 2 wds.
48 Approximately: 2 wds.

Down

1 Acadia National Park's state
2 Take by force, as a territory
3 Mexican entree: 2 wds.
4 ___-Caps
5 First female House Speaker
6 Functions
7 Sports figures
8 Owned
9 Western tribe for whom a U.S. state is named
10 Apiece
16 Fox comedy show
18 Wish you could take back
20 Alcoholic beverage: 2 wds.
21 ___ Marie Saint
22 "I see!"
24 Carries
26 Not many
27 Number of years
29 Fountain or ink
32 Began
34 It rings in the kitchen
36 "Reversal of Fortune" star Jeremy
37 Catch with a rope
39 Leave stunned
41 ABC rival
42 Miner's find
43 French word in wedding announcements
44 "What I think," when texting

Across

1 Submachine gun
4 Cartoon "devil"
7 Golf course score
8 ___ code (5- or 9-digit number)
11 Bird: prefix
12 One of four in a deck
13 ___ Lanka
14 Before ninth
16 Camp water
17 Get older
18 From ___ (completely): 3 wds.
20 Charon's river
21 Stirred up
24 Little dog, for short
25 "Ciao!"
26 "___ Maria"
27 Mt. ___ (where Noah landed)
29 Worker's weekend shout
30 "Lovely" Beatles girl
31 "2001" computer
32 Canine cry
34 "Absolutely!": 2 wds.
37 "___ you there?"
38 100 percent
39 Olive ___ (Popeye's love)
40 Lock opener
41 Ground cover
42 ___ center
43 Apr. addressee

Down

1 ___ the crack of dawn: 2 wds.
2 12th president: 2 wds.
3 Anger
4 ___ Bo (exercise system)
5 Flying ace
6 Son of reggae star Bob, who sang "Tomorrow People": 2 wds.
8 Hungarian who slapped a cop in L.A.: 3 wds.
9 Aggravate
10 Apple or cherry
15 Bewitch
16 Singer Rawls
19 One of five on a foot
20 Day ___ (place for a pedicure)
22 Curse: 2 wds.
23 Dict. entry
25 Louisville Slugger, e.g.
28 Tear
29 Thanksgiving, e.g.: abbr.
32 Talk and talk
33 Before
35 Former GM car
36 Special attention, for short
38 "___ Lay Me Down": 2 wds.

Across

1 Breakfast food
4 Small amount
7 Neither fish ___ fowl
8 Singer Grant or novelist Tan
9 Grocery store holder
12 Make neat: 2 wds.
14 Ending for Japan or Surinam
15 Way, way off
16 U-Haul rival
18 Allots, with "out"
20 Soul great Redding
21 Not post-
22 Baseball announcer's phrase when a home run is hit: 2 wds.
25 Hole in your car
27 Fun on a lake: 2 wds.
29 Santa ___, Calif.
32 Advil target
33 More competent
35 Arsenic, e.g.
38 Border
39 Little pest
40 Nature's "opponent"
42 Discouraging words
43 Hawaiian instrument, for short
44 Ruin
45 Prepared
46 Untrustworthy

Down

1 Set up tents, e.g.
2 Jack Nicklaus or Tiger Woods
3 Top tunes for a band: 2 wds.
4 Blackout
5 "It's my turn!": 2 wds.
6 Sort
9 Where 3-down often appear: 3 wds.
10 Invite to the house: 2 wds.
11 "Silly" birds
13 "___ we having fun yet?"
17 Canceled: 2 wds.
19 Make, as a putt
23 The first "T" of TNT
24 Sammy of baseball fame
26 Functions
27 Tokyo's country
28 ___ Lodge (motel chain)
30 Nerve-related
31 Blood route
34 Baseball equipment
36 Burden
37 Put in the microwave
41 Not working any longer: abbr.

52

Across

1 Circus performers

7 Once around the track

10 Lasso

11 Woman of the house

12 Marcos with a lot of shoes

13 Sign of the future

14 "The Da Vinci Code" author: 2 wds.

16 Gush (forth)

19 Actor Mineo of "Rebel Without a Cause"

20 Scientist Marie or Pierre

22 Badge with a photo on it, for short: 2 wds.

26 Walk ___ in someone else's shoes: 2 wds.

27 It's tougher than string

28 Time away from work, for short: 3 wds.

29 ___ & Garfunkel

30 Fake hair

32 Fender-bender result

33 One of five "Great" bodies of water: 2 wds.

37 Allies' foes, in WWII

38 "___ and upward!"

42 40-day period

43 Music system

44 Throw in at no extra cost

45 "Amen!": 3 wds.

Down

1 151, in Roman numerals

2 On the ___ (fleeing the police)

3 Valuable mineral deposit

4 1999 Will Smith/Kevin Kline movie: 3 wds.

5 Zippo

6 Musial and Laurel

7 Big car for a celeb

8 Several: 2 wds.

9 Sean of "Mystic River"

11 Internet: 3 wds.

15 Puts worms on a hook, e.g.

16 Damage permanently

17 Mountain lion

18 "___ Brockovich"

21 Creepy

23 Magazine that chooses a Person of the Year

24 With an unknown author: abbr.

25 Fellow

31 Disgusting

33 Random chorus syllables

34 Fired, in slang

35 Gentle

36 "___ the Groove" (Madonna hit)

39 "Where ___ we?"

40 Outdoor sports chain

41 Period

53

Across

1 Sticker on a windshield
6 Clearly surprised
11 Clear, as a disk
12 Far from fresh
13 Be off-target: 3 wds.
15 Chemical suffix
16 Long-term spy
17 Valuable stone
18 Couch
22 Groups of words
26 Brooks of "The Producers"
27 TV doctor
28 "Don't get any funny ___!"
30 "___ say!"
31 Corrode: 2 wds.
33 Onion's cousin
35 Carpet
36 Swedish retailer
38 Dove's sound
41 Country singer from Canada: 2 wds.
45 Groups of cattle
46 Symbol of the US
47 Live
48 Prom wear

Down

1 Moore of "G.I. Jane"
2 Andrews or Brockovich
3 Beer amount
4 Fool
5 "Hmmmm...": 3 wds.
6 Cain's brother
7 Chess and checkers
8 Santa ___ Winds
9 Golf score
10 Animal found in Finland
14 "Where the heart is"
17 Neon or argon

19 Sign of the future
20 Accomplishment
21 "Not to mention ..."
22 TV's Dr. ___
23 One of 18 on a golf course
24 Be a monarch
25 Placed
29 Archaeological site
32 Part of town
34 Varieties
37 Star___ (tuna brand)
38 Hamster's home
39 Sesame and olive
40 Mind ___ manners
41 That woman
42 Put a spell on
43 "Entourage" role
44 Armed conflict

Across

1 Does one's fly
5 Canada's capital
11 McGregor of "Trainspotting"
12 Van Gogh painting of flowers
13 Former "Saturday Night Live" player Dunn
14 Nooks
15 Candy bar in a red wrapper: 2 wds.
17 iPhone company
19 Little bits
22 Mexican restaurant condiment
23 F. ___ Fitzgerald
25 Glass of NPR
26 "That's relaxing!"
27 Tree found in people's houses
30 North Dakota city that's also a movie
32 Video game brand name
33 Tell the waiter what you want
34 President Jackson
36 Items for a meeting
39 California valley known for its wine
42 On ___ knee (proposing marriage, perhaps)
43 Baldwin of "30 Rock"
44 Earns after expenses
45 Campfire entertainment

Down

1 Buddhist sect
2 "Sands of ___ Jima"
3 Second-most expensive property in Monopoly: 2 wds.
4 French dish some find icky
5 Pig's sound
6 Groups of three
7 "The 1 1/2 calorie breath mint"
8 Cigar detritus
9 Tiny
10 Rude person
16 Darjeeling or oolong
17 "Yeah, I'm so sure!": 2 wds.
18 The Eiffel Tower's city
20 Most expensive property in Monopoly
21 Part of a theater
24 Norse god played by Chris Hemsworth in a 2011 movie
28 African nation once run by Idi Amin
29 Machine that makes wood smooth
30 In favor of
31 Stadiums
35 Pops
36 "Dancing with the Stars" network
37 Alternative to shaving cream
38 Compass dir.
40 Architect I.M. ___
41 Pretend

Across

1 Pub orders
6 Weapons
10 Fit for a king
11 Unlike the kiddie pool
12 Baby's garment
14 Roy's wife
15 Finishes up
16 Without walls
17 Send a message to
19 Dusk
21 One of Frank's exes
22 Hail Mary, e.g.
23 Nice stone
24 Affirmative vote
25 Church bench
28 Snack for an aardvark
29 Mining metal
30 Respectful greeting
33 Didn't dillydally
34 Coagulate
35 Former center O'Neal, casually
37 "Portnoy's Complaint" author Philip
38 Professor's guarantee
41 "Do ___ others as..."
42 Noun-forming suffix
43 Grizzly, e.g.
44 Naps

Down

1 Sib for sis
2 Director ___ Howard
3 An optometrist administers it: 2 wds.
4 Failed to be
5 Went down in a hurry
6 Extras
7 Brings in
8 Brouhaha
9 Exhausted
13 A teacher administers it: 2 wds.
17 Make "it," on the playground
18 Night before
20 Finds a niche for
22 Breathe hard
25 A teacher administers it: 2 wds.
26 Prior to
27 Join in holy matrimony
28 Name on a book's spine
30 Wash thoroughly
31 "Home ___"
32 "Whole ___ Shakin' Goin' On"
33 ___ Domingo (capital of the Dominican Republic)
36 Principal
39 Salmon ___ (sushi bar stuff)
40 Navy rank: abbr.

Across

1 50% there
8 Tree whose wood is used to make baseball bats
11 The U.S.
12 Cow's sound
13 Gather, as a ground ball: 2 wds.
14 Play on words
15 "___ the ramparts..."
16 In addition
17 City on the sea or a river
20 Show up
22 Ice skating maneuver
23 Little bit of a drink
24 Hot chocolate
26 Drink holder
30 Ancient
32 Actor Estrada of "CHiPs"
33 Not that complicated
36 "Return of the ___" ("Star Wars" sequel)
37 ___ Spunkmeyer cookies
38 Org. including the Knicks, Lakers, Bulls, etc.
40 "Angels & Demons" author ___ Brown
41 Guacamole ingredient
45 Pale ___ (kind of beer)
46 Becomes more alert, as from coffee: 2 wds.
47 Part of DOS
48 Locks of hair

Down

1 Is in possession of
2 Cable channel that shows old films
3 Only three-letter zodiac sign
4 Circular kids' cereal: 2 wds.
5 Clean, as a windshield
6 Popular Hondas
7 Talk non-stop
8 Sufficient
9 "The March King" John Philip ___
10 Sing the praises of
16 Circular kids' cereal: 2 wds.
17 ___-Man (1980s video game)
18 Palindromic cookware company
19 Word before room or center
21 Animal that makes bacon
25 Every bit
27 "___ you kidding?"
28 Old school comedian ___ Caesar
29 Go down the mountain
31 Colorado's biggest city
33 Pops
34 Country that completely surrounds Vatican City
35 Where people find gold
39 Uninteresting person
41 Fitting
42 Jerk
43 Word on bills
44 Photo-___ (politician's events)

Across

1 Actor O'Shea
5 Late singer Michael's nickname
10 Hardly any: 2 wds.
11 Additional
12 Pleasant, imaginary route: 2 wds.
14 The States
15 Wedding figure: 2 wds.
20 Cup
24 Motif
25 R-rated, maybe
26 Give off, as light
27 Words of agreement in church
29 Garden hassles
30 Eyelash stuff
32 Arnold Schwarzenegger lifts them
37 Pleasant, imaginary route: 2 wds.
40 Not sour
41 Two-color cookie
42 Jury members
43 Stinging insect

Down

1 Papa's mate
2 Thing
3 Flimsy, as an excuse
4 Aroma
5 "Ulysses" novelist James ___
6 "Finally!": 2 wds.
7 When doubled, a dance
8 Barbie's guy
9 Iron ___
13 Barbecue entree
16 Quaker's "you"
17 Enthusiastic volunteer's shout: 2 wds.
18 During
19 Brings home
20 Less than an ounce
21 Dalai ___
22 Air force heroes
23 Harmony
28 Mark Twain's Tom
29 "Hold it!"
31 Breaks
33 Cultivate
34 Greek goddess
35 Pegs carried by caddies
36 "Cut it out!"
37 Clairvoyance, e.g.
38 Leave in wonder
39 "Get it?"

58

Across

1 "That's really funny!"
5 Mother ___ (noted humanitarian)
11 Opposite of good
12 Finally finish: 2 wds.
13 Fixes, like an election
14 Complete
15 ___ Wednesday
16 "Aladdin" prince
17 109, in Roman numerals
18 Fidgety person's problem
21 Immediately: 2 wds.
23 See 25-down
27 Golf great Tiger
28 Snippy, as remarks
29 Half of Mork's sign-off,
   on "Mork & Mindy"
30 Bested
31 1980s video game with a little
   yellow guy eating dots
33 Hesitant syllables
36 "Alice" waitress
37 "May ___ excused?": 2 wds.
40 Mr. ___ Head (kid's toy)
42 A long, long time
43 "Hold on!": 2 wds.
44 Fellow
45 New Jersey city
46 Shock

Down

1 Zeus's wife and sister
2 Rival rent-a-car company of
   Dollar and Enterprise
3 Classic Gary Cooper western: 2 wds.
4 Green and Franken
5 With 30-down, another term for
   the two times in this puzzle
6 Bert's puppet pal
7 Animal that carries the plague
8 ___ fail (big blunder)
9 Tom and Katie's kid
10 Peak point
16 Semicircles
19 Finish: 2 wds.
20 Christmas guy
21 Wheat covering
22 Come ___ standstill: 2 wds.
24 When the day begins
25 With 23-across, former dictator of Uganda
26 Mr. Flanders, on "The Simpsons"
28 Japanese wrestling
30 See 5-down
32 Not before
33 "Once ___ a time..."
34 Sharpen
35 Hungarian goulash, e.g.
38 Male companion
39 Sports channel
41 Solid ___ rock: 2 wds.
42 Summertime coolers, for short

59

Across

1 Fearless

5 Cash or gold coins, e.g.

10 "I had no ___!"

11 Food in a "cook-off"

12 "Some Like It Hot" actor: 2 wds.

14 Operation with a pencil

15 Clint Eastwood TV show

20 Search for water

24 Satan

25 Opera tune

26 General or corporal

27 "___ in the Night" (Fleetwood Mac album)

29 Numbers

30 One way to cook pasta: 2 wds.

32 Puget Sound city

37 Hot dog brand: 2 wds.

40 Camelot, to Arthur

41 Go a few rounds

42 Hotel posting

43 Some male dolls

Down

1 Quick meal

2 Aroma

3 Olin of "Chocolat"

4 Quite a while

5 Integra automaker

6 Sharp, as a businessman

7 Be in session

8 Inventor ___ Whitney

9 "___ the season ..."

13 Fix

16 "My ___!"

17 "Terrible" czar

18 Little dent

19 Fraternal organization

20 Pieces of info

21 Spoken

22 Leaf-scattering force

23 Popular herb

28 Discounted: 2 wds.

29 Baseball feature

31 "___ of Endearment"

33 Job at hand

34 Sort

35 Slender

36 Blows it

37 Bobby of Boston Bruins fame

38 Baltic or Black

39 Pet with whiskers

Across

1 Annoyingly self-confident
5 Military overthrow
9 Places to live
11 Had possession of
13 Russian unit of currency
14 Pitching great Martinez
15 He beat Frazier in "The Thrilla in Manila"
16 Sales agent, for short
18 Flightless bird from Down Under
19 Zero, in soccer scores
20 Sis's sibling
21 Fix, as an election
22 Make a sweater, maybe
24 Votes into office
26 Third-largest city in the U.S.
28 Show off, as wealth
30 Shape of the president's office
33 "You've got mail" company
34 Traffic lane you need passengers to use
36 Actress ___ Marie Saint
37 Director Jean-___ Godard
38 Semicircle
39 Tombstone letters
40 They're too good for you
42 Summary
44 Everglades bird
45 Killed, in the Bible
46 Border
47 Persuasive piece in the newspaper, for short

Down

1 Got smaller
2 "___ Rouge!" (2001 Nicole Kidman movie)
3 Source of a fetus's food: 2 wds.
4 Shaving option
5 "The Godfather" director
6 Have debts
7 Agent with an assumed name: 2 wds.
8 Allow
10 Belgrade resident
12 Flutie and Llewellyn
17 ___ Set (kid's building toy)
23 Day after Wed.
25 Self-importance
27 Too quickly: 2 wds.
28 Not true
29 One of the rooms in the board game Clue
31 Fly
32 Passed on the track
35 Old-school movie players
41 Ask for alms
43 Comedian Philips

61

Across

1 Stylish
5 Capital of France
10 Zeus's wife
11 ___ in (overflowing with)
12 1992 Edward James Olmos movie: 2 wds.
14 Completed
15 One way to fall in love
18 Legislate
23 Individual
24 "Hey there!"
25 What parents may "put up" with their kids: 2 wds.
28 Detroit baseball team
29 "Do the Right Thing" director
30 Therefore
31 Salad green
33 Train's sound
35 Mississippi music: 2 wds.
41 Wedding
42 Biblical birthright seller
43 Brewskis
44 Belgrade native

Down

1 When doubled, a dance
2 ___ and haw (stall)
3 Anger
4 Christmas ___
5 Rate
6 Not in the dark about: 2 wds.
7 Took off quickly
8 School of thought
9 "___-Devil" (Meryl Streep movie)
13 Climbing plant
15 Tooth's home
16 "Tomorrow" musical
17 Condescend
19 Swed. neighbor
20 "Fixing ___" (Beatles song): 2 wds.
21 Ice cream holders
22 Carries
24 Running backs gain them: abbr.
26 P.I., in old slang
27 ___ Set (kid's toy)
31 Corn holder
32 Cameos, e.g.
34 ___ Christian Andersen
35 Do a voice-over
36 One way to go: abbr.
37 Deception
38 "It's no ___!"
39 Swimmer's ___
40 Big sandwich

Across

1 Pretended (as though)
6 Teens who wear black makeup, e.g.
11 What a plane or ship carries
12 Not urban
13 Friend, in Mexico
14 Cheri formerly of "Saturday Night Live"
15 Word before room or center
16 "Tic-tac-toe, three in a ___"
18 iPhone program
19 Reindeer's relative
20 Newsman Rather
21 Spinning kid's toy
22 Walk off the job
24 Chunk of ice floating in the sea
25 Reason
27 Daily ___ (the same old thing at work)
28 Section
29 Be a chef
30 Reading and Short Line, in Monopoly: abbr.
31 In addition
32 Clairvoyant's ability, supposedly
35 Back muscle, for short
36 Unusual
37 Narcotics watchdog: abbr.
38 Vegetable that makes you cry
40 Having debts
42 Extreme suffering
43 Like the gods Thor and Odin
44 Car imperfections
45 Try to win, as a contest

Down

1 Without ___ in the world: 2 wds.
2 Desert animal with humps
3 "Who's buried in Grant's tomb?" for example: 2 wds.
4 Omelet ingredient
5 Critical, as a situation: 3 wds.
6 No longer a child
7 Not safe, in baseball
8 Abuse: 3 wds.
9 Whale hunter's weapon
10 Succumbed to a wet floor
17 Cracklin' ___ Bran (Kellogg's cereal)
23 Country north of Mex.
24 To and ___
25 Amount that can fit in a Ford, say
26 Put in order
27 "That was a funny joke!": 2 wds.
29 Popular fish for fish 'n' chips
31 Awards for Broadway actors
33 Hearing, taste or touch
34 Beeper
39 Canadian province: abbr.
41 Took first place

Across

1 Delay
4 Mel of baseball fame
7 "___ Maria"
8 Bank offering
9 In good shape
12 Scary snake
14 Solid ___ rock: 2 wds.
15 Otherwise
16 "Welcome Back, Kotter" star
18 Was sweet (on)
20 Oil of ___
21 Lennon's lady
22 "West Side Story" song
25 Exact revenge: 2 wds.
27 Like some country roads
29 "Scram!"
32 Miles per hour, e.g.
33 Prepared
35 Stick (to)
38 Each
39 Even score
40 Unthankful person
42 "To ___ is human ..."
43 Coloring fluid
44 "Winnie-the-Pooh" baby
45 "Casablanca" pianist
46 2,000 lb.

Down

1 Texas city on the Rio Grande
2 Toyota model
3 Meets up: 2 wds.
4 Black gold
5 Arduous journey
6 "Gone With the Wind" plantation
9 Not doing well emotionally: 2 wds.
10 Bartender on "The Love Boat"
11 Roberts of "That '70s Show"
13 Golf peg
17 Small hole
19 Computer info
23 Guys
24 "... lived happily ___ after"
26 Robert ___: 2 wds.
27 Give a speech
28 Low point
30 "Same here!": 3 wds.
31 Use, as a computer: 2 wds.
34 Listening organ
36 Clears
37 Irish singing great
41 Beauty

Across

1 Arms and legs
6 "Beat it!"
11 Honda brand
12 Texas food
13 Have a temper tantrum, maybe: 2 wds.
15 Holed up
16 Prior to
17 Go-___ (1980s band)
18 "___ you serious?"
19 Faint
20 Anger
21 "Beetle Bailey" creator Walker
23 Hit with a baseball
25 Waken from slumber
27 Hidden
30 Janitor's tools
34 Valuable mineral
35 "Dig in!"
37 By way of
38 High card
39 ___ Lanka
40 Christmas present wrapper, maybe
41 XXXIII
44 Kind of dye
45 Doozies
46 ___ Allan Poe
47 Pharaoh's land

Down

1 English poet John
2 Suzuki of baseball
3 "___ on the Orient Express"
4 "My man!"
5 Did a lumberjack's job
6 Plans
7 Greek letter
8 Try to answer on "Jeopardy!": 2 wds.
9 Former vice president: 2 wds.
10 Didn't hit
14 Small river, often
22 Three: It.
24 Store convenience, for short
26 Lousy, like a movie
27 Hate
28 Tried to appear larger, as a cat
29 ___ up (preparing to drive a golf ball)
31 Too
32 Get larger, as a workload: 2 wds.
33 Least risky
36 Deed
42 Biology abbr.
43 Embrace

65

Across

1 Where Adam and Eve were
5 Bobby Fischer's game
10 Block for kids
11 Part of a TV feed
12 Young wedding participant: 2 wds.
14 Plus
15 Speaks with the higher power
18 October birthstone
22 Chair part
23 Garden-variety
26 Mobile's state: abbr.
27 Sweet potato cousin
28 Novelist Levin
29 "Peace," in yoga class
31 Cabernet, for one
32 Board member, for short
33 Valentine's Day dozen
35 Difficult
38 Young wedding participant: 2 wds.
43 Love to pieces
44 Wander far and wide
45 Authority
46 Rival of NYSE

Down

1 One of Santa's little helpers
2 Md. neighbor
3 "I" problem?
4 "Forget it!": 2 wds.
5 Cadillacs and Chevrolets
6 Bigger than big
7 Newspaper worker
8 Respectful title
9 The sun
13 Some magazine pieces
15 Boeing 747, e.g.
16 "Calm down!"
17 "It's only ___!": 2 wds.
19 Couples
20 See eye to eye
21 Sporting advantages
24 Big wine holder
25 Arise
30 TV ad phrase: 2 wds.
34 "Gone With the Wind" last name
36 Shrek, e.g.
37 Coolest of the cool
38 Urban music style
39 Altar words: 2 wds.
40 CD-___
41 "The Three Faces of ___"
42 Man's name that means "king" in Latin

66

Across

1 Do the laundry
5 Golfer's bag carrier
11 Money before a poker hand
12 Get there
13 Celebrity
14 Person who loves books
15 Brad of "Thelma & Louise"
16 Apple computer
17 Poet ___ Pound
19 Doing: 2 wds.
23 One of Santa's Little Helpers
25 Clarify in detail
27 Soccer scores
29 More than on time
30 Pilot
32 ___-Mex cuisine
33 Actress Laura of "Rambling Rose"
34 "___ Tuesday" (Rolling Stones hit)
36 Cow's food
38 In the distance
41 Money for putting a song on the radio
44 ___ Parks of the civil rights movement
45 Graduates from a school
46 Witty words
47 Put down
48 Board in a bed

Down

1 Stinging insect
2 Against: pref.
3 Fun place to go on rides and eat food: 2 wds.
4 Rival of Avis, Enterprise and Budget
5 Company that sells used autos
6 Section
7 Famous vampire
8 Performed
9 "___ been thinking about you!"
10 Suffix with mountain or musket
18 Relax
20 Spilling a beer, for example: 2 wds.
21 Scrabble piece
22 Dark mineral
23 "My goodness!"
24 Valentine's Day celebrates it
26 South American country whose capital is Lima
28 Cosmetics brand
31 Certify, as a priest
35 Root beer brand
37 Arm bone
39 Largest of the continents
40 At full attention
41 Tablet
42 Samuel Adams Summer ___
43 "That tastes good!"

Across

1 ___ on the back
4 "Polythene ___" (Beatles song)
7 Stomach muscles
10 Paul Newman role
11 Vain person's issue
12 Montana or Biden
13 "The Little Drummer Boy" syllable
14 ATM code
15 Museum pieces
16 "Act your ___!"
17 Finds out new things
19 Deborah's "The King and I" co-star
20 Attention-getting shouts
21 Similar
23 "Kapow!"
25 Paquin or Chlumsky
26 Verve
28 Thin fish
29 Permitted
31 Coup d'___
33 "What ___ doing?": 2 wds.
34 Waves, perhaps: 2 wds.
37 Deeply philosophical
38 Fuss
39 Enjoy a Winter Olympics sport
41 "Lord, is ___?": 2 wds.
42 Word before gift or reflex
43 Chest muscle, for short
44 Photographer Goldin
45 Doc bloc
46 "Is it ___ wonder?"
47 Food from a hen

Down

1 Tropical fruit
2 Salad vegetable
3 Facebook format
4 Vigor
5 Catlike
6 Tourist's wear: 2 wds.
7 Almost closed, like a door
8 "___ in the USA" (Springsteen album)
9 Adjusts, as a clock
18 Make ___ (be a good vendor): 2 wds.
20 Place to get a massage: 2 wds.
22 Bending pair
24 What each of the three long entries in this puzzle begins with
27 Convention ID
30 Cloud with a silver ___
32 Clay of "American Idol" fame
34 Epic story
35 Sandler of "Big Daddy"
36 Exercise discipline with lots of stretching
40 Cold

Across

1 ___ talk (encouraging words)
4 The Colonel's restaurant
7 Software program, briefly
10 Mine stuff
11 Rounded shape
13 She won the U.S. Open in 1979 and 1981: 2 wds.
15 Common flower
16 Possesses, in the Bible
19 Quickly
23 Role for Paul
24 Try it out: 3 wds.
27 "Bloom County" character: 2 wds.
29 Metal named for an animal: 2 wds.
30 Compete
31 Gets a look at
32 Cravings
33 "Who's there?" reply: 2 wds.
37 1980s show about a detective from Texas: 2 wds.
43 Pencil parts
44 Amaze
45 Fly catcher
46 Came into contact with
47 Drops in the morning meadow

Down

1 Daisy holder
2 Go wrong
3 Little green vegetable
4 Lock openers
5 Apartment
6 Game with Colonel Mustard
7 Appropriate
8 Greek consonant
9 Writing instrument
12 Tel Aviv's nation
14 Meowing pet
16 Lock parts

17 Bandleader Shaw
18 Military tactic
20 Medical application
21 "Encore!"
22 Mugs for the camera
24 Not his
25 "Without further ___..."
26 Delivery vehicle
28 Drops in on
32 "Absolutely!"
34 Not us
35 Achy
36 Has to
37 Kitty's sound
38 "You ___ so right!"
39 Bill at a bar
40 Tiny amount
41 Have to repay
42 "What's ___?"

Across

1 Cry like a baby
5 "Two Women" Oscar-winner Sophia
10 Ashtabula's lake
11 "Hearts ___"
12 President after Richard Nixon: 2 wds.
14 "___ moment, please"
15 Affirmative vote
16 Electric shooter
18 Challenger
23 Lunch holder, maybe
25 Dash
26 What both 12-across and 41-across have brands of in their names
30 Body covering
31 AMA members
32 Nairobi's country
34 Scarlett of "Gone With the Wind"
38 Animal house
40 Herbert of the "Pink Panther" movies
41 Comic actor known for portraying 12-across: 2 wds.
45 Certain bellybutton
46 Black cat, maybe
47 Bargains
48 Chuck

Down

1 Brought forth
2 "Gladiator" setting
3 Sends money, perhaps
4 Actress Salonga or Thompson
5 Gentleman's counterpart
6 Bid
7 2016 Olympics city
8 Make a mistake
9 Actor Beatty
13 Former NFL player in Calif.
17 Black
19 Like someone from Dublin
20 Kilmer of "The Doors"
21 Part of a royal flush
22 Guitar great ___ Paul
24 George Burns role
26 "Don't ___!"
27 Don Ho instrument
28 Metallic element
29 Untamed horse
33 Tylenol alternative
35 "Remember the ___!"
36 "The Subject Was ___"
37 Church words
39 Peepers
41 Atlantic fish
42 Color
43 In-flight info
44 Burning

70

Across

1 Medieval weapon, or modern spray weapon
5 Different
10 Milky gemstones
12 "Hand over the money!": 2 wds.
13 "Be quiet!": 2 wds.
14 Kick out
15 Concealed
16 Sought office
18 Period of time
19 "Nevertheless..."
21 Will Smith musical genre
22 Moan and groan
24 Pacino and Capone
25 ___ cards (spooky deck)
27 First five of 26
29 Chicken ___ king: 2 wds.
30 Walk proudly
32 Little doggy
33 Part of a baseball game
36 Mischief maker
37 Big primate
38 "C'est la ___!"
39 Shaquille or Tatum
41 Piece of pizza
43 Some teachers grade on one
44 Lugs (around)
45 Obnoxious people
46 Funeral fire

Down

1 Kind of coffee
2 Be ___ in the neck: 2 wds.
3 You see a lot of them on November 1st: 2 wds.
4 Quarterback Manning
5 Ready for business
6 Money for the government
7 Behavior some kids may exhibit on November 1st
8 The ___ City (capital of the Land of Oz)
9 Fall back, as into a bad pattern of behavior
11 Narrow waterways
17 "The Fountainhead" novelist Rand
20 "Which person?"
23 Honest and sincere
25 Kind of pudding
26 Male graduate
28 Part of a hamburger
31 Waiter's money
34 More pleasant
35 Silly birds
37 Ginger ___ (some soft drinks)
40 Wide road: abbr.
42 Cut (off)

Across

1 Publicity, casually
4 "Raiders of the Lost ___"
7 Six-pack muscles
10 Got outta Dodge
11 ___ and Jerry's (ice cream brand)
12 ___ Tuesday (Mardi Gras)
13 Neighbor of Canada
15 Time of the past
16 "Dig in!"
17 Authority
19 Cheat, in a way
21 "Don't ___!"
22 Palindromic woman's name
23 Hershey's candy bar
27 Spearheaded
28 "ER" network
29 Scottish "no"
30 Saw wrongly
32 Believer's suffix
33 DVD player's predecessor
34 Frosts, as a cake
35 Secret booze container
38 Strong tree
39 Calif. airport
40 Breakfast food
44 Good club?
45 Prefix with lateral
46 Baseball card stat
47 Take down the aisle
48 Athletes Cobb and Warner
49 Gelled

Down

1 Lyricist Gershwin
2 "China Beach" setting
3 Volleyball player's equipment
4 Not much: 2 wds.
5 ___ center
6 Backpack
7 Not many: 2 wds.
8 Empty, like a cupboard
9 Part of a constellation
14 Sunbeam
18 Plains city, for short
19 Placid
20 "The ___ Love": 2 wds.
21 Ann ___, Mich.
23 Flatten: 2 wds.
24 Fancy pants
25 Lessen
26 "___ go!"
31 Flat-screens, e.g.
34 "How Dry ___": 2 wds.
35 Blemish
36 Shoestring
37 Fired
38 Elevator name
41 "___ Which Way But Loose"
42 Honest prez
43 Ignited

Across

1 Aria, e.g.
5 Was just kidding around
11 "___ Brockovich"
12 Strike caller
13 Fishing equipment
14 Put in order
15 "The lady ___ protest too much"
16 Finale
17 Kinks hit
19 Site for bidders
23 Look through a peephole: 2 wds.
26 Beer variety
27 Fencing swords
28 Fit for a queen
30 Second-century date
31 Make a misstep
33 Old Chrysler
35 "Can ___ serious for a moment?": 2 wds.
36 "It's no ___!"
38 Song and dance, e.g.
41 "Goodness!": 2 wds.
44 Increase, with "up"
45 Two dots over a vowel, in German
46 Former NYC stadium
47 Courtroom plea
48 Thanksgiving dish

Down

1 E-mail, e.g.
2 Cookie often twisted
3 "The Loco-Motion" singer: 2 wds.
4 Off the cruise ship for a while: 2 wds.
5 Alaska's capital
6 Sign of the future
7 Not a heart, club or diamond
8 Bestseller
9 Before
10 Room where work gets done
18 Red ink amount
20 Nickname for a WWI weapon: 2 wds.
21 "Come on, be ___!": 2 wds.
22 Ivy League school
23 Eat like a bird
24 Long saga
25 Not false
29 Government outpost
32 Cartoon bird
34 Of the country
37 Blue books?
39 Abound
40 Fitness centers
41 Used a shovel
42 Australian runner
43 Role for Will Smith

Across

1 Parking ___
4 Underwater warship
7 Bar for beers
10 "I ___ Man of Constant Sorrow": 2 wds.
11 ___ Today (colorful newspaper)
12 Pollution-fighting branch of govt.
13 Medical procedure named for a Greek physician: 2 wds.
15 Fork over the cash
16 "Whoops!"
17 Butler of "Gone With the Wind"
19 Testifying group of experts
21 Ringo of the Beatles
23 Page in an atlas
25 Miss ___ (TV psychic)
26 Urban music genre
29 Come out on top
31 Lock opener
32 Soothing plant
34 Master Mind game piece
36 Nation of ninjas
38 Put pen to paper
42 Take it all off
44 Supercelebrity, like Oprah or Madonna
45 Letters before a criminal's alter ago
46 Small camping shelter: 2 wds.
48 Wheels
49 In favor of
50 Devoured
51 Explosives in Angry Birds
52 Up to this point
53 Neither here ___ there

Down

1 Drink, as a cat does milk: 2 wds.
2 Nebraska's largest city
3 Strike lightly, as a window pane: 2 wds.
4 Take to court
5 "Back in the ___" (Beatles song)
6 Tubs
7 Words to encourage the team: 2 wds.
8 Cornered, like a cat: 3 wds.
9 Chesapeake or Charleston
14 Not us
18 And so forth
20 "___ & Order"
22 Cowboy singer Rogers
24 Spot on a die
26 British rule in India
27 Person from Anchorage or Juneau
28 Kellogg's breakfast food
30 "What's ___?"
33 Head attachment
35 "True ___" (1969 movie remade in 2010)
37 A little cold outside
39 Arctic or Atlantic
40 The Lone Ranger's kemo sabe
41 Oversized computer key
43 100%
45 Memorize lines and hit the stage
47 Place to plant plants

Across

1 Beeped
6 Close, as a race
11 Amtrak service
12 Baseball blunder
13 Orson Welles classic: 2 wds.
15 Masthead names, briefly
16 Buddhist discipline
17 Born, in wedding announcements
18 Working together
20 Bicker
23 Full of lip
26 Amount of work
27 Drag
28 Danger
30 Red Square man
31 "Please enter!": 3 wds.
33 Chinese dictator
35 Bunk
36 Nile snake
39 Words before "Get your elbows off the table": 3 wds.
42 Blabs
43 Automaton
44 Send out a short message, maybe
45 Online call site

Down

1 Clip
2 Battery contents
3 Understands
4 QB Manning
5 Really wow
6 Court sport
7 Bother
8 Person with a III after their name
9 Sharpen
10 Elm or oak
14 Moray, e.g.
18 Video's counterpart
19 Consumed
20 Matterhorn or Mont Blanc
21 Fish eggs
22 Scary statue on top of a building
24 Go down a mountain
25 Japanese currency
29 Reappearing insect
30 Beverage bottle amounts
32 Neither's partner
33 Mr. Romney
34 Not many: 2 wds.
36 "Dear" lady with advice
37 Pig's food
38 Baseball great Rose
40 "Wonderful job!"
41 Just fine

75

Across

1 Sheltered little bays
6 Easy victories
11 Popular printing font
12 Actor Hirsch of "Into the Wild"
13 Word before Christmas or Pranksters
14 Full of too much energy
15 Food that comes in a dozen
16 Flag
17 King, to the French
18 ___-Mex cuisine
19 Before, in poems
20 Occurring every year, as an event
22 "Hey, you!"
23 Inside the womb: 2 wds.
25 "See ya!" in Rome (or Hollywood)
27 "...that saved a ___ like me" ("Amazing Grace" line)
30 Extra pds. of a basketball game
31 Container for peanut butter
32 Exist
33 Silicon ___ (high-tech part of California)
35 In the distance
36 Cuban kid ___ Gonzalez in 2000 headlines
37 Escapee on the Underground Railroad
38 Shakespeare's "___ of Athens"
39 Greek letters
40 Likely to talk back
41 Irritable

Down

1 Picture taker
2 Portland's state
3 Cigarette brand that used to sponsor tennis tournaments: 2 wds.
4 Vincent van Gogh cut one of his off
5 Sneaky
6 Real estate company with a hot air balloon as its logo
7 Country on the Arabian Peninsula
8 Famed pool player: 2 wds.
9 Toolbox tool
10 Something only a few people know
16 Road that runs around a big city, like Washington, D.C.
18 Another Greek letter
21 One, in Mexico
22 Not post-
24 Make a mistake
25 Is jealous of
26 Rome's country, to Romans
28 Necktie alternative
29 Speaking against the church's beliefs
31 Weight loss expert ___ Craig
34 Country that borders Vietnam and Thailand
35 Soothing plant
37 "Take a chair!"

76

Across

1 Biblical shepherd
5 Ali and Frazier, e.g.
11 Brazilian soccer legend
12 Outfit for baby
13 "___ on Down the Road"
14 Malicious
15 "A Is for Alibi" author: 2 wds.
17 Actress Russo
18 Break down
21 Humpback, e.g.
26 "Pumping ___"
27 "Here comes trouble!"
28 Dancer's boss?
30 Big tests
31 What ice does if you leave it out
33 Largest city in South Dakota: 2 wds.
39 Fight back against
40 Extremely tired
41 "Catch-22" author Joseph
42 Peru's capital
43 Seaport of the Ukraine
44 "Baseball Tonight" channel

Down

1 "Planet of the ___"
2 Boyfriend
3 Different
4 Oscar winner for "Shampoo": 2 wds.
5 Martin's "Laugh-In" partner
6 Soon: 3 wds.
7 Blow off steam
8 About: 2 wds.
9 Animal with a mane
10 One of 100 in D.C.
16 King: Sp.
18 Criticize, slangily
19 Victorian, for one
20 Not a pro
22 Family last name on "The Cosby Show"
23 "Bingo!"
24 "Pink Panther" films actor
25 Hesitant syllables
29 Makes laugh
30 Will Ferrell comedy about Christmas
32 Additional
33 Future flower
34 Speck in the Pacific, e.g.
35 Peanut and vegetable
36 Hawaiian necklaces
37 Light
38 "South Park" boy
39 Greek letter

Across

1 Chichen Itza builders
6 Long, long time
10 Mexican brick
11 ___ Plus (shampoo brand)
12 Baseball feat: 2 wds.
14 Otherwise
15 Art class material
18 Store with a bull's-eye logo
23 Backstabber
24 Dentist's direction
25 "I had no ___!"
27 Forest growth
28 Gross dinner sound
30 Shook hands with
31 ___ tank
33 Alluring
34 Lady ___ (pop star)
36 Track and field sport: 2 wds.
42 "Take this!"
43 Newswoman Shriver
44 All tied up
45 Expertise

Down

1 "Spy vs. Spy" magazine
2 Fuss
3 "What did ___ say?"
4 "___ Road" (Beatles album)
5 Unload, as stock
6 Enter the picture
7 Come together
8 Historian's period
9 Oinker's place
13 Guess: abbr.
15 Magician ___ Angel
16 Soup server
17 Consumed quickly: 2 wds.
19 Hoop
20 Garden statue, sometime
21 County of England
22 Cantankerous
26 Paintings, photography, etc.
29 See 9-down
32 "Silent" prez
33 Pat of "Wheel of Fortune"
35 Nice rocks
36 Word in many movie titles
37 Show off, on a Harley
38 Wrath
39 Spoon-bender Geller
40 Dot follower, in some e-mail addresses
41 Amigo

Across

1 Back of the neck
5 Insignia
11 Biblical twin
12 African nation whose capital is Lilongwe
13 Drink quickly
14 Flying high
15 MacLachlan of "Twin Peaks"
16 Backboard attachment
17 Not pro
19 Bidding site
23 "Forget about it": 2 wds.
25 Song for one
26 Iron ___
27 Sandwich order, for short
29 Awful
30 Functionalities
32 Saudi ___
34 Taboo act
35 Indiana city, or a man's name
36 Meadow
38 ___-Caribbean music
41 Grooms' mates
44 Hard punch
45 Has a good time
46 Weak, as an excuse
47 Disinclined
48 "For Your ___ Only"

Down

1 Adam's apple spot
2 Far from ruddy
3 TV celebrity chef from Savannah: 2 wds.
4 Oregon city
5 TV celebrity chef from Louisiana: 2 wds.
6 African nation
7 Charges
8 Back muscle, familiarly
9 She's a sheep
10 ___-Atlantic
18 Check
20 TV celebrity chef from New York City: 2 wds.
21 Jai ___
22 "Star Wars" role
23 It may be proper
24 About: 2 wds.
28 "La la" preceder
31 Fuse two pieces of metal
33 Fit for farming
37 Congers
39 City of the Coliseum
40 Has a mortgage
41 Undergarment
42 Holy title: abbr.
43 "___ got it!"

Across

1 Not macho at all
6 Sailing on the ocean: 2 wds.
11 Italian for "love"
12 P.F. ___'s
13 Taboo acts
14 Dull photography finish
15 Finishes up
16 Go back
17 Day: Sp.
18 "For ___ a jolly good fellow..."
19 Traffic light color
20 Hits the keyboard
22 Conception
23 Tennis great Navratilova
25 "Glee" or "Mad Men"
27 Persuades
29 Cadillac or Porsche
30 Cattle call?
31 Quick sip, as of brandy
33 Indicate that you know the answer, on a game show: 2 wds.
35 One of Columbus's ships
36 Creature from outer space
37 Pup
38 Tube-shaped pasta
39 Without color
40 Defeats by a little
41 London measurement, a bit more than a yard

Down

1 Lessened
2 "The problem is being taken care of!": 3 wds.
3 Worst time of the week, in a 1966 Mamas & Papas #1 hit: 2 wds.
4 Experts
5 "What can I do for you?"
6 High points
7 "How is ___ my problem?"
8 Best time of the week, in a 1976 Bay City Rollers #1 hit: 2 wds.
9 Main course
10 Items to be discussed at a meeting
16 Uses for support: 2 wds.
18 Billy Joel's "Tell ___ About It"
21 Cat's foot
22 One ___ million chance: 2 wds.
24 ___ Jima (WWII battle site)
25 Use a spatula, sometimes
26 Flagged down, as a taxi
28 Madonna or Lady Gaga
30 Gold and silver sources
32 Last name that sounds hurtful
34 Trait carrier
35 Sniffer
37 River blocker

Across

1 "___ Rich Pageant" (R.E.M. album)
6 About: 2 wds.
10 James Bond, for one
11 Practice boxing
12 "Golden Girls" actress: 2 wds.
14 Celebrity
15 Female lobster
16 "This ___ travesty!": 2 wds.
18 Epic tale
22 Takes willingly
26 Common container
27 Not better
28 Sharp, as a pain
30 Time of the past
31 The ___ (upper Great Plains region)
33 Audition tape
35 Each
36 Chop (off)
38 Cookie since 1912
42 Country music great: 2 wds.
45 Be the owner of
46 First Greek letter
47 Bad day for Caesar
48 Dapper

Down

1 Friendly dogs, for short
2 "___ it now!": 2 wds.
3 Greek cheese
4 Contest submissions
5 Pig's home
6 Arthur of tennis fame
7 Whirls
8 Piece of body art
9 Taconite, e.g.
13 "Come again?"
17 Went fast
19 Be next to
20 "I've ___ Secret": 2 wds.
21 Cancels
22 Blown away
23 Apple center
24 Shove (in)
25 Benefit
29 Popular Toyota
32 Datebook abbr.
34 Mediterranean food
37 Small bills
39 Totally engrossed (by)
40 Real: Ger.
41 Just fine
42 Greek letter
43 Young fella
44 Forbid

81

Across

1 "Seinfeld" uncle
4 Marvelous, like the Beatles
7 Tombstone letters
10 Christmas creature
11 Anger
12 "First..."
13 ___ sprouts
15 Attorney's field
16 Last name that sounds hurtful
17 Vulcan mind tricks
19 Mel who hit 511 home runs
20 "... happily ___ after"
21 "Hop on Pop" author
23 Had the nerve
25 Score for Tiger Woods
26 Rolls-Royce or Maserati
27 Cupid's projectile
30 Spacious
32 John Paul II, e.g.
33 Historical time
34 Jasmine and basmati
35 Fancy pool shot
38 "A rat!"
39 Overly formal
41 Highest heart
42 Control
43 ___ foo yung
44 The P in MPG
45 "Yes" indication
46 Funny Romano

Down

1 Ballet move
2 "___ Enchanted"
3 Nuts: 3 wds.
4 Choice cuts
5 Kennel sound
6 Broadcast
7 Amusement park fun: 2 wds.
8 Imagined: 3 wds.
9 Seats with kneelers
14 Aardvark food
18 Actress ___ Marie Saint
21 Health resort
22 Secret Service agent's wear
24 Arid
28 "Well done!"
29 Vegetable oil brand
30 Tell again
31 Face-to-face exam
34 Do farm work
36 Big name in computer games
37 Hip
40 One roll of the dice

82

Across

1 Singing great ___ Horne
5 1980s pop singer ___ E.
11 Innovative Apple computer
12 ___ beef and cabbage (Irish dish)
13 Lion's hair
14 Makes changes to, as the Constitution
15 Pedaled vehicle
17 Sneaky
18 Chocolate tycoon Milton
23 Action
25 Birthday dessert
26 Cylinder to suck a drink through
28 Opens (one's soul)
29 God of war
30 Brain
31 Albany's state: 2 wds.
33 More than months: abbr.
36 Fruity alternative to ice cream
38 Confusing
42 Obama 2008 campaign word
43 Take off a pickup truck
44 "Jane ___"
45 In abundance
46 "Unto us ___ is given": 2 wds.

Down

1 Arms and legs
2 Click "send"
3 Fictional female detective: 2 wds.
4 ___-deucey (backgammon variant)
5 ___ back (downsized)
6 Bart Simpson's dad
7 "Able was I ___ I saw Elba" (famous palindrome)
8 Motel
9 Quarterbacked
10 Magazines run them
16 Munch (on)
19 Look over quickly
20 Fictional male detectives, with "The": 2 wds.
21 Squeeze (out a living)
22 Not no
24 Simple
26 ___ Francisco
27 Three: It.
28 Short form of 15-across
30 Dr. Jekyll's counterpart: 2 wds.
32 Schindler of "Schindler's List"
34 Copy, for short
35 Dutch painter Jan ___
37 Perlman of "Cheers"
38 Yank
39 Genetic material
40 "___ tell you what..."
41 Make a dove's sound

Across

1 Took care of: 2 wds.
6 "___ la vista!"
11 Get ready for a marathon
12 Part of "the works"
13 Where you'll see seven dwarfs running around
15 Vietnam's capital
16 Sneaky
17 "May ___ excused?": 2 wds.
19 Biblical paradise
21 She turned people to stone
23 Kind of gemstone
27 Grads
28 Funeral song
29 "Li'l Abner" cartoonist
30 Kitchen gadgets
31 C-___ (political channel)
33 Took a chair
34 A pint, maybe
37 Antipasto piece
39 Where you'll see lots of elves running around: 2 wds.
43 Inbox contents
44 Largest organ in the body
45 John, Jane and Judy
46 Coasters

Down

1 Normal: abbr.
2 "Exodus" character
3 No longer in fine form: 2 wds.
4 Louise of "Gilligan's Island"
5 Harmony
6 Mandel of "Deal or No Deal"
7 "I'll take that as ___": 2 wds.
8 Respected gentlemen
9 Cost to drive on a road
10 Rooney or Roddick
14 Little green man in film
17 Apple product
18 Actor Lugosi
20 Pinot ___ (kind of wine)
22 Baseball referees, for short
24 Keep for the future
25 The Taj Mahal's city
26 "___ we forget"
28 Boone and Day-Lewis
30 Ashy
32 Surveys
34 "Absolutely!"
35 ___ beans
36 Dutch cheese
38 Colorado resort
40 Conk out
41 Kennedy or Williams
42 "48 ___"

Across

1 David Copperfield's field
6 Sleeps in a tent
11 Destructive hurricane of 2011
12 Scarlett's last name, in "Gone With the Wind"
13 Puff on a cigar
14 Items being sold
15 Way off in the distance
16 High tennis shot
18 Cobb of baseball fame et al.
19 Verb suffix
20 ___ whim: 2 wds.
21 Gardening tool
22 Even scores
24 Task done outside the house
26 Customers
28 Maryland or Massachusetts, once
30 Put one foot in front of the other
33 Gold: Sp.
34 Cut, as a tree
36 Flightless bird of Australia
37 ___ de Janeiro (Olympics city of 2016)
38 Ending for lime or lemon
39 Soaked
40 Biology classification
42 Separate
44 Non-reactive, like some gases
45 On the ___ of (about to)
46 Way of doing something
47 Computer key

Down

1 Person without a social group
2 Big name in men's suits
3 "Syriana" and "Ocean's Eleven" actor
4 Sign, as a contract
5 Half of the band Gnarls Barkley (anagram of ECOLE)
6 House for mooers
7 "Now I've got you!'
8 Billionaire with her own "Living" magazine
9 Attack, as a predator does: 2 wds.
10 Talked back to
17 Like two of the jacks in a deck of cards
23 ___-mo camera
25 Some football linemen: abbr.
27 Hurriedly: 2 wds.
28 Welsh ___ (cute dogs)
29 "Murder on the ___ Express"
31 Come to the forefront
32 Golf club used on the green
35 Work with a loom
41 Web address: abbr.
43 Be the author

Across

1 Country karaoke came from
6 Astound
11 Cognizant
12 Sprite flavor
13 Brawl
14 Lend ___ (assist): 2 wds.
15 Respected lady
17 Hi-___ graphics
18 "I ___ you one"
20 Baggy
22 Toy company
24 Tiny particle
27 Chips in
28 Foreword, for short
29 Advertising sign gas
30 Negates
31 Begin
33 "Help!"
34 Butter amount
36 Old Oldsmobile
38 Broadcasting: 2 wds.
40 Dutch cheese
43 Back in style
44 Bucolic
45 Sixth-grader, maybe
46 Sailing: 2 wds.

Down

1 Improvise musically
2 Leave astonished
3 South Carolina's nickname: 2 wds.
4 Length times width, for a square
5 Pokes fun at
6 San Antone landmark
7 Just OK
8 Bar drinks: 2 wds.
9 Area
10 Ultimate goals
16 "You've got mail" co.
18 Arab League member
19 Decline
21 Beach grains
23 Camping gear
25 Cookie often eaten with milk
26 What a rolling stone doesn't gather
28 Acura model
30 Website address, for short
32 Hank with 755 home runs
34 After-dinner drink
35 Again
37 Beat badly
39 Anger
41 Actor Daniel ___ Kim
42 Miss. neighbor

86

Across

1 Zines
5 Burning
10 Biol. subject
11 Travel book
12 "Young Frankenstein" woman
13 Not pen
14 Scary knives
16 Finale
17 ___ Mujeres, Mexico
18 Amiss
20 Motel
22 President before LBJ
25 Soaked
26 Go downhill
27 Portland's st.
28 Norton and Wood
29 "The Name of the Rose" author Umberto ___
30 Relatives
31 ___-bodied
33 Play on words
36 Run-down hotel
39 Sloth or panda
41 Forbidden act
42 Egyptian peninsula
43 Inflict upon: 2 wds.
44 Ringo of the Beatles
45 By the ___ of one's teeth

Down

1 Domestic
2 Late model ___ Nicole Smith
3 Funny presents: 2 wds.
4 Bucks
5 Long, long time
6 Pistol, e.g.
7 Hair critters
8 Norse god
9 Fuse
13 Bart Simpson specialty: 2 wds.
15 "Fur ___" (Beethoven work)
18 Have debts to
19 Gave grub to
21 Mythical weeper
22 It's full of funny things: 2 wds.
23 Thu. follower
24 Barbie's guy
32 Comes down to Earth
33 Quarterback's throw
34 Apartment
35 One of Columbus's ships
36 Just OK
37 Not pro-
38 Continue: 2 wds.
40 Ruin

87

Across

1 Dust remover
4 Bill
7 Automobile
10 Singer Yoko ____
11 Peyton's brother
12 "I ____ you one"
13 Cats and dogs
15 Club ____
16 Big house
17 Prefix meaning "three"
19 African antelope
20 Sought help from: 2 wds.
23 Jazz genre
25 Weary cry: 2 wds.
26 Juan Peron's wife
27 Gave chow to
28 Fiesta food
31 Go to the other side of the street
33 Bracelet site, sometimes
34 Balloon filler
35 Marry
36 "Forget it!": 2 wds.
39 Health resort
41 Make all riled up
43 Not just him
44 Brown shade
45 Howard of "Happy Days"
46 Finale
47 Keep watch on
48 Two-out plays, in baseball stats

Down

1 Be itinerant
2 Palindromic woman's name
3 Regressing: 2 wds.
4 Get weepy: 2 wds.
5 100%
6 Casual eatery
7 Volunteering: 2 wds.
8 Leave in wonder
9 Traffic light color
14 Uni-
18 "Go team!"
21 Little piggies, so to speak
22 Chances
23 ____ carotene
24 Twitter co-founder Williams
29 "Bravo!"
30 Calm
31 Dog
32 Brawl
37 Above
38 Cravings
39 That lady
40 Be the author
42 Happy

Across

1 Arthur ___ Stadium (NYC tennis locale)
5 Entered: 2 wds.
11 "Black diamonds"
12 Immediately: 2 wds.
13 Pet food brand
14 Held (over someone's head)
15 Overthrowing, like a dictator
17 Vote in favor
18 "The ___ Has Landed"
22 President Roosevelt
24 Go looking in other people's stuff
25 Baseball stat
26 "First off..."
27 Country the Nile flows through
30 Econo ___ (motel chain)
32 Army reply to a superior officer: 2 wds.
33 Frequently, in poems
34 Fuel for a Ford
38 Misbehave for attention: 2 wds.
41 Part of USA
42 Start back up again
43 Eye drop?
44 Beat-keeping movement
45 Guesses: abbr.

Down

1 "There's more than one way to skin ___": 2 wds.
2 Song for one voice
3 1970s-80s sitcom with Ron Howard: 2 wds.
4 Ran off to get married
5 San Diego's state, casually
6 Makes up (for)
7 "The Shawshank Redemption" actor Freeman
8 Last part
9 Surface for Wayne Gretzky
10 Mr. Flanders, on "The Simpsons"
16 Produce eggs
19 1970s sitcom with Esther Rolle
20 Taking up a lot of time, like a speech
21 Sword used in an Olympic event
22 High school student, usually
23 Therefore
28 Eat way more than you should: 2 wds.
29 Shock to the system
30 Lavatory, in London
31 Recently: 2 wds.
35 "___ right up!"
36 Not messy
37 Goes astray
38 Music, paintings, etc.
39 Company head, for short
40 Mao ___-tung

Across

1 To the ___ degree
4 To and ___
7 Karlsbad, for one
10 Nest egg money
11 Ending for velvet
12 ___ and cheese sandwich
13 "E.T." actor: 2 wds.
16 ___ oil
17 Ready for business
18 Make cleaner: 2 wds.
20 Big truck
23 Stands for painters
26 ___ Lodge
28 One of the Osmonds
29 Language
31 Emerald ___ (Ireland's nickname)
32 Became angry: 2 wds.
34 Since: 2 wds.
36 Mass holder
40 Longtime CNN newsman: 2 wds.
42 First name in the NFL
43 Aurora's counterpart
44 ___ Speedwagon
45 Caspian or North
46 Make a different color, like hair
47 Actress Poehler

Down

1 Small sips, as of booze
2 Oak or hickory
3 Head covers
4 Physics Nobelist Enrico ___
5 Ebb
6 Former partner of Lennon
7 Mall visitors
8 Cracker spread
9 "Absolutely!"
14 Using, as plates: 2 wds.
15 "Amen!": 3 wds.
19 Starchy food
20 TV ___
21 Green prefix
22 Country landlocked by China and Russia
24 "___ Abner"
25 "Understand?"
27 Away
30 Find work for
33 Come to mind
34 Amazes
35 Exclusive
37 Poet ___ Pound
38 Appear
39 QB Aikman
41 Four-poster, for example

90

Across

1 ___ up (invigorates)
5 Patrick of "Dirty Dancing" and "Ghost"
11 Shade of blue that means "water" in Latin
12 More comfortable and cozy
13 There are two in a pint
14 Make ___ (apologize)
15 Capsizes: 2 wds.
17 Secret agent
18 Deer meat
22 Metal the pipe is made of in the board game Clue
24 Give up, as territory
25 Coral island
27 Polished one's car
28 Neanderthal's "house"
29 Fur for a coat
30 Kicked out
32 Savings plan
35 With natural-born skill
37 Follower of an Eastern philosophy
40 Razor brand
41 Famous: 2 wds.
42 Feature of blue jeans or a baseball
43 High on marijuana
44 Clothing designer Taylor and TV newswoman Curry

Down

1 Agreements between nations
2 Give material to
3 Innocent romantic crush: 2 wds.
4 Be disrespectful to
5 Used a 40-across
6 Ladies
7 Word before cheese, Indian, or "Idol"
8 Yang's counterpart, to a 37-across
9 Last letter of the alphabet, in England
10 Hospital areas: abbr.
16 Curved geometric shape
19 Seductive lady: 2 wds.
20 "___ to a Nightingale"
21 Actor Beatty
23 Voting event
25 Highest card in the deck
26 ___ Mahal
27 Far and ___ (all over the place)
29 Like the cheese on a grilled cheese
31 Have a bite of
33 Showed again on TV
34 Second U.S. president
36 Govt. arm that put up the space shuttles
37 Talking-___ (admonishments)
38 Back part of a boat
39 John Lennon's love

91

Across

1 "___, humbug!"
4 Narc's org.
7 "Mogambo" actress Gardner
8 Bobby of hockey fame
9 "Exodus" character
12 Singer Valens
14 Gen-___
15 "Goldberg Variations" composer
16 Nikon or Konica
18 Old anesthetic
20 Share a border with
21 Sandra ___ of "Gidget"
22 Every last thing: 2 wds.
25 Kind of newspaper
27 Halftime encouragement from the coach: 2 wds.
29 Football measurements: abbr.
32 Double-___ (kind of tournament, for short)
33 1950's Ford flop
35 Binds: 2 wds.
38 Grand Ole ___
39 "Yada, yada, yada"
40 Diet number
42 "Understand?"
43 Deception
44 Infomercials, e.g.
45 "Go on ..."
46 "Are we there ___?"

Down

1 ___ wire (stuff on a fence)
2 Fly a plane
3 Unfair article by a journalist: 2 wds.
4 "Stupid me!"
5 Clapton who sang "Layla"
6 Section
9 Product with sexy TV ads: 3 wds.
10 Show shown again on TV
11 Really mad
13 "Evita" role
17 When repeated, a fish
19 Country great McEntire
23 Every bit
24 Pepsi rival
26 24-hr. conveniences
27 "For ___ sake!"
28 A-list
30 Talk bad about
31 Most sneaky
34 Scooby-___ (cartoon dog)
36 The Bruins' sch.
37 Hurt
41 Was winning

Across

1 Colonial-era musical instrument
5 Word before "party" or "bottoms"
11 Spoken
12 Tooth covering
13 Musical genre with its Hall of Fame in Cleveland: 3 wds.
15 Tiny crawler
16 "___ not the end of the world!"
17 Sports org. that includes the Houston Rockets
18 Gunk
19 Twosome
20 Like people who are "out"
21 Makes a blunder
23 Weasel's sound, in a song
25 Put back to zero
27 Slithery lizards
31 "A mouse!"
33 Too sweet
34 Stuff tapped off a cigarette
37 Marked a ballot, maybe
39 Not a "nay" vote
40 Highest card in the deck
41 Prefix meaning "three"
42 Cigarette additive
43 Beer that comes in a green bottle: 2 wds.
46 Black, white and orange bird
47 Stare
48 Cell phone giant bought by Sprint in 2005
49 Active person

Down

1 Someone who scours for food
2 Its mined in Minnesota's Mesabi Range: 2 wds.
3 Things to consider
4 Animal with antlers
5 Kept inside, as rage
6 Et cetera: 3 wds.
7 Peanut butter container
8 Surrounded by
9 Peach ___ (kind of dessert)
10 Soothe, as fears
14 Band-___ (scrape cover)
22 Get a look at
24 Puppy or kitten
26 Fabric
28 "Nice job!": 3 wds.
29 Sweet syrup served in England
30 More unadorned
32 Piece of unpopped popcorn
34 First name in the Bible, alphabetically
35 Make a goal or a basket
36 Curving line, like of DNA strands
38 Like, to a hippie
44 Parking place
45 Fishing pole

Across

1 Forearm bone
5 Prepared a salad
11 Screwdriver or hammer
12 Baltimore base-stealer or bunter
13 In addition
14 Chosen by luck
15 Scoring three goals in one game of soccer or hockey: 2 wds.
17 Steal from
18 Russian Revolution leader
22 Genre for "Battlestar Galactica"
24 Eat away at slowly
25 Has the power to
26 Put a patch on jeans, e.g.
27 It may be 90 degrees in geometry class
30 Wonderful
32 Put back to 000000, as an odometer
33 Suffix with cloth or cash
34 It's worth ten times more than a "red cent": 2 wds.
38 Irish language
41 Stocking trouble
42 Intention to do harm
43 Waffle brand fought over in ads
44 Least risky
45 Condition of sale at garage sales: 2 wds.

Down

1 Six-sided state
2 Hit for The Kinks
3 They're "attached" in commitment-free deals: 2 wds.
4 Many: 3 wds.
5 Spelling of "Beverly Hills, 90210"
6 Microsoft rival, or an ancient source of knowledge
7 Tricky baseball pitch
8 Do the lawn
9 1970s band that sang "Do Ya"
10 Obama, e.g.
16 Baseball statistic that's higher for heavy hitters
19 Goth kids wear them: 2 wds.
20 Concept
21 2012 presidential candidate Gingrich
22 Hurt badly
23 Walking aid
28 Allow to rest, like sleeping dogs: 2 wds.
29 Morality subject
30 Alcoholic drink that's also a card game
31 Moses parted it: 2 wds.
35 "Law & Order: SVU" actor
36 "The Gift of the ___"
37 They may clash
38 Chess experts: abbr.
39 Small battery
40 Christmas creature

94

Across

1 Actor Damon of "Rounders" and "The Bourne Ultimatum"
5 Hollywood awards
11 Burden
12 Perfect society
13 Restaurant list
14 City of Ohio or Spain
15 "Black ___" (Natalie Portman film)
16 Place for a manicure or a massage
17 "___ understand it...": 2 wds.
19 Hit with the hand
23 Atlantic island with a triangle named for it
27 "Nicely done!"
28 Journalist's information: 2 wds.
30 "Mazel ___!"
31 Underhanded plans
32 Sports channel
34 Female chicken
35 "Cat ___ Hot Tin Roof": 2 wds.
37 "And there we have it!"
41 Put down
44 Computer owner
45 Unexpected, as a plot twist
46 It's thrown at a wedding
47 Thread holder
48 Talks incessantly

Down

1 Not dads
2 From the beginning
3 Fish in a salad or a can
4 Tidal wave, to the Japanese
5 Long shot possibility: 2 wds.
6 Grind to a halt
7 Pepsi, Coke and RC
8 Mimic
9 Cleansed (of)
10 ___ Paulo, Brazil
18 Beer, casually
20 Hang ominously on the horizon
21 ___ vera (lotion ingredient)
22 ___ up (invigorates)
23 Crunch down on
24 Deputy ___ Strate ("The Dukes of Hazzard" bumbler)
25 Say whether you're going to the party
26 Arthur who won the U.S. Open in 1968
29 100 years
33 Eternally: 2 wds.
36 Hammer's target
38 Where China and India are
39 52 cards
40 God of war
41 Noise
42 Prior to, palindromically
43 One of the Three Stooges

95

Across

1 Last name of Russian czars
8 "That's hilarious," when texting
11 Texas city
12 Columbus coll.
13 Black TV cartoon animal: 3 wds.
15 Side facing the street
16 Public perception
17 Hazy history
18 Symbol of Libra
19 Tight ___ (football position)
20 "___ of the Field" (Sidney Poitier movie)
21 Dot on a computer screen
22 Shipping boxes
24 Capture, like a crook
27 Containers sometimes made of cedar
28 Additional
29 It makes waste
30 Small string instrument
31 Academy Award recipient, like Julia Roberts or Matt Damon: 2 wds.
33 Man's name made of three consecutive letters
34 Section of London: 2 wds.
35 Wide shoe size
36 Prom outfits

Down

1 Contest with a drawing
2 "A Midsummer Night's Dream" role
3 Not milady
4 Draw ___ in the sand: 2 wds.
5 Immediately following
6 Toronto's province: abbr.
7 Cars, trucks, etc.
8 Site
9 Oklahoma Indians
10 Old stringed instruments
14 Letter, these days
18 Followers of fives
20 Threw trash on the ground
21 Spaghetti or tortellini
22 Pure
23 Save
24 Not belonging to anybody
25 Woman's name that rhymes with 11-across
26 They cover faces
27 Selected
28 Altoids or tic tacs
30 Holding tool in shop class
32 Armed conflict

Across

1 Janitor's tool
4 Ask for a higher court to hear your case
10 Big shot in the office
12 Word before Mist or Madre
13 In the vicinity of
14 Substantial, as a meal
15 Civil ___ (riot conditions)
17 Admit: 2 wds.
19 Peeper
22 Apprehend (a crook)
24 "I'm ___ Boat" ("SNL" short film): 2 wds.
25 Was winning
26 Owner of the Kwik-E-Mart, on "The Simpsons"
27 Gives approval to
28 Glossy publication, for short
29 "Hold on a ___!"
30 Jean-___ Godard (French-Swiss director)
31 Prior to
32 Pose a question to
33 Ringo on drums
35 Arts & ___ (summer camp activity)
38 Unleavened bread eaten during Passover
43 Make someone healthy again
44 Stick (to)
45 Garden of ___ (Biblical site)
46 Oklahoman
47 Michigan's biggest city: abbr.

Down

1 What a waiter hands you
2 Animals with yokes
3 "The Good Earth" author: 2 wds.
4 "That '70s Show" star: 2 wds.
5 Cherry or lemon meringue
6 Round, green vegetable
7 Go wrong
8 Field for Manet and Monet
9 Set (down)
11 Largest Canadian tribe
16 Bar seats
18 Org. for speedy drivers
19 Bugs Bunny's nemesis: 2 wds.
20 Leap ___ (2012 or 2016)
21 Border
22 Org. that sent up the space shuttles
23 Baboon cousins
34 Event for 18-down
36 Each of this puzzle's three theme entries starts with one
37 Fired off, as an e-mail
38 More: Sp.
39 "Much ___ About Nothing"
40 Despite, in poems
41 Kind of Buddhism
42 State that "Portlandia" is filmed in: abbr.

97

Across

1 Get up on your feet
6 "Sense and Sensibility" author Austen
10 One of the two cheeses traditionally used in American cheese
11 Hair for lions
12 Being social on the town: 3 wds.
14 Next-to-last Greek letter
15 Make a mistake
16 Its R stands for "retirement"
17 Common street name
18 Its U stands for "utility"
19 Washington baseball team member, for short
20 Stitching line
22 Kind and sweet
24 Supermarket path
26 Missing, like from class
29 Lights-out song played on a bugle
33 Not working anymore: abbr.
34 Cruise of "Mission: Impossible III"
36 Well-worn path, like at work
37 Chinese dictator
38 Former Bush spokesman Fleischer
39 African antelope that doesn't sound old
40 Stylishly successful: 3 wds.
43 Nephew's sister
44 Nice cut of steak
45 Trait carrier
46 Plant store packet

Down

1 ___ Monkey Trial
2 Muss up, as someone's hair
3 Popular Nissan
4 Jeremy Lin's sports org.
5 Units of force
6 Quick punch, to boxers
7 Name, as a successor
8 Nerve-related
9 Huge house and its grounds
11 Comic book company
13 Where to buy ibuprofen
21 West who said "I generally avoid temptation unless I can't resist it"
23 It's topped by tape, on a tennis court
25 Consumption
26 Giving guns to
27 ___ Babies (popular dolls)
28 Taken without asking
30 Style of socks or sweaters
31 Made a wordplay funny
32 Evel Knievel achievements
35 Irritates
41 Cubes in the freezer
42 Say something that's not true

Across

1 Painting holder
6 Throws, as a stone
11 ___ noodles (cheap instant meal)
12 Ask (for a loan): 2 wds.
13 Not acceptable: 3 wds.
15 Popular wine, for short
16 ___ room (place to play in the house)
17 "That's interesting!"
18 Final part, as of a movie
19 Animal whose name also means "to talk nonstop"
20 Dirt plus water
21 Empty ___ syndrome (when the kids leave home)
23 Summarizes
25 The Jetsons' dog
27 "That's fine!": 2 wds.
30 City on the water, like New Orleans or Los Angeles
34 Govt. arm involved in green issues
35 Word after spelling or quilting
37 Each
38 Color on the Canadian flag
39 Polish off, like pancakes
40 Take advantage of
41 Song from "The Little Mermaid": 3 wds.
44 John ___ tractors
45 "___ you the one who said..."
46 Tacked on
47 More than mean

Down

1 Like TV dinners, when purchased
2 Gully
3 Make ___ (apologize to those you've hurt)
4 Mal de ___ (seasickness)
5 Attempt to win a contest
6 Piece in the game where you say "king me!"
7 Be sick
8 Societal disapproval
9 Auto garage service
10 Goes too fast on the highway
14 Sound heard by a stethoscope
22 ___ and feather
24 Policeman
26 ___ up (let the liquor wear off)
27 Poet Pablo ___
28 Took the wrapping paper off
29 Put questionable expenses on, like a report
31 Masterworks
32 Find offensive, as someone's words
33 Agreement between nations
36 Patriot ___ Allen
42 Before
43 Historical time

Across

1 Gets outta here
6 Coffin holders
11 Like knit sweaters
12 Dot in the Pacific or Atlantic
13 Pawn to king's four in chess, for example: 2 wds.
15 Wood or Paul
16 Common weather in London
17 Sliced dessert
18 Used a shovel
19 Jacksonville's state: abbr.
20 Mentalist's ability
21 Meal prepared in a pot
23 Entertains
25 Holder of the title
27 Magic ___
30 "Apollo 13" org.
34 Imitate
35 Keep tabs on
37 Largest city in Mich.
38 One of Snow White's buddies
39 Bachelor's home
40 Fink
41 It's soon after last call: 2 wds.
44 Similar
45 Roof section
46 ___ bear (white animal)
47 Exhausted, as resources

Down

1 Knights fought with them
2 Weak excuse: 2 wds.
3 Get someone back for
4 Lowest two-digit number
5 Get a noseful of
6 The Super Bowl, e.g.: 2 wds.
7 Ending for a school of thought
8 Runs off to get married
9 Make many changes to, as a text
10 Prepares tea
14 He pitched seven no-hitters: 2 wds.
22 Pan used in Chinese cooking
24 Cremains holder
26 More tearful
27 Wacky, as antics
28 Greek god for whom a theater in New York is named
29 Draw back in horror
31 Where floppy disks went: 2 wds.
32 Sailors
33 Vouch for, with "to"
36 Defeats, but just barely
42 Musical genre from Jamaica
43 ___ water (it's from the faucet)

100

Across

1 President between Grant and Garfield
6 Much higher than before: 2 wds.
11 By oneself
12 White ___ (where 1-across lived)
13 Flying transportation, in mythical tales: 2 wds.
15 Stocking problem
16 Computer key that's usually next to the space bar
17 Leave town for good: 2 wds.
22 Demi Moore movie about the military: 3 wds.
25 Ginger ___ (soft drink)
26 Came up, as a topic of conversation
27 One of Columbus's ships
29 Pan used in Chinese cooking
30 Bird that's a symbol of the Andes Mountains
31 Volleyball players' equipment
34 Martin ___ Buren (8th president)
35 Take the peel off, as an apple
39 Where scandals may be "swept": 3 wds.
43 Brief and to the point
44 Stuff on a cake
45 Kills, in the Bible
46 RBI or ERA, e.g.

Down

1 Pork products
2 Alda or Arkin
3 Exercise from India
4 Puzzles
5 "Hold on a ___!"
6 Mammal of the sea
7 Largest artery
8 "Uh-huh!"
9 Purpose
10 Kitty or puppy
14 Bear's home

18 Dollar bill
19 Magician's stick
20 Palo ___, Calif.
21 365 days, usually
22 Stare
23 Tool for getting wrinkles out of clothes
24 It may start "knock-knock"
27 Like two peas in a ___
28 Look over closely
30 Lacks the ability to
32 Each
33 Roles
36 Opera song
37 Smallest of the litter
38 They're colored at Easter
39 Letters on navy boats
40 The Toronto Maple Leafs, the Los Angeles Kings, etc.
41 Classic 1950 film noir movie remade in 1988
42 Not hers

101

Across

1 Quick-spreading ideas
6 Brazilian dance, or its music
11 "That's ___ excuse!": 2 wds.
12 Characteristic
13 Copy machine company
14 Corrosive liquids
15 Wall-climbing vine
16 Make a mistake
18 Born, in wedding announcements
19 Bad: Fr.
20 Performed
21 Airport guess: abbr.
22 One of the Four Corners states
24 Pre-election survey
26 Servers hand them out
28 Demi or Dudley
31 God: Lat.
33 Microsoft game console
34 "Lord of the Rings" bad guy
36 4.0 is a perfect one
38 Dallas sch.
39 Golf course score
40 Talk and talk
41 World Chess Champion of the 1960's Mikhail ___ (hidden in CRYSTALLINE)
42 Keep away from
44 Spy
46 Picture puzzle
47 Marie who won two Nobel Prizes
48 Plus
49 "This has me down in the dumps!": 2 wds.

Down

1 Largest possible amount
2 Raise up
3 Seafood pulled from the Chesapeake Bay: 2 wds.
4 Depressing, like music
5 Junior high class: 2 wds.
6 Celebrity's reality
7 Three-point line in basketball, for example
8 Seafood pulled from Casco Bay: 2 wds.
9 Giggle-evoking bathroom fixture
10 Far from the coast: 2 wds.
17 Gravestone letters
23 Tint
25 Smoked salmon
27 Hint at
29 European country whose capital is Bucharest
30 Rejoiced
32 Where to get a facial
34 Bizet's "Carmen" is one
35 Very positive reviews
37 Ancient counting devices
43 Word on bills
45 Hubba Bubba or Bubblicious

Across

1 Lack of war
6 Assistants
11 Edgar ___ Poe
12 Child's coughing
13 Coins often given away: 2 wds.
15 Professor's helpers: abbr.
16 West of Old Hollywood
17 Male doll
18 Inquire
19 State south of Mich.
20 Finale
21 Wetter than wet
23 Pro votes
24 Up to now: 2 wds.
26 "Hey, you!"
29 French port on the English Channel
33 Charged particle
34 Pet you may brush
35 Longtime NBC show
36 Gunk
37 Mono-
38 First word of countless book titles
39 Umpire's shout before "You're out!": 2 wds.
42 Not here
43 German WWI menace
44 Approving replies
45 Blog entries

Down

1 Tortellini, rigatoni, etc.
2 Texas city on the border with Mexico: 2 wds.
3 Anchorage's state
4 Jaguar or Jeep
5 Foes
6 Suffered from soreness
7 Tax shelter
8 Shrek's buddy
9 Oregon city, or a man's name
10 Throws around, as money
14 Christmas treat: 2 wds.
22 Kit ___ (candy bar)
23 Ocean that Portugal is on: abbr.
25 Accept flattery eagerly: 3 wds.
26 Where you'll hear oinks
27 Be calming
28 Sleeping sounds
30 Houston's baseball team
31 Ready to reproduce, like dogs: 2 wds.
32 Comes down hard from the sky
34 Green vegetables, casually
40 Wrath
41 "Entourage" channel

103

Across

1 Big handfuls, as of cash
5 Rat out, as to Mom or Dad: 2 wds.
11 Bring on at the company
12 Black, white and orange bird
13 Father of Thor
14 Told a lie
15 "___ the Fockers"
16 Tina of "30 Rock"
17 "Okey-___!"
19 Tall hairstyle
23 Java and Kona, for two
26 Totally cool
27 Bring together
28 Express a viewpoint
30 Ask for charity
31 U2's "Where the ___ Have No Name"
33 Helper: abbr.
35 Robert of "The Brady Bunch"
36 Have bills
38 One of Jacob's wives
41 Kind of soup on Chinese menus: 2 wds.
44 Stare
45 "All ___!" (conductor's shout)
46 Jamaican fruit
47 "Thelma & Louise" director ___ Scott
48 Former ruler of Russia

Down

1 "To ___ It May Concern:"
2 Helper
3 Snack from the Middle East: 2 wds.
4 Dispatched, as an envoy: 2 wds.
5 Candy type
6 Cleveland's lake
7 North African nation whose capital is Tripoli
8 Tennis shot that should have topspin
9 "Nicely done!"
10 Actor Beatty
18 Florida archipelago
20 They may be ordered sunny side-up: 2 wds.
21 Long-winded tirade
22 Some poetry
23 Caribbean island that gave us mojitos and mambo music
24 Small bills
25 Achy
29 Drive away in a hurry: 2 wds.
32 All the rage
34 Breakfast cereal in a blue box
37 Had on
39 "It's ___ big misunderstanding!": 2 wds.
40 Person mentioned in a will
41 Armed conflict
42 ___-Wan Kenobi (Alec Guinness role)
43 Indicate that you agree

104

Across

1 "Over There" composer George M. ___
6 Hate intensely
11 Make a speech
12 Keaton of "Annie Hall"
13 More ready for plucking
14 "___ of God" (Jane Fonda movie)
15 Bursting balloon's sound
16 High-ranking person
18 Function
19 Sneaky
20 Ending for insist
21 People related to you
22 Canadian sentence-enders
24 Was very stinky
26 North African nation bordering Libya
28 State of Mexico
30 Chicago Blackhawks, Toronto Maple Leafs, etc.
32 Shiba ___ (cute dog breed)
33 Part of a play
35 Santa's shouts
37 Animal with antlers
38 The woman over there
39 Three-point line's shape, in basketball
40 "Zorba the Greek" author ___ Kazantzakis
42 See it the same way
44 Author Zora ___ Hurston
45 Showed again
46 Campfire remains
47 Flair

Down

1 Peace ___
2 Baltimore ___ (state bird of Maryland)
3 Greeting for Jews, beginning tonight: 2 wds.
4 Chowed down on
5 Gumption
6 Electrical device
7 Ginormous
8 Jon Lovitz character from "Saturday Night Live"
9 Baby's garment
10 Try again, as to deliver an e-mail
17 Attainable
23 ___-mo cameras
25 "Ich bin ___ Berliner"
27 Green growths
28 Burnt ___ (Crayola color)
29 Kids with no siblings, in slang
31 Makeup company
34 Drops on your face?
36 Public fight
41 "Wonderful job!"
43 Comprehend

105

Across

1 Minnelli of "Cabaret"
5 Get a closer shot with your camera: 2 wds.
11 Clapton who sang "Change the World"
12 Introduce by force, as laws
13 Cried
14 Mortar and ___
15 Lady
17 Williams or Turner
18 Teamed (up with)
20 Pig's home
21 Make a mistake
22 New member of society, for short
24 Tiny
25 Ending for cloth or bombard
26 Put in the microwave
29 Oklahoma city
30 Kind of beer
31 ___-tac-toe
34 Productivity
36 Yoko who loved John Lennon
37 Gin and ___
38 No longer edible, as butter
40 ___ Lisa (famed painting)
43 Portuguese-speaking African nation
44 Garden of ___ (Biblical paradise)
45 Physical well-being
46 Covered in morning moisture, as a meadow

Down

1 Alcindor or Ayres
2 Wrath
3 Fun way down from a tree: 2 wds.
4 Tom Cruise or John Travolta
5 Song with the line "Mr. Bluebird's on my shoulder"
6 Sign of the future
7 Photo-___ (politician's engagements)
8 Apple juice brand
9 Small dot in the ocean
10 Impoverished
16 Newspapers, magazines, etc.
18 Church bench
19 "___ you kidding me?"
23 Coffee maker brand
26 Part of a mailing address: 2 wds.
27 "The Simpsons" character
28 Butter amount
31 Jewish holy book
32 Nonsensical
33 Cuban dance
35 Against the clock
37 Pinball infraction
39 Rank below gen.
41 ___ Hampshire
42 "Did you have ___ luck?"

Across

1 Feature of a nice hotel
4 Inaccurate
7 ___ rally (high school event)
8 Holbrook nominated for a 2007 Oscar for "Into the Wild"
9 James Bond creator ___ Fleming
12 Installment, as of a TV show
14 Die-rolling possibility
15 Sword used in Olympic competition
16 Bothers persistently: 2 wds.
18 Coffee that won't keep you up
20 "Present and accounted for"
21 Word after iron or lead
22 Progress, metaphorically
25 Captain ___ (person who proudly states something everyone already knows)
27 Where the shortstop and second baseman play
29 Be a chatterbox
32 ___ tape (powerful adhesive)
33 "We ___ Overcome"
35 Uses one end of a pencil
38 Actress Fisher of "Wedding Crashers"
39 Pose a question
40 Track and field event that uses a heavy ball: 2 wds.
42 General whose father was a general
43 Palindromic music genre
44 Great anger
45 Badminton barrier
46 Suffix with employ or induct

Down

1 Revealing swimsuit brand
2 Salt's pal
3 "So simple!": 4 wds.
4 "So that's your game!"
5 Become less famous over time
6 Dog's irritation
9 "So simple!": 4 wds.
10 Emmy or Tony
11 Margin markings
13 Big body of water
17 Old-school word for "you"
19 Number of fingers
23 Zero, in soccer scores
24 Fishing store selection
26 Tiny pieces
27 Perfect
28 Drink slowly, as a beer
30 Attraction
31 Kitchen cupboard items
34 Popular song
36 Cable channel that sometimes shows bowling
37 Sock cover
41 Decide

107

Across

1 Adorable animal that's a symbol of China
6 Beauty queen's crown
11 Expend, as resources: 2 wds.
12 Did some math, maybe
13 Multi-purpose living room furniture: 2 wds.
15 Owned
16 California's largest newspaper, for short
17 Fix, like an election
18 Make bigger, as a photo: abbr.
19 Juan Peron's wife
20 180 degrees from WSW
21 Part of a process
23 Undoes, as pencil marks
25 Last name of twin actresses Ashley and Mary-Kate
27 Swapped
30 Show no respect for
34 Lipstick color, often
35 Pablo Picasso's field
37 Eat well
38 Part of speech like "happy" or "wonderful": abbr.
39 Overly
40 Brazilian city that will host the 2016 Summer Olympics, for short
41 Expert with the remote control: 2 wds.
44 Come after
45 12-year-old, say
46 Put off
47 Embraces

Down

1 Shoves
2 Leaning
3 Sewing item
4 Deserving
5 Fruit that's also a computer
6 Steak ___ (raw dish)
7 Passports, driver's licenses, etc.
8 Loves to pieces
9 Process sugar
10 Wise sayings
14 Listen in
22 Place for peas
24 "What else?"
26 Moccasin material
27 Didn't draw freehand
28 Renovated
29 Tweak
31 Neighbor of Lebanon and Egypt
32 Both having hearts or diamonds, like a pair of cards
33 Silverware drawer slot
36 Canine or molar
42 Signal for an actor
43 Possible roll of the die

Across

1 Predatory birds
6 Album parts
11 To no ___ (pointlessly)
12 Pageant winner's crown
13 Inflammation suffered by athletes: 2 wds.
15 Finish
16 ___ talk (inspiring speech)
17 Man of the future?
18 Regret
19 Roads: abbr.
20 Christmas ___
21 Worker with few rights
23 Join two pieces of metal
25 Lee or Levi's, for jeans
27 ___ of water (lakes, rivers, etc.)
30 Impromptu singing style
34 U.S. state on the Pacific Ocean: abbr.
35 Gillman in the Pro Football Hall of Fame
37 Genetic matter
38 Come out on top
39 Wedding day phrase: 2 wds.
40 Its T stands for "teller"
41 South Dakota creek where Crazy Horse was killed: 2 wds.
44 Tune from the past
45 Biological classification
46 "While My Guitar Gently ___"
47 Cairo's country

Down

1 Not fanboys
2 Connecticut ___ (Monopoly property)
3 Travel around with no destination
4 Relatives
5 Falls on a banana peel
6 Family member by marriage
7 Peanut or grapeseed
8 Caught, like a criminal
9 Vinyl record feature
10 Mark Twain's Tom
14 Saves for later: 2 wds.
22 J. Edgar Hoover once led it
24 The Mormon church, for short
26 Lives
27 Dog's sound
28 Yankee's rival, in the American League East
29 Remove clothing from
31 Small pocket, as in an English muffin
32 Get the poker pot started: 2 wds.
33 Least wild
36 Get out of the way of
42 ___ in the bud (catch a problem early)
43 Beer holder, at a fraternity house

109

Across

1 Computer key for emergencies
4 Friend of the French
7 Scholastic org.
10 Zero, to soccer players
11 Shortest room in the house?
12 "What can I do for you?"
13 Drink that may be black
14 Magazine pages, often
15 Congressperson: abbr.
16 Ninny
17 Harvard rival
18 Copy
19 "___ Too Late"
20 ___-fi movies
21 Dudes
22 Girl of Glasgow
24 Confederates
26 How to serve white wine
28 Capital city named for a Greek goddess
30 Scandinavian city
33 Guevara on T-shirts
34 Precursor to the DVD player
36 Not pro
37 Series of talks, or a man's name
38 "I knew it all along!"
39 Tool with a long handle
40 Hosp. section
41 Actor Chaney, Jr.
42 Finish
43 Kilmer of "The Doors"
44 Part of many German surnames
45 Ryan of Hollywood
46 Compass pt.
47 Ron who played Tarzan
48 Peeper

Down

1 Consist of
2 Nap
3 Student's week: 2 wds.
4 Second president
5 Where doctors went: 2 wds.
6 Firmly establish, as values
7 Unsustainable swindle: 2 wds.
8 Cone-shaped home
9 Trees that may grow at high altitudes
23 Not he
25 Only three-letter zodiac sign
27 Make a part of
28 Participating
29 Prison, in slang: 2 wds.
31 "___ Tunes"
32 Not relaxed: 2 wds.
35 Actor Cox

Across

1 Deep valley
6 Tennis star Rafael ___
11 Rent-a-truck company
12 Last name on the TV show "Dallas"
13 Make petty comments
14 Slacks
15 London for the 2012 Olympics and Rio de Janeiro for 2016, e.g.: 2 wds.
17 Visit a restaurant: 2 wds.
18 Do some math
20 In need of a steamroller, as a road
24 People, places or things
27 Mrs. Archie Bunker
28 Train stations
30 North Carolina city: abbr.
31 It steeps in hot water: 2 wds.
34 Archaeologists often rediscover them, like Chichen Itza or Mohenjo Daro: 2 wds.
38 Boyfriends
39 Karan of DKNY
40 Nostalgia-evoking
41 One side in the Civil War
42 Pale-looking
43 "___ porridge hot..."

Down

1 Spew, like an oil well
2 "I shouldn't have done that!": 2 wds.
3 Lifted: 2 wds.
4 "Paging Dr. ___" (CNN show)
5 Put into office
6 Uranus neighbor
7 Looked forward to
8 Have a sumptuous meal
9 Insects that form colonies
10 T-shirt sizes: abbr.
16 Three vowels that mean "you'll get your money"
18 Additionally
19 Anonymous John or Jane
21 Staunton's state
22 Greek letter
23 The Los Angeles Kings, the Edmonton Oilers, etc.
25 Unwilling to bet on it: 2 wds.
26 Cowboy's hat
29 ___ fly (baseball play)
32 Cause to get higher, as a price at auction: 2 wds.
33 Make up (for)
34 Spike and Ang
35 Promising words
36 First son of Seth, in Genesis
37 Not nuts
38 Victoria's Secret product

111

Across

1 Plagued, as by problems
6 Colorado ski resort, or a tree you might find there
11 Oldsmobile model
12 Switzerland's capital
13 Rude comments, in hipster-speak
14 Dr. Frankenstein's assistant, and namesakes
15 Title of respect for a man
16 Brynner of "The King and I"
18 Automated performer of computer tasks
19 Put in, as with a letter
21 Every bit
22 Section of Manhattan or London
23 Make possible
25 Farmer and author ___ Berry
27 Language spoken in Egypt and Morocco
29 Hi-Q pieces
32 Canadian city where the Blue Jays play: abbr.
33 X-ray type: 2 wds.
35 World ___ II
36 Prior to
37 Number of years you've been alive
38 State that borders Wyoming
40 Baton ___ (Louisiana's capital)
42 Sheets, pillowcases, etc.
43 Extremely stingy person
44 "It would be my honor": 2 wds.
45 Kids go down hills on them in the winter

Down

1 Deep voices
2 Weather phenomenon that means "the boy" in Spanish: 2 wds.
3 What the police need to look through your house: 2 wds.
4 Make a mistake
5 Largest city in Japan
6 Texas city
7 Part of a line, in geometry: abbr.
8 What the police need to get 3-down: 2 wds.
9 Sign up, as for a class
10 Chocolate company that makes Quik
17 Auto dealership purchase: 2 wds.
20 Pop singer Lisa
24 Swiss mountains
26 "Excellent job!": 2 wds.
27 Whenever you're ready: 2 wds.
28 Person who sets up equipment for rock concerts
30 Couldn't handle the doctor's tongue depressor
31 Mocking, evil looks
34 They're six years for senators
39 ___ and haw (stall for time)
41 Word after olive or sesame

Across

1 Gross growth, but not from toads
5 Walk with confidence
11 Fleshy plant
12 Tempt
13 Votes against
14 Sounds
15 Embarrassing info, to the tabloids
16 Quality ___ (hotel chain)
17 Approximately: 2 wds.
19 Steffi who won 22 Grand Slam tennis tournaments
23 "Jerry ___" (Tom Cruise movie)
26 Body spray brand
27 "___ you forgetting something?"
28 Verve
30 Part of MPH
31 Roman, Inca and British
33 Talk back
35 "I'm ___ you!" ("You don't fool me!")
36 Dude
38 Run ___ (go wild)
41 Money for finding something
44 Cold War enemy of the Warsaw Pact
45 Country with the cities of Roma and Milano
46 "___ the Wild" (Jon Krakauer book)
47 Let it ride, in gambling
48 Make the food

Down

1 Stick for a magician
2 Jai ___ (fast-moving sport)
3 Title cowboy in an Elton John song: 2 wds.
4 Dress rehearsal: 2 wds.
5 Sophomore plus two years
6 Unsigned, for short
7 British singer who was head of The Police
8 Not hers
9 Flying expert
10 "What can I do for you?"
18 Web location
20 Queens-born comedian/sitcom actor: 2 wds.
21 Rod that holds tires
22 Charges
23 Google ___
24 Vicinity
25 Sports channel
29 Best Picture set at sea
32 Long before the weekend
34 Microscopic
37 Opera tune
39 Palindromic name
40 Weirdo
41 Tear
42 Two letters after epsilon
43 More than a battle

113

Across

1 Mexican food, sometimes
6 Elevator's home
11 Video game company that made Asteroids
12 Sarah from Alaska
13 Jovial O'Brien
14 Fail to be
15 Souvenir, often
17 Green vegetables used in potato soup
18 Business with rolling pins
21 Hide and go ___
25 Boxer known for verbal jabs with Howard Cosell
26 Christmas movie starring Will Ferrell
27 Send a message to, over the phone
29 Unexpected
32 Academy Award
34 Kind of joke
39 Look into
40 Bird on the U.S. Great Seal
41 Powerful person, or a kind of Greek god
42 "___ its course": 2 wds.
43 For later use
44 Requirements

Down

1 Pushpin alternative
2 Plenty: 2 wds.
3 "Would you allow me to do that?": 2 wds.
4 Source of wisdom
5 Tricky baseball pitch
6 Defeat soundly, in slang
7 Bother continuously
8 Baldwin of "Malice"
9 He rats people out to the fuzz
10 Explosive palindrome
16 Lock unlocker
18 Piece of baseball equipment
19 Bar order
20 Cereal that's "Kid-Tested, Mother-Approved"
22 Ending for velvet
23 QB Manning
24 McDonald's rival
28 "So sorry to hear that!": 2 wds.
29 "Gross!"
30 Earn, as a large sum of money: 2 wds.
31 Finely decorated
33 Part of a movie
34 Singer/actor Kristofferson
35 Phrase of denial: 2 wds.
36 Shrek is one
37 Dressed (in)
38 Jennings and Burns
39 Elementary school group, for short

Across

1 Dictionary entries, for short
5 Did another version of, as an old movie
11 Rapper who stars in "Law & Order: SVU"
12 In a fair way
13 Old stadium for the New York Mets
14 One under par on a hole in golf
15 "My goodness!": 2 wds.
17 Paddle's cousin
18 Similar to
22 Shimmering beads on a dress
26 Become droopy
27 Clumsy person
28 One of Christopher Columbus's three ships
30 "...then ___ monkey's uncle!": 2 wds.
31 Kicked out (of an apartment)
33 Extinct bird
35 High card in the deck
36 Cute and chubby: 2 wds.
41 Black belt's specialty
44 Where China and India are
45 "Understood!": 3 wds.
46 Cat's weapon
47 Equally: 2 wds.
48 Rock group that sounds like a vegetable

Down

1 Plate
2 Natural "recording" of a sound
3 Touch
4 "Don't come in here!": 2 wds.
5 Given a new life
6 Just plain bad
7 Streep of "It's Complicated"
8 "What else?"
9 551, in Ancient Rome
10 It may be blue or hazel
16 Native American crop
19 "___ that funny?"
20 Winslet of "Titanic"
21 "Oh my!"
22 Hit the brakes quickly
23 Red puppet on "Sesame Street"
24 Area of a college campus surrounded by buildings
25 Hot
29 You put it on an injury to stop the swelling: 2 wds.
32 Car parkers
34 Give a speech
37 Milo's dog buddy, in a movie title
38 Capital city on a fjord
39 "That's not true and you know it!"
40 Sign that someone's tired or bored
41 Relatives
42 Long ___ (way back when)
43 Catholicism or Hinduism: abbr.

Across

1 Mr. Mineo
4 Make a misstep
7 Legume holder
10 U.N. member nation
11 "___ is me!"
12 "Now I see!"
13 Proves untrue, as a rumor
15 Knight's honorific
16 Rescue
17 Teacher's unit
19 Arm benders
21 "Darkness on the ___ Town" (Bruce Springsteen album): 2 wds.
23 "My goodness!"
27 Actress Thompson
28 Bank feature
30 Need to pay back
31 Table formation seen in the Southwest
33 They save the day
35 Used one's teeth
37 Gave a shock
40 Poetry event
43 Mimic
44 Combination
46 Spy novelist Follett
47 Cold, as a stare
48 KGB's former rival
49 Finish
50 Pince-___ glasses
51 Kit ___ (candy bar)

Down

1 Beer, casually
2 Largest continent
3 City for gamblers: 2 wds.
4 Woolly female
5 What your fate may depend on in 3-down: 4 wds.
6 Stitch again
7 Decide not to take your turn

8 Cincinnati's river
9 "Shoot!"
14 One-named soccer great
18 Not NNW
20 Feathery neckwear
21 Common street name
22 Actor Billy ___ Williams
24 What you say to people in 3-down: 2 wds.
25 Amaze
26 ___ Moines (Iowa's capital)
29 Kitten's noise
32 Make believe
34 Take a breather
36 Crowd uncomfortably: 2 wds.
37 Maggie Gyllenhaal's brother
38 Kind of tournament
39 Give for a while
41 Opera number
42 Mutton or venison
45 Last of the alphabet

116

Across

1 They go with knives and spoons
6 Marla of "The Jeffersons"
11 Goodbye, to the French
12 Scarlett ___ of "Gone With the Wind"
13 What students take in class
14 Coin for the bus or subway
15 Stationery with horizontal and vertical lines: 2 wds.
17 Puts on the radio
18 Several: 2 wds.
21 Color of the Beatles' submarine
26 Ravi Shankar's musical instrument
28 Leader of a sports team
29 Didn't leave
31 Palindromic bus driver on "The Simpsons"
32 Piece of furniture in an office
34 Puzzles that can be created on 15-across
40 Loud, metallic sound
41 Turn away, as one's gaze
42 Caribbean island nation that speaks French
43 Newspapers, magazines, etc.
44 Give the house a new room: 2 wds.
45 Theater items

Down

1 Long tooth, as on a vampire
2 Unpleasant scent
3 Hayworth or Marley
4 Steer clear: 2 wds.
5 Raw fish from Japan
6 "Can I talk to you?": 3 wds.
7 Breakfast-all-day chain, for short
8 Put in the oven
9 ___ Rabbit (tricky literary character)
10 ___ Francisco
16 Ask nosy questions
18 Beast of burden
19 In good shape
20 Airport guess: abbr.
22 Examine: 2 wds.
23 California's largest newspaper, for short
24 Month between Sept. and Nov.
25 "Which person?"
27 Washington football player
30 ___ Moines (Iowa's capital)
33 Place for an alligator
34 Dressed (in)
35 Quick, unexpected attack
36 Not fooled by
37 Try again
38 Faucet problem
39 Train stops: abbr.
40 "___-ching!"

117

Across

1 Mischief makers
5 Chicken houses
10 Not cooked very much, like a steak
11 Firetruck feature
12 Item for getting wrinkles out of clothes
13 Restaurant choices
14 Timetable
16 Month after Sept.
17 Academy Award
21 "Star Wars" director George
23 Vodka brand, for short
24 Pose a question to
25 Apprehend, like a crook
26 Sesame ___
29 Looks over quickly
31 "See what you think!": 2 wds.
32 Make a mistake
33 It shows how much something costs: 2 wds.
37 Hand-manipulated character
40 Herb used with salmon
41 Evaluate
42 Capital of Norway
43 Lions' homes
44 Pierce with a knife

Down

1 Purple flower
2 Painter Chagall
3 What Wayne Gretzky played: 2 wds.
4 One of the five tribes of the Iroquois Confederacy
5 Guitarist Santana
6 Most unusual
7 "___ to a Nightingale"
8 Each
9 Some H.S. students
11 Baseball great Brock or Gehrig
15 Some football positions: abbr.
18 Scammer: 2 wds.
19 Alda of "M*A*S*H"
20 Spare ___ (barbecue dish)
21 Final
22 Computer owner
27 The Big ___ (constellation)
28 Emphasize
29 "Hold on a ___!"
30 Statements of belief
34 That thing's
35 "It's ___ big misunderstanding!": 2 wds.
36 Amorphous amount
37 Buddy
38 Calif. and Conn. are part of it
39 Greek letter

118

Across

1 Homer Simpson exclamations
5 ___ Spring (soap brand)
10 Palin or Ferguson
11 Newspapers, magazines, etc.
12 San Antonio landmark
13 Extremely famous people
14 Bedroom chatter: 2 wds.
16 Hawke of "Training Day"
17 Slithering creature
20 Show up for
24 Be in arrears
25 Enjoyed oysters
26 Cow's sound
27 Birthed anew
29 With no clothing
30 Totally out of cash
32 What a musician reads: 2 wds.
37 Baby kangaroos
38 Make amends (for)
39 "No more for me, thanks": 2 wds.
40 Amber, once
41 Necklace parts, maybe
42 Run like a horse

Down

1 Surreal Spanish painter
2 Taken by mouth
3 Shakespeare title character
4 "Darn it!"
5 Copy
6 Take back, as words
7 "American ___"
8 Bathroom fixture
9 Is in possession of
10 Maple syrup stuff
15 This and that
17 Neither fish ___ fowl
18 Female in a flock
19 Internet
21 Big bird
22 Doze (off)
23 A deer, a female deer
25 Hauls down to the station
28 Toed the line
29 Like "das" words in German
31 Store that once had Blue Light Specials
32 Not all
33 "For ___ jolly good...": 2 wds.
34 Average
35 "What's ___ for me?": 2 wds.
36 100 yrs.
37 Triangular sail

119

Across

1 Leap in the air
5 Have big goals
11 Bills with George Washington on them
12 Exactly right
13 Sicilian mountain an insurance company is named for
14 Texas city, or a TV show
15 African-American woman, in 1970's slang: 2 wds.
17 Person under 18
18 Engage in a Renaissance Fair sport
21 Synthetic material for stockings
25 Strong tree
26 Lamb's mom
27 Say hi to
30 Complete and total
32 ___ Cheesier! (Doritos flavor)
34 Overly large government, in George Orwell's phrase: 2 wds.
39 Easy to control
40 Use a swimming pool, sometimes
41 Worker bees
42 Some poems
43 Deeply held beliefs
44 Fellow, for short

Down

1 Montana, Pesci and Frazier
2 "Do ___ others..."
3 What a server hands you
4 Book of the Bible
5 Recipe phrase: 2 wds.
6 Spring or summer
7 Hardly worth mentioning
8 Not being productive
9 Lion's "meow"
10 Printing measures
16 Take a chair
18 Do a few laps around the track
19 Rower's need
20 Hawaiian "guitar," for short
22 Astrological sign for Lucille Ball or Ben Affleck
23 Bird in the Harry Potter books
24 French word before a maiden name
28 Motor
29 iPad, for example
30 "___ am I kidding?"
31 Picnic food in a bun: 2 wds.
33 Winter ___ (flowering plant)
34 Uninteresting type
35 Person everyone has heard of
36 ___ and seek
37 Like 2, 22 or 2,000,000
38 Take it easy
39 Pesticide banned in the 1970s

120

Across

1 Washington hockey team, casually
5 Medieval drinks
10 Find ___ for the common cold: 2 wds.
12 See eye to eye
13 Appetizer on Chinese menus: 2 wds.
15 "Rocky ___"
16 "Dig in!"
17 Small amount
18 Pioneering game console, for short
19 Four Monopoly properties: abbr.
20 Extreme anger
21 Nicaraguan leader Daniel
23 Computer brand...
24 ...and those who help people navigate them
26 French author Emile ___
29 "Very funny!": 3 wds.
33 Laundry detergent brand
34 Beer drinker's stomach
35 Mr. Flanders
36 Intent
37 Past tense of 16-across
38 Wander (about), looking for fun
39 Maine course?: 2 wds.
42 Time-tested tune
43 Binge
44 Drops of sadness
45 Earth neighbor

Down

1 Place to play poker
2 More sore
3 Not one to embrace the new
4 ___ Lanka (Asian island nation)
5 LeBlanc and Damon
6 Driving force
7 Language of the Koran
8 Wish
9 Irish ___ (breed of dog)
11 Come to the forefront
14 Skydiving need
22 Greek H
23 Tap one's cigar
25 Not fans at all
26 Ardent supporter
27 American League East bird
28 Four after 22-down
30 Kind of cat or sweater
31 Medicine man
32 Confuses
34 Microsoft's Bill
40 "Can I help you, ___?"
41 Car tire abbr.

Across

1 Go down in defeat
5 Chocolate substitute
10 Lobbing Lendl
11 Crescent-shaped fruit
12 Bridge play
13 Part of 28-across
14 Hillside, in Scotland
15 QB Tebow
16 It's thrown in a bar
18 Nile snakes
22 Get out of jail: 2 wds.
24 Theater magnate Marcus
25 "Now I see!"
26 "___ Robinson"
28 1994 World Cup host
29 Swallow or hawk
31 Continue: 2 wds.
33 John Lennon's "Dear ___"
34 The latest
35 "That's more than I needed to hear!"
37 Popular tablet
40 Greatest hits: 2 wds.
43 Zero
44 "Where are you?" response: 2 wds.
45 Vanished
46 Bonnie's partner in crime
47 Keep the beat, maybe

Down

1 Arm or leg
2 Finito
3 What to eat greens with: 2 wds.
4 Make liked
5 "Would you allow me...?": 2 wds.
6 Raccoon or racehorse
7 Critter on the Chinese calendar
8 "First..."
9 Awful
11 What to cut pats with: 2 wds.
17 "Stand" band
19 What to eat bouillabaisse with: 2 wds.
20 Mexican money
21 "Black ___" (Natalie Portman movie)
22 Elapse, as time: 2 wds.
23 Cincy's state
27 Get a look at
30 Like lowercase i's and j's
32 "Dallas" family
36 Extra
38 "___ Karenina"
39 Like the pool beneath a diving board
40 Pen or lighter brand
41 Make bigger, like a photo: abbr.
42 Like wallflowers

122

Across

1 Polishes, as a car
6 June 6th, 1944
10 Dark, as a passageway
11 Rich cake
12 Hit hard
13 Largest city in Nebraska
14 Spinning toy
15 First ___ kit
17 World ___ I
18 Cut (off)
19 Genetic material
20 Quality ___ (hotel chain)
21 Actor Estrada
23 Gets on one's feet
25 Money saved for retirement: 2 wds.
27 Laughing a lot
29 Sports channel
32 More genetic material
33 North African nation: abbr.
35 One of a foot's five
36 "Lost" network
37 Drink with scones
38 Aisle
39 Bullwinkle, e.g.
41 Duane ___ (drugstore chain)
43 Asked nosy questions
44 Tries to make a strike or a spare
45 "___ Karenina"
46 Beginning

Down

1 Hustle and ___
2 Bring up anchor
3 Way to randomly choose between two things: 3 wds.
4 In good shape
5 Word with farm or home
6 ___ Perignon champagne
7 Way to randomly choose a person for an unpleasant task: 2 wds.
8 Readily available: 2 wds.
9 Has a longing (for)
11 So far: 2 wds.
16 Fashionable: 2 wds.
22 Fraternity party container
24 Number of years
26 Scheduled
27 Nana's man
28 Not learned after birth
30 Dog that might be named Fifi
31 Most recent
34 Great Greta
40 Baltic or Irish
42 Long period of time

123

Across

1 Restaurant requests

7 ___ spumante (Italian sparkling wine)

11 Not wide

12 Pig that's wild

13 Emphasize the similarities between

14 1970s group that sang "Waterloo"

15 Closest star to us

16 Poem often about a person

18 Peyton Manning's brother/rival

19 "Mice!!!"

20 Puts on a pedestal

22 Oyster's cousin

24 Undo

25 Girl of the house

27 Rejecting replies

28 "Alright with you?": 2 wds.

31 Backtalk

34 Fruit used to make tea and jelly: 2 wds.

36 One of the Brady kids

37 Just fine and dandy

38 Yoko born in Tokyo

39 Coll. founded by Thomas Jefferson

40 "___ and away!": 2 wds.

42 Tarantula, e.g.

44 Fix, like fences or clothes

45 Checkers demand: 2 wds.

46 Big boats

47 Poverty stricken: 2 wds.

Down

1 "Hold on": 2 wds.

2 Sex symbol Welch

3 Completely wasted: 4 wds.

4 Dishwasher detergent brand

5 Moving part of an engine

6 Neighbor of Norway

7 Lawyers' org.

8 Not wasted at all: 4 wds.

9 Small computer, like an iPad

10 Poker announcement: 2 wds.

17 All square

21 They might clash

23 Tiny bit

26 Trendy area of London

28 Major shock to the system

29 1978 Burt Reynolds comedy

30 Nastassja of "Tess"

32 "Help!": 2 wds.

33 Caught in a trap

35 Visit briefly and without warning: 2 wds.

41 There are three in a hockey game: abbr.

43 Roadside stopover

124

Across

1 Shrimp ___
7 Late humor writer Bombeck
11 Andy Warhol's field: 2 wds.
12 Continue: 2 wds.
13 Common compliment: 3 wds.
15 Black, to poets
16 Married woman
17 No longer in style
20 Computer company
22 Scary snake
23 Burning
26 "What an improvement!": 2 wds.
29 Like Superman's actions
30 Dark and depressing, as music
31 Frat party need
32 Jerks
34 ___ talk
36 Space shuttle org.
38 "Can't make any promises": 4 wds.
43 One of the primary colors
44 Herman of movies and TV
45 Word after trash or sandwich
46 River's little cousin

Down

1 Secret agent
2 Dove's sound
3 "The Simpsons" role
4 Guys
5 Investigation
6 "Was ___ harsh?": 2 wds.
7 One of twelve
8 Rent sharers
9 Anchor
10 "No ifs, ___ or buts!"
14 Weapon in the game Clue

17 Route
18 1975 Wimbledon champ Arthur
19 Car part: 2 wds.
21 Diner sandwich
23 First three of 26
24 Idea
25 God of love
27 Foot "finger"
28 Prince album "___ the Times": 2 wds.
32 Up to now: 2 wds.
33 Scary sword
34 ___ Xtra (soft drink)
35 Singing great Fitzgerald
37 Band equipment
39 ___ Moines, Ia.
40 She's a sheep
41 The Red or the Med
42 President pro ___

Across

1 Country whose largest island is Honshu
6 Two-wheeled vehicles
11 Stadium
12 Country whose largest island is Sicily
13 Traditional healer: 2 wds.
15 Robe closer
16 Cigarette stub stuff
17 "That hurts!!!"
19 Place to work out
23 Nunnery
27 Internet company that merged
   with Time Warner in 2000
28 Does what one's told
29 To the left or right
31 Big snake that squeezes its prey
32 Takes down, in football
34 Wagers
36 "Little ol' me?!"
37 Scientist's workplace, or a kind of dog
39 Big book
43 Traditional healer: 2 wds.
47 Dodge
48 Cousin of the guitar
49 John and Jane
50 Not quite right

Down

1 1975 movie about sharks
2 Las Vegas casino, or a kind of song
3 You feed them and hug them
4 Pungent fish put on pizza
5 "I don't think so"
6 Life stories, for short
7 In need of scratching
8 Kit ___ (candy bar)
9 Band that sang "Don't Bring Me Down"
10 Country whose capital is
   Damascus: abbr.
14 When the sun comes up

18 Where the sun goes down
20 Letters, bills, flyers, etc.
21 Secret language
22 Bar orders
23 Kind of salad that's also a baseball great
24 Instrument in an orchestra
25 In good order
26 ___ Bell (Mexican fast-food chain)
30 They go downhill in a hurry: 2 wds.
33 Prefix with dextrous
35 Popular piece of playground equipment
38 Cards with a letter on them
40 Prefix meaning "all"
41 Army members below col.
42 Genesis name
43 Fellows
44 ___ Marie Saint ("North by Northwest" actress)
45 Hydroelectricity source
46 Hoops player's org.

Across

1 Becomes weather-beaten, as an old car
6 Head monk, at a monastery
11 God, to Muslims
12 Spaghetti sauce brand that means "you're welcome" in Italian
13 Rattler or water moccasin
14 "The Power of Positive Thinking" author Norman Vincent ___
15 Dish you eat off at a picnic: 2 wds.
17 Sneaks a look
18 Software company named for a colorful piece of clothing: 2 wds.
22 Number of Beatles or Teletubbies
25 Nabisco cookies
26 Sporty car
27 Nicely organized
28 Kind of charge listed on a receipt
29 Dorky type
31 Glass you drink out of at a picnic: 2 wds.
36 Accomplishments
37 Chevy ___ (comic actor)
38 Sailing the waters: 2 wds.
39 One of the simple machines
40 Give it another go
41 Put forth, as energy

Down

1 Woodworking tool
2 Arm bone
3 Hit with the hand
4 Grab
5 Guides to Mt. Everest
6 Fruit that's also a computer
7 Suddenly run towards, as an exit: 2 wds.
8 Defeats, as for a part in a play: 2 wds.
9 Stare
10 One of five on a foot
16 Cat or dog, often
18 Howard or Paul
19 Before, in poems
20 Ahead of no one, in a competition: 2 wds.
21 What a tea bag goes in: 2 wds.
23 ___ tree (trapped): 2 wds.
24 Tyrannosaurus ___ (big dinosaur)
26 Office worker's area
28 All prepared
30 Opinion pages piece
31 Tennis great Sampras
32 Cereal brand that goes in party mixes
33 Neanderthal's home
34 Computer owner
35 ___ Plus (shampoo brand)
36 A long way away

127

Across

1 Clever people
5 Attraction
11 "That's funny!" sound
12 Play a simple instrument
13 Actor Sharif of "Funny Girl"
14 Sweet and soothing, ironically
15 Dutch spy of WWI: 2 wds.
17 Cole ___ (picnic side dish)
18 Is in possession of
22 Summer workers, often unpaid
25 Cool
26 ___ and aahed
27 Earth-shaking event
29 Patriotic letters
30 Said "1, 2, 3..."
32 Becomes solid, like concrete
34 Friends
35 Refreshing item given in spas: 2 wds.
39 Italian sausage
42 Tea you can order at Starbucks
43 Not what you'd think
44 Model Moss or actress Winslet
45 Is the father of, in the Bible
46 Baseball great Musial

Down

1 "To ___ it may concern..."
2 "___ Man of Constant Sorrow": 3 wds.
3 Words to wind things up: 2 wds.
4 Baked goods brand that "Nobody doesn't like": 2 wds.
5 When the sun comes up: 2 wds.
6 Come down hard
7 FDR's affliction
8 And so forth
9 Kind of beer
10 Allow
16 First letter in "California" or "Colorado": 2 wds.
19 The general situation: 2 wds.
20 Shoe company with a swoosh as its symbol
21 Went too fast
22 Notes for those in debt
23 It smells
24 Sit in a crouching position
28 Opens, as a door
31 Fiber ___ (telecommunications technology)
33 1953 Alan Ladd movie
36 Leave out
37 "I'm so hungry, I could ___ horse!": 2 wds.
38 Financial claim, as on a house
39 Bro or sis
40 "You ___ Not Alone" (Michael Jackson song)
41 Fireplace piece

Across

1 "Now I see!"
4 Gift of ____ (ability to talk to people)
7 Pose a question
10 Fish often batter-dipped
11 "Bravissimo!"
12 School org.
13 With 40-across, hit CBS sitcom that debuted in 2003: 5 wds.
15 Politician's "no" vote
16 Super-cool
17 Period of history
18 Zsa Zsa or Eva
21 What you look for on a first date
23 Inch or foot
24 ABC morning show, for short
25 Hit ABC and then CBS sitcom that debuted in 1960: 3 wds.
30 "Electric" creature
31 Take to the seas
32 Japanese car
35 How some things are contested
36 Took off quickly
37 Restaurant big shot
39 "____ and Nancy"
40 See 13-across
44 Mineral deposit
45 All Hallow's ____ (another name for Halloween)
46 Sailor's agreement
47 Neither this ____ that
48 Home for lions or thieves
49 Tree that doesn't sound like me

Down

1 Make believe
2 "In what way?"
3 Shakespearean fuss
4 Doomed individual
5 Alan of "Sweet Liberty"
6 "I have no idea!": 2 wds.
7 Sleeping condition
8 Oldest of the Beatles
9 Quick little watercraft
14 One more
18 Chewing ____
19 "Is it ____ wonder?"
20 Piece of information
22 Falsely present (something as): 2 wds.
24 Some shaving cream
26 Attained
27 Little piece in a feedbag
28 Zero
29 Sneaky
32 Starting a destructive fire on purpose
33 Capital city on the Nile
34 Beneath
35 Keller or Hunt
38 Own
41 Fifth month
42 It blinks and winks
43 ____ Mexico

Across

1 Non-reactive to other gases
6 Place to play racquetball, or a 1979 hit song
10 At no time
11 Necklace component
12 Overly authoritarian
14 Do the math, maybe
15 Come into contact with
16 Hairy mammal
17 Confederate general
18 Enjoy oysters, say
19 Sea: Fr.
20 Whirlpool
22 Catches a few Z's
24 Scene of battle
26 "___ and Confused"
28 Golf scores
32 Turner who founded CNN
33 Barker or Marley
35 Two after tee
36 Palindromic woman's name
37 Mystery in the sky
38 Card with a letter on it
39 Speedy
42 Two-color cookies
43 Swap
44 Body part nicknamed the "schnoz"
45 Brought on board

Down

1 Breathe
2 Had to have
3 Avoided, as the law
4 Fire up (the motor)
5 "Give it a shot": 2 wds.
6 Money in Tokyo
7 Proper address for a lady, in France
8 Brunch items
9 Kind of tree whose wood is used to smoke salmon
11 General played to an Oscar by George C. Scott
13 Averted, as a disaster: 2 wds.
21 Nickname of Red Sox great Carl
23 Put in the microwave, for short
25 Offers counterarguments against
26 Actor in "Goodfellas" and "Casino"
27 Wise old sayings
29 2009 James Cameron movie
30 Go back, as a hairline
31 Expected to place, as in a tournament
32 Claw
34 Kind of restaurant table
40 Work with the soil
41 "Either you do it, ___ will!": 2 wds.

130

Across

1 Some desktops
4 Arena where the Knicks play, for short
7 "Now I understand!"
8 Every last bit
9 Place for a pea
12 Nameless man, in court: 2 wds.
14 Comic Gasteyer
15 Middle Easterner, often
16 Warning signal
18 Painting on a wall
20 Raise
21 Nutty ___ fruitcake: 2 wds.
22 Georgia known for painting flowers
25 Mona Lisa painter
27 Make believe
29 "Survivor" network
32 Show set on an island
33 Reproductive structure, in biology
35 Makes changes to, as a piece of legislation
38 Financial field, for short
39 ___ and feather
40 Stock analyst's arrow, in good times
42 Critter found in a messy kitchen
43 Ruin
44 High card, in many games
45 Ask nosy questions
46 Neither here ___ there

Down

1 Word before party or bottoms
2 Singing group
3 Big hot place: 2 wds.
4 Magazine with Alfred E. Neuman
5 No neat freak
6 Singing show set in Ohio
9 Big wet place: 2 wds.
10 Light switch choices: 2 wds.
11 "The Divine Comedy" author
13 Heat, Nuggets, etc.
17 Actor Guinness
19 Adore
23 Relatives
24 Winds up
26 Letters on business envelopes
27 Silver: Sp.
28 Like Julius Caesar
30 Untamed horse
31 "Return to ___"
34 Each
36 Pour (out)
37 Practice boxing
41 Attempt

131

Across

1 Put one foot in front of the other
5 The San Diego Chicken, e.g.
11 Spoken
12 Video game place
13 Homer Simpson's older daughter
14 Make less messy
15 Connect-the-___ (pencil and paper game)
16 Has the power to
17 Work with acid
19 Get-rich-quick scheme
23 Many different kinds of
26 Pie ___ mode: 2 wds.
27 Put up, as a building
28 Camera company
30 Fix, as an election
31 Material for a cyclist's clothing
33 Grocery store containers
35 Highfalutin'
36 Not her
38 Reverberating sound
41 Evaluate
44 Smear, like paint
45 Sewing kit item
46 "Do ___ others..."
47 Made fun of
48 Townshend or Sampras

Down

1 Auctioneer's shout
2 Threesome
3 Food eaten on a spring holiday: 2 wds.
4 Credit card material
5 Fu ___ (kind of mustache)
6 Section
7 Looks over
8 Meowing pet
9 Kind of poem
10 ___-down (this answer)
18 Simple beds
20 Food eaten on a winter holiday: 2 wds.
21 ___ vera (lotion ingredient)
22 8-down with no tail
23 Action word
24 Song for one, in an opera
25 Damage permanently
29 Wanted in on the poker hand: 2 wds.
32 Sped by, on the highway
34 Backyard structures
37 Small piece of land in the water
39 Jabba the ___ (villain in "Return of the Jedi")
40 Woodwind instrument
41 Tiny crawler
42 Catch a glimpse of
43 Hemingway book "The Old Man and the ___"

Across

1 Blinking pair
5 Light bulb inventor
11 Wander far and wide
12 River that Vienna and Budapest are on
13 Concept
14 Fresh water entering a lake, e.g.
15 Dessert made from an orange vegetable: 2 wds.
17 "Hallelujah" singer Leonard ___
18 State known for its potatoes
21 Vampire's killer
25 Not many
26 Gun (the motor)
27 Perspire
30 Embarrassing public fight
32 "___ Business" (Tom Cruise movie)
34 Dessert made from an orange vegetable: 2 wds.
39 Indicate
40 State known for its corn
41 Financial arrangement involving a neutral third party
42 Blood problem
43 Defeats
44 Some kids

Down

1 Mr. Clapton
2 Little green guy in "The Empire Strikes Back"
3 At any time
4 Look (for)
5 Archie Bunker's wife
6 High school social events
7 Baby
8 Mope
9 One of the woodwind instruments
10 ___ and improved
16 Tic-tac-toe line
18 Variables
19 Grass's morning cover
20 Amazement
22 "___ you joking?"
23 Barbie's buddy
24 Christmas ___
28 Puts metal plates on
29 Walk very quietly
30 Go downhill in a hurry?
31 Doubting Thomases
33 Throws off, like poll results
34 Mexican currency
35 Auntie's mates
36 Sport associated with Ralph Lauren clothing
37 Victorious cry: 2 wds.
38 Chows down on
39 Neighbor of Md.

133

Across

1 "Very funny!"

5 Las Vegas business

11 Actor Sharif

12 Lessened

13 40-day period

14 Didn't just throw away

15 Doesn't leave any hard feelings: 2 wds.

17 Be the father

18 "Take ___ Train": 2 wds.

22 Essentially: 2 wds.

25 Golfer Ernie

26 Not dull

27 Wanders far and wide

29 Fine and dandy

30 Use, as a ladder: 2 wds.

32 LBJ or JFK

34 Untouched serves, in tennis

35 Carpenter's place

39 At the dinner table

42 "And there you have it!"

43 Quick look

44 Related (to)

45 Gizmo

46 Monthly bill

Down

1 Golfer's target

2 "I agree completely!"

3 Act of agreement

4 More pretentious, as a painting

5 Life's work

6 Cain's brother

7 ___ Ste. Marie, Mich.

8 "___ just what I wanted!"

9 French word before a maiden name

10 Like the numbers 3, 5 and 7

16 Alternatives to sandwiches

19 Act of disagreement

20 "St. ___'s Fire"

21 Org.

22 Letters that mean "very fast"

23 Norse god, son of 37-down

24 Train's path

28 Low-rated, as a movie or a hotel

31 Wal-Mart rival

33 Try to hit a baseball

36 Just a single time

37 Norse god, father of 23-down

38 Gasp for air

39 ___ McMuffin

40 Pie ___ mode

41 Tiny bit

134

Across

1 Another name for the buffalo
6 Tennis great Rod
11 Right as expected: 2 wds.
12 Singer Cara or Actress Dunne
13 "I've never seen its like before!": 3 wds.
15 ___ and feather
16 Letters on exploding crates, in Angry Birds
17 Designer Anna ___ (hidden in PURSUING)
18 "Excellent!"
19 "Help!"
20 Before, to bards
21 Kid's room, often
23 Checkers of vital signs
25 Online call service
27 Self-___
30 Big containers at a winery
34 Only three-letter zodiac sign
35 Negative replies
37 Use a needle and thread
38 Driver's licenses, e.g.
39 "Tastes good!"
40 Bruce or Spike
41 "Hold on!": 3 wds.
44 ___ the hole: 2 wds.
45 Failure
46 Receive a ___ welcome
47 3s, in cards

Down

1 Underside
2 Absorb oxygen
3 Terrifies
4 Umpire's shout
5 Eagles' homes
6 Raises: 2 wds.
7 Former Bush spokesman Fleischer
8 Poetry divisions
9 Make certain
10 Tries the laces again
14 Unsigned by the author
22 Compass pt.
24 Show off, as a motorcycle's engine
26 Nairobi residents
27 Actor Wood of "The Lord of the Rings"
28 Tempt successfully
29 Person who throws something
31 Not level
32 Itty-bitty
33 People of Stockholm
36 Work with iron
42 Uncle: Sp.
43 Ride

Across

1 Cooper cars

6 Be born, like a chick

11 Illogical

12 Mr. T & pals

13 Drink insertion

14 Kingdom

15 Get it in the goal!: 2 wds.

17 "Hasta la vista, baby"

18 Rotate

21 Light wind

25 Baseball number

26 Top

27 "Who's the Boss?" role

31 Goes down temporarily

32 Perhaps

34 Get it in the goal!: 2 wds.

39 Fracas

40 Claw

41 Tell the server what you want

42 Els of golf

43 Prom purchase

44 Not fresh

Down

1 Loretta Lynn's "___ Being Mrs."

2 Liking

3 Rat (on)

4 One way Coke comes: 3 wds.

5 Mended clothing

6 Safe place

7 "Relax," in the military: 2 wds.

8 Blue shade

9 "Safe!" or "Strike two!"

10 "Makes you wonder..."

16 Spare part?

18 English breakfast, e.g.

19 Kind of vase

20 Cloth for cleaning

22 Mr. Manning

23 24401 or 29340

24 NYT workers

28 Hosts

29 L.A. squad

30 Sailor's "sure"

31 Leave

33 Data units

34 No Frau

35 Time-tested, in cheesy store names

36 Arm bone

37 Cobra's configuration

38 Body part with a cap

39 Forum administrator, for short

136

Across

1 Practices boxing
6 Like some films or change
11 Attacks: 2 wds.
12 Safe place
13 Girl who visits Wonderland
14 "___ we all?"
15 One's home country
17 Olympic Games weapons
18 First letter of "freedom" but not "Friday": 2 wds.
21 Not real quick
25 Superman's enemy ___ Luthor
26 "This tastes awesome!"
28 Amaze
29 Miss ___ (TV psychic)
31 Showed shock
33 Brother's daughter, say
35 Twinned metropolis: 2 wds.
40 ___ Rica
41 "The Governator"
42 Cereal in a blue box
43 Holiest city to Muslims
44 Tale
45 Old anesthetic

Down

1 Dog and pony show
2 ___ Alto, Calif.
3 "___ happens...": 2 wds.
4 "Friends" character
5 How prices may rise
6 Sedimentary rock
7 Bother repeatedly
8 Kitchen cooker
9 Tear apart
10 Dynamite letters
16 Tom Petty hit of 1980
18 Utah's capital, initially
19 Torme or Gibson
20 Fire
22 You lose it when you stand
23 Have red ink to clear up
24 Lead down the aisle
27 Technique with knots
30 GM brand
32 Something only a handful of people know
34 Milan's country
35 It blackens a chimney
36 Ratio phrase: 2 wds.
37 Move slowly
38 Former Vikings coach Mike
39 2011 or 2012
40 Places for trials: abbr.

137

Across

1 1970s music style
6 Not able to serve, as with the military
11 Different
12 "___ the Greek"
13 Throws up a red flag
14 Poker announcement: 2 wds.
15 Reveal (that you know something): 2 wds.
17 Sailing on the ocean
18 eBay attempts
19 Inch, foot or yard
21 Young fella
22 Big fans
25 Between zero and two
26 Central
27 Scooby-___ (mystery-solving TV dog)
28 Aphrodite or Artemis
30 The latest craze
31 Towards the sunset
32 Alan of "M*A*S*H"
33 "That's so funny!"
35 Of the sun
37 Use, as influence
39 Senegal's capital city
41 Animal that starts with a double consonant
42 Last Greek letter
43 Director Jackson or singer Gabriel
44 Valentine's Day flowers

Down

1 ___ Jones Industrial Average
2 From Rome or Florence, to someone from Rome or Florence
3 Classic breakfast cereal: 2 wds.
4 Pennies
5 Approximately: 2 wds.
6 Machine gun type
7 "That's cheating!": 2 wds.
8 Classic breakfast cereal: 2 wds.
9 Ending for convert or digest
10 "And there you have it!"
16 People who like to walk around naked
18 Online journal
20 Indicates "yes"
22 City where Iowa's straw poll is
23 Angry's driver's "condition": 2 wds.
24 Pop
29 "Oh goodness!": 2 wds.
32 San Antonio building, with "The"
33 Assistance
34 Rod in a car
36 Unpleasant smell
38 Cigarette additive
40 Dormitory heads, for short

138

Across

1 Picture puzzle
6 Athlete who uses performance-enhancing drugs
11 First letter, in Israel
12 Eat away
13 It often comes with tortilla chips
14 Become fully understood, as an idea: 2 wds.
15 Marlboro, for short
16 Sporty British cars
18 Devoured
19 Singer DiFranco
20 Take to court
21 Pull behind, as a boat
22 Advantage, in sports
24 Mistakes
26 Without a connecting flight
28 Looks for water with a stick
30 Float, as an aroma
33 One ___ million: 2 wds.
34 Snake that killed Cleopatra
36 Prefix with conservative or classical
37 Football official, for short
38 One of five on a foot
39 Has the power to
40 Embarrassing mistake
42 "Don't be a hog!"
44 Actress Page of "Juno"
45 Selfish person
46 They go downhill fast
47 Storage structures

Down

1 Mischievous type
2 "Seinfeld" role
3 Breakfast food named for a European country: 2 wds.
4 Shipping company whose nickname is "Brown"
5 Bogus proceedings
6 Last part of the meal
7 Miner's stuff
8 Food also called a "latke": 2 wds.
9 Newspaper employee
10 Extends, as a magazine subscription
17 "Seems to be the case": 2 wds.
23 Two, in Spanish
25 Aisle
27 Makes more orderly
28 Funeral songs
29 Common tie score, in baseball or soccer: 2 wds.
31 Was scared of
32 Copy machine powders
35 Irritants
41 Gave grub to
43 "Yeah, right!"

139

Across

1 Letter between rho and tau
6 Lawyer's org.
9 Goodbye, in France
10 Large holder of coffee
11 Soft drink company known for ginger ale: 2 wds.
13 Reason you couldn't have committed the crime
14 Actors Holbrook and Linden
17 Cheri formerly of "Saturday Night Live"
21 "Can ___ now?": 2 wds.
22 Hosted at one's house: 2 wds.
24 Beauty pageant title: 2 wds.
26 Mrs. ___ cow (animal that caused the Great Chicago Fire)
27 Little kid
28 Streep of "Julie & Julia"
29 Piece of glass in a window
30 Underground place for waste
33 State between Texas and Arizona: 2 wds.
37 Sound made by someone entering a hot tub
38 Coffee that won't keep you awake
39 In favor of
40 Pleasant smell

Down

1 ___ fly (baseball play, for short)
2 State whose capital is Boise: abbr.
3 Gershon and Carano
4 Dinner, lunch or brunch
5 German automaker
6 IRS employee
7 "It's so cold!"
8 "Is it ___ wonder?"
12 Humble homes
14 It's shouted by people who are only on TV for a few seconds: 2 wds.
15 Nimble, like a gymnast
16 Winner's victim
18 Broadway musical about a leader of Argentina
19 Spy's activity, for short
20 Very, very angry
22 Home to basketball's Globetrotters
23 Late singer Winehouse
25 "Oh yeah?": 2 wds.
29 Cost
31 Gets married to
32 Part of CEO
33 Afternoon snooze
34 One of two on your head
35 Has the power to
36 Frequently, for short

140

Across

1 Mighty trees
5 Purity units, to goldsmiths
11 Made a picture of
12 Roma's country
13 Eat well
14 Silver, tin, etc.
15 "For Pete's ___!"
16 Not just hugs
17 Hawke of Hollywood
19 "Absolutely, general!": 2 wds.
21 Mauna ___ (Hawaiian volcano)
24 Exist
25 iPhone, e.g.
27 Fluid in a pen
28 Be nosy
29 Actress Bynes of "What a Girl Wants"
31 "___ a Song of Bethlehem": 2 wds.
32 Like a mischievous child
36 ___ out a living (barely gets by)
39 Polynesian cocktail: 2 wds.
40 Long-term spy
41 Nicaraguan leader Daniel
42 Part of MIT
43 Male tennis players, sometimes
44 Long period of time

Down

1 Vegas calculations
2 Song for one
3 "One Flew Over the Cuckoo's Nest" author: 2 wds.
4 Candy and such
5 Member of a California reality TV family: 2 wds.
6 Had food at home: 2 wds.
7 "Darn it!"
8 "Woe is me!"
9 Scrabble piece
10 Backtalk
18 Cool and edgy, like Brooklyn kids
19 Talk and talk and talk
20 Make a blunder
21 Movie ape: 2 wds.
22 Wind up
23 Letters before a crook's alias
26 "What ___ going to do?": 2 wds.
30 Blood condition
31 Indian tribe
32 "It's my turn!": 2 wds.
33 Adult female horse
34 Brad of "Thelma & Louise"
35 Thingy
37 Different
38 Becomes hard, as concrete

141

Across

1 Left work for the day: 2 wds.
7 House: Sp.
11 Rome's country, to Romans
12 Without attribution, as a poem: abbr.
13 "Stopping by Woods on a Snowy Evening" poet: 2 wds.
15 Currency unit of the U.S.
16 Aegean, Red or Adriatic
17 Calf's laugh
18 Put into office
20 Offspring, or a popular Toyota
22 Try again
23 Plato's city
24 Coke rival
26 Lorne of "Bonanza"
29 St. Louis football team
33 Do the numbers again
34 Sound of a melon hitting the ground
35 Lang. you speak
36 "That's amazing!"
38 Number in Nicaragua
39 "Song of Myself" poet: 2 wds.
42 Hint of the future
43 Fruit that's also a color
44 Where a sparrow sleeps
45 More physically alluring

Down

1 Big beam in a building
2 Peter of "Lawrence of Arabia"
3 Put off for later, as a discussion
4 "Well done!"
5 Leading the pack
6 Destiny
7 Mazda or Mitsubishi
8 Societal rootlessness (anagram of ONE AIM)
9 "Leaving already?": 2 wds.
10 Playwright Chekhov and actor Yelchin
14 Doesn't eat, for religious reasons
19 Dealt (with), as a problem
21 Sing like a bird
23 Big primate
25 Give money to, as a university
26 Became charming to, over time: 2 wds.
27 Call something else
28 Philadelphia's NFL team
30 Grads of a school
31 Oversee
32 Pothead
34 County, in English place names
37 Cries of discovery
40 Dynamite letters
41 Money for the IRS

142

Across

1 Should it happen that
7 Palindromic title of respect
11 Bone ___ transplant
12 "Assuming yes..."
13 Alfred Hitchcock classic
14 Stitched
15 Hardy and Asner
16 Gives approval to
18 Dripping
19 Country between Vietnam and Thailand
21 Consistent
23 Leg exercise
25 To any degree
26 Baseball stat
27 Carew or Stewart
28 Resident in heaven
30 Quick on the uptake
33 Ruined
35 Gush (forth)
36 Actress Longoria
37 Hemingway's "The Old Man and the ___"
39 Greek letter
40 Valley known for its wine
42 Family tree men
44 Spun the records
45 Persuasive
46 Just average
47 Is

Down

1 Forces
2 NYSE rival
3 Say "I didn't want that anyway!"
4 Semicircle's shape
5 Area of NYC
6 "Return of the Jedi" cuties
7 Prefix with apprehension
8 They spoil the bunch, it's said
9 Additionally
10 Talk show host Williams
17 Celebs
20 ___-toothed tiger
22 Tiny particles
24 Scrabble pieces
28 Changes, like the Constitution
29 Indian tribe near the Grand Canyon
31 Hold against
32 Unexpected plot events
34 Two, in cards
38 Strong as ___
41 Shakespearean hubbub
43 Special effects letters

143

Across

1 Quick punch
4 In the past
7 "___ I known..."
10 Letters seen in red, white and blue
11 Scientist's workspace
12 2001 boxing pic
13 Title for a knight
14 Write in code?
16 Bakery buy
18 Brings up
19 "Moving on..."
21 Little kid
23 Feature of some diaries
24 Reagan and Clinton
25 Card in the hole
27 Touch on the shoulder
29 Ending for persist
30 Affectionate letter closing
32 Long story
34 LSD
35 It's in your blood
38 Baker or Hill
40 A long way from wealthy
41 Bug
43 ___ de guerre
44 Game with Skip cards
45 Lad
46 Preceding
47 Room where work gets done
48 Many a Monopoly property: abbr.
49 Communist

Down

1 "___ second!"
2 _____-Americans
3 Director of "Diner" and "Rain Man"
4 Swiss peak
5 World Chess Champion from 1985-2000
6 Instrument also called the "hautbois"
7 Co-founding journalist of "60 Minutes"
8 Sarah Palin, e.g.
9 About to go out, as a light bulb
15 Way through a fence
17 "Secondly..."
20 Pretend
22 Superlative suffix
25 In the manner of
26 Sherlock Holmes's drug
28 Buddy
31 Make changes to a book
33 Age ___ (feature of some relationships)
36 Sexy Demi
37 Not just dangerous
39 Big brass instrument
41 Fizzling firecracker
42 Free round in a tournament

Across

1 Army rank
6 Amassed, like a big bar tab
11 Flying solo
12 Make up (for)
13 Sends to the canvas
14 Presidential periods
15 Computer key with its "ape" cut off
16 Historical period
18 Gymnastics cushion
19 Mike and ___ (candy brand)
20 Palindromic holiday
21 Ending for orange or Gator
22 Keep ___ on (watch)
24 Demeanor
26 Non-thinking
28 Pothead
30 Winnie-the-___
33 Museum pieces
34 Scary snake
36 Card game whose name is Spanish
37 ___-di-dah (pretentious)
38 Hair styling goop
39 Presidential candidate, often: abbr.
40 Perfect
42 To the left or right
44 On the ___ of (about to)
45 Gets with a good one-liner
46 Fools
47 Plus thing

Down

1 Succeed
2 State purchased from the Russians
3 Psychologist who was a frequent guest of Johnny Carson
4 Lennon's love
5 Put back to zero
6 Tapping sound
7 Consumed
8 Famed proponent of nuclear disarmament
9 Like some beds
10 Irritate repeatedly
17 Rueful feeling
23 Pop's boy
25 Quick sip
27 Dogs like Snoopy
28 Spit, to doctors
29 Swaps
31 Feeling restless
32 Sure to tell the truth
35 Shopping center
41 Lady's secret, often
43 Certain sibling, affectionately

145

Across

1 Candy bar option

6 One of 435 in DC

9 Lisa and Bart's sister

10 Metric system prefix

11 January 1st

13 Shows appreciation (for)

14 One of many in the Pacific

15 Working hard

16 Hour sixtieth

18 "___ understand it..."

19 Des Moines residents, for example

20 Roman numeral for this weekend

21 Fasten securely, perhaps

23 Place for a manicure

26 Scattered

27 Not us

28 Drink quickly

29 Not what you'd expect

30 They're made on January 1st

33 Exist

34 Recently

35 Round green vegetable

36 They measure support

Down

1 Diamond Head's state

2 Home to the Sphinx

3 Seemingly forever

4 Aunt: Sp.

5 That woman's

6 Feature of Japan's flag

7 Places on a pedestal

8 Check recipient

9 Reacts like ice in the sun

11 Elite Eight and Final Four org.

12 African peninsula

16 Gumption

17 Victorious claim

19 Mischief makers

20 Bette Davis's role in "All About Eve"

21 Area of activity

22 Sickened feeling

23 Gets on film

24 Pasta often with ridges

25 Tan and Carter

26 Word before metal or paper

27 Proceeding in court

29 "___ have to do"

31 Cut (off)

32 What a lenticular cloud may be mistaken for

146

Across

1 Where dandruff forms
6 Word in many Florida city names
11 FDR's affliction
12 Bird on the U.S. Great Seal
13 Fictional detective, or pseudonym of his creators
15 Playing hard to get
16 Greek letter after sigma
17 Palindromic woman's name
18 Singer Kristofferson
20 Of the coldest season
22 Period after Mardi Gras
23 Prefix with classical
24 Defeats by a small amount
26 Law school class
30 Total: abbr.
32 Boat's underside
33 Loud noisemaking
36 Indian woman's clothing
37 Put on TV
38 Drink made from leaves
40 Study
41 Creepy author from Maine
44 Bert's puppet buddy
45 Family tree female
46 Put off
47 Scary snake

Down

1 Dotted pattern
2 Used crayons
3 Teaming up (with)
4 It isn't true
5 Seattle or St. Louis
6 "Hush!"
7 ___ de toilette (perfume)
8 Real estate ___
9 Obvious
10 Old-school comedian Youngman
14 Show signs of being tired
19 Power for old trains
21 Breakfast corners
25 Put out a fire, one way
27 Prepared
28 Stamp or Trent D'Arby
29 Word after hash or gun
31 Elm or oak
33 Prepared to rob, as a house
34 Petrol amount
35 "___ we all?"
39 Another palindromic woman's name
42 Apple or cherry
43 Joke around with

147

Across

1 Game show host who lets people buy vowels
6 Easily-fooled folks
11 Send to cloud nine
12 Warn
13 Dangerous and unpredictable, as a situation
14 Flyer that extended its name in 1997
15 Make an inquiry
16 "I'm afraid that's impossible"
18 #s
19 Fifty divided by fifty
20 George Bush's brother
21 Pig noses
23 Feliciano or Canseco
24 Dir. away from SSW
25 "The Cask of Amontillado" author
26 Havana's island
28 Hang
31 Hockey great Bobby
32 U.S. currency unit: abbr.
33 Man's name that means "king" in Latin
34 Go through hell, as when making a decision
36 Ability to read minds
37 Decorate with sequins, as a jacket
38 Greek letter that becomes another Greek letter when you remove its first two letters
40 Kid's truck name
41 Palindromic word that means "belief"
42 Hateful look
43 Big pitchers for water

Down

1 Family cars
2 Bluegrass singer Krauss
3 "Running on Empty" and "Doctor My Eyes" singer
4 Stuffed in one's piehole

5 ___ speaker (convention participant)
6 Pesto or marinara
7 Ingrid's role in "Casablanca"
8 Pittsburgh Steelers tackle in a famous 1970s Coca-Cola commercial
9 Groups of lions
10 Flashy light
17 Roll-___ (some deodorant sticks)
22 A, in Mexico
23 "The Daily Show" host Stewart
25 Colors for an artist
26 East and West, in the U.S.
27 Encourage
28 12: abbr.
29 TV newsman Holt
30 People who've moved away from the U.S., say
32 Middle eastern currency unit
35 Adidas rival
39 Cut, as trees

148

Across

1 Food served in slices
6 Shaving need
11 Conceptions
12 Part of a martini
13 Undercover policemen, e.g.
14 Pepe ___ (cartoon skunk)
15 "Just as I thought!"
16 Hawaiian instrument, for short
18 In favor of
19 Rushed person's problem
21 Your and my
22 Giving approval to
24 1960s drug
25 "Manhattan" and "Manhattan Murder Mystery" director
27 Sign of the zodiac
29 Confederate leader
30 Soviet prison system
32 Place to get some drinks
33 Understand
36 Palindromic woman's name
37 Salmon on a bagel
38 Prefix with angle
39 Japanese dressed in black
41 Clarifying words
43 Machu Picchu builders
44 Country singer Steve (sounds like a nobleman)
45 FBI employee
46 No manly man

Down

1 Blame for, as a crime
2 State famous for potatoes
3 Rigid enforcement of rules
4 Efron of "High School Musical"
5 Taking for granted
6 Part for an actor
7 Beer
8 Silver-colored fire sources
9 Say too much, as a catchphrase
10 Finds a new way to express
17 Barbie's buddy
20 Pres. Eisenhower
23 The Milky Way, and others
25 European country next to Greece
26 Like the famous tower in Pisa, Italy
28 Year of the ___ (2008, to the Chinese)
31 Mysterious sight in the sky
34 Spoken exams
35 "Eeny-meeny-___-mo..."
37 Final
40 One of the Brady kids
42 ___ tai (drink)

149

Across

1 Cigarette remains
6 Condition of sale, sometimes
10 Old love
11 End of ___
12 1998 Robert De Niro movie
13 Element that's tested for in people's basements
14 Charged particle
15 Lake maker, sometimes
17 First off
18 Worker busy in Apr.
19 ___-cones
20 Rejections
21 Arthur who won the U.S. Open in 1968
23 Kid who's skipping school
25 Actress Gilbert or singer Manchester
27 Longtime colleague of Jennings and Rather
29 ___ and crafts
32 Actor Chaney
33 Sheep's greeting
35 Great anger
36 Toronto's province: abbr.
37 Heavenly sphere
38 Popular kind of Buddhism
39 Lighted sign at a radio station
41 Splotches, as of paint
43 Junior ___ (movie theater candy)
44 Zellweger of "Jerry Maguire"
45 Caspian and Caribbean
46 Makes very wet

Down

1 Cameroon's continent
2 Boats with one mast
3 TV character played by Miley Cyrus
4 Big record label
5 Mails
6 Palindromic woman's name
7 Resort city south of the Grand Canyon
8 Like some patches
9 Least crazy
11 Protective covers
16 Pacifist
22 "I just saw a mouse!"
24 Neighbor of Canada: abbr.
26 The 12 ___ of Hercules
27 Flowers
28 Reagan nickname
30 "Jeopardy!" host
31 Gets the feeling (that)
34 Short forms, for short
40 "___ no problem!"
42 Shortest sign of the zodiac

Across

1 Gives a darn
6 Burly
11 Coral island
12 Eskimo's house
13 Stylish
15 Creature in a colony
16 Fish used in fish & chips
17 Suffix with Seattle or Manhattan
18 Drink cooler
19 Prior to
20 Salt: Fr.
21 Medieval peon
23 Does a plant owner's job
25 Triangular road sign
27 Measuring medicine
30 Takes a chair
34 Iron ___
35 Little bit, as of coffee
37 Negating word
38 Have the title
39 Fork cash over to
40 17-17 in football, e.g.
41 Healthy
44 Stomach issue
45 Kind of mushroom
46 Online magazine once owned by Microsoft
47 Busybody

Down

1 French coastal city
2 Instantly
3 Roto-___
4 Antlered animal
5 Piece of pizza or pie
6 "Who cares!"
7 Ingredient in an omelette
8 Nancy Drew's aunt
9 Twenty-___ (kind of putt)
10 Sings from the mountaintops
14 Scandinavian language
22 "Just so it's known..."
24 6-pointers, in football stats
26 Put big ideas in the head of
27 Idiot
28 "1984" author
29 One of the tribes of the Iroquois Confederacy
31 Summer worker
32 John
33 ___ Artois (beer brand)
36 Short African tribesman
42 Permit
43 Trouble

151

Across

1 Charles of investment advice
7 Massages
11 John of "A Fish Called Wanda"
12 Jacob's twin, in the Bible
13 Construction site vehicles
15 Pen tip
16 Thin fish eaten as sushi
17 Hospital workers: abbr.
18 Ensnares
20 Comedian Anderson
22 Push, as merchandise
23 Drank small amounts of
24 Old anesthetic
26 Sweet, like soft drinks
29 Mimics
33 Make ___ of (highlight)
34 Feeling of regret
35 Thompson of "Caroline in the City"
36 Univ.
38 Lowest two-digit number
39 Items on restaurant tables
42 Largest of the continents
43 Retaliate for
44 Flower of the future
45 Damaged, as a car's body

Down

1 Odors
2 Actress Danes or Forlani
3 Like some remedies or medicine
4 Soaking
5 Remnants of a cigar
6 "That Should ___" (Justin Bieber song)
7 Gun (the motor)
8 Exhausted
9 "Peter Pan" author
10 Figured (out)
14 North of the Iran-Contra scandal
19 Skirt part
21 Wealthy Winfrey
23 Not outgoing
25 Lock of hair
26 Mexican restaurant condiments
27 Feeling of discomfort
28 Hands-on soccer player
30 Inventor's claim
31 Come to the forefront
32 Had the idea
34 Get rid of one's beard
37 African nation that's also a man's name
40 Little bit
41 "One Flew Over the Cuckoo's Nest" author Kesey

152

Across

1 Money given under the table
7 Victory
10 Seatmate of a clarinetist or flautist
11 Woman
12 Serenade
13 Multivitamin component, often
14 In a harmless manner
16 Yell in a shrill way
18 One of the colors of the rainbow
19 Irish ___ (dog breed)
23 Pat of "Wheel of Fortune"
25 Replay camera
26 Person who asks "Got a light?"
28 Condominium, to real estate brokers
29 "I will save the day!"
31 ___ City (New Jersey resort)
34 Not that
35 Dummies
39 Not worth discussing
40 Pacific, Indian, or 31-across
41 Moon's counterpart
42 Japanese automaker

Down

1 Mass. city
2 Baseball stat
3 Charged particle
4 McDonald's order with eggs, sausage, a biscuit, etc.
5 Lauder of perfume
6 Rocks, or a rock band
7 Raise a red flag
8 Show that made Taylor Hicks famous, for short
9 Biggest city in the USA
11 What people often eat a few hours after 4-down
15 Finishes off a cake
16 Criticize harshly
17 Stephen King title dog
18 Some coll. degrees
20 ___ avail (unsuccessfully)
21 Give off
22 Spoil, as food
24 Sharp
27 Turns in to the cops (or to Mom)
30 Christina of "The Addams Family"
31 They give out $20 bills
32 You, old-style
33 Animal with a mane
36 More, in Mexico
37 ___ roll (doing well)
38 Nine-digit ID

153

Across

1 Types online notes to, for short
4 Piece of equipment for a rock band
7 "___ was that masked man?"
10 Understand
11 Rank below gen.
12 Mate for a ewe
13 ___ hot streak (doing well)
14 Actress ___ Marie Saint
15 "May ___ excused?"
16 Score a touchdown rushing the ball
18 ___ the cows come home
19 Singer Celine and namesakes
20 Suffix with Wisconsin
21 Sport in the snow
23 Pecan or cashew
24 Raggedy ___
25 D followers
27 Gangster's gun, for short
28 Interest on a loan shark's money
29 Seer into the future
31 It may be poached or deviled
32 Painting holder
33 Day after Wed.
34 Shade providers
37 "Give ___ try!"
38 Playground game
39 Body art, for short
40 Mal de ___ (seasickness)
41 "___ you almost ready?"
42 One of two that view
43 TV announcer Hall
44 The Mormon Church, in initials
45 Rock band that broke up in 2011

Down

1 Composer Stravinsky
2 Restaurant options
3 Watching things closely
4 Polish remover
5 "Let's get beyond this topic..."
6 Intends
7 College area usually run by the English department
8 As a matter of routine
9 Brunch food
17 Roman numeral added to names
21 Find a shortcut
22 Gave a "sir" title to
26 Country estates
30 Friend, to the French
32 Deadly
35 Marvin who sang "What's Going On"
36 Part of a tulip

154

Across

1 Tiger's ex
5 Libra's symbol
11 TV "Warrior Princess"
12 Dictatorial ruler
13 Muhammad Ali's old name
15 Newton of gravitational fame
16 Mia of soccer
17 When some local news starts
18 Starch often candied
21 Hawaiian necklace
22 Biblical garden site
24 Girl or woman
26 "White Album" ballad
28 Talk
31 Some fast-food places
35 Pie ___ mode
36 Mountain ___ (green soft drink)
38 Money for later years
39 Fictitious Cincinnati radio station
41 The ___ Brothers ("Shout" singers)
43 Traditional part of Lent
46 Juneau's state
47 Attractive
48 Flower that's dying
49 "Planet of the ___"

Down

1 Bring a thrill to
2 Didn't buy, as a car
3 Totally nuts
4 Letters on the space shuttles
5 Good name for a guy who makes gumbo?
6 Baseball great Young et al.
7 St. Louis landmark
8 Random chorus syllables
9 Tooth covering
10 One of the Little Rascals
14 More than cool
19 Blazing
20 Gibson or Blanc
23 ___-picking
25 January honoree, for short
27 Take down the aisle
28 Appalachian fruit
29 Base that dissolves in water
30 Of the ankle
32 Put gas in, as your tank
33 Make
34 Agree
37 Come out on top
40 "Hey, you!"
42 Pet-lover's org.
44 Pres. Eisenhower
45 Paddle's cousin

Across

1 Neither fem. nor neut.

5 Architectural feature usually found over columns

11 Concerning

12 Threw the dice

13 She played Diane Chambers on "Cheers"

15 Americans' Cold War rivals

16 Boston cream ___

17 Author Jong

18 Goes down, like the sun

19 Get a good look at

20 Vegetable related to the turnip

23 Mad person's emotion

24 Ending for hell

26 Tenth month: abbr.

29 1990s pop group Color Me ___

30 "I agree completely!"

32 Hubbub

33 Let pass, as a storm

35 "The Three Amigos" actor

37 Largest piece at KFC

38 "Where ___ could it be?"

39 Hot topics of the day

40 Skeezy look

Down

1 Catholic services

2 On dry land

3 Wonder who sang "Overjoyed"

4 Baby's affliction

5 Guitar neck marking

6 Rogers and Cohn

7 Sickly

8 Runs off to get married

9 High point

10 Rims

14 Finds out

18 Male customer, to a polite store clerk

21 Get along in years

22 Layer of skin

23 First ___ kit

24 Airplane locators

25 Loves to pieces

26 Peter of "My Favorite Year"

27 18 holes

28 Teeter-___ (seesaw)

29 Dear deer of film

31 Great aunt of Drew Barrymore

33 Prudent

34 They can ruin picnics

36 Greek letter

Across

1 Big pieces, as of meat or marble
6 Celebrity
10 Slander's cousin
11 Not reacting
12 Walk casually
13 Session after a speaker's talk, for short
14 Frenchwoman who won two Nobel Prizes
16 Protestant work ___
17 Since
20 "Where are you?" response
24 Use needle and thread
25 Take to the stage
26 Like people who are "out"
27 Montana's capital
29 Not all
30 Uneasy feeling
32 New York's governor, 1983-94
37 Pasta with ridges
38 Goodbye, to the French
39 Carries (around)
40 Medium-distance runner
41 Blown away
42 Blog write-ups

Down

1 Poetry ___ (literary competition)
2 Peru's capital
3 Shortened form, for short
4 Faith
5 Dangerous winter weather
6 Collar stuff
7 "Beloved" author Morrison
8 Assistant
9 Letters on some TVs
11 Strain to view something
15 Largest city in the Midwest
17 Cigarette stuff
18 "What did I tell you?"
19 Bird in the Harry Potter books
21 Driving force
22 Aries is one
23 Palindromic body part
25 Oakley and Leibovitz
28 Made, as money
29 Place to record an album
31 Rascal
32 Cat's sound
33 Money before a poker hand
34 Some paints
35 Shake hands with
36 Yours and mine
37 School org.

157

Across

1 Nights before holidays

5 Does a housecleaning task

10 Half a quart

11 Repeated phrase

12 Thought

13 "I agree completely!"

14 Exact replica

16 ____-free diet

17 Vail visitor, usually

19 Evil spirit

23 Candy with its own dispenser

24 Yoko from Tokyo

25 Place for gladiators

28 People of Copenhagen

30 Defeating by a small margin

32 Overtime rule in soccer where the first team to score wins immediately

36 Deteriorate

37 Red Muppet

38 "Please play some more songs!"

39 Financial claim, as on a house

40 Side dish in a Mexican restaurant

41 Perfectly rational

Down

1 Of historic importance

2 "Livin' la ____ Loca"

3 Inspire

4 Home to horses

5 Boogied down

6 Negated, as work

7 Use your feet

8 3, in cards

9 Pathetic

11 Herb used in making tea

15 Not just my

17 Masseuse's employer, sometimes

18 "____-plunk"

20 Big country between China and Russia

21 "First..."

22 Words of rejection

26 ____ Rockefeller, vice president under Ford

27 Venomous snakes

28 Commotion

29 Heavenly harpists

31 Trait carrier

32 Vanished

33 Killer whale

34 Sunday shout

35 Solo

36 Spider's home

158

Across

1 "Don't take that ___ with me!"
5 Succeed
11 Masterwork
12 Instantly
13 Non-permanent employee
14 Stuffed (oneself)
15 Before, in poems
16 Huge heap
17 Third of 12
19 Did up, as one's sneakers
23 Tic-tac-toe line
24 Untrustworthy person
25 Whine when you don't get your way
27 Small bird
28 Ladies of the family
30 Big roll of cash
31 Sing like Sinatra
32 Church instrument
35 Breakfast area
37 Baboon's cousin
38 Washington neighbor
41 Big speakers at a rock concert
42 English-speaking country of Central America
43 Animal fur
44 Backbones
45 Finds work for

Down

1 ___ pole
2 Mozart's "Don Giovanni," e.g.
3 The best of the best
4 Ability tested by Zener cards
5 "The Gift of the ___"
6 Coral islands
7 1950's conflict
8 Language you speak: abbr.
9 Freezer cubes
10 Turner who founded CNN
16 Vietnamese soup
18 Eli Whitney invented it
20 What this puzzle's three theme entries end in
21 Manage (a living)
22 Room in the Brady Bunch household
25 Ms. ___-Man (video game)
26 Your and my
29 Button many hit in the morning
30 Pan used in China
33 Steve Jobs' company
34 Bird houses
36 Small bills
38 No longer used, as a word: abbr.
39 Dem. rival in DC
40 ___ Lilly pharmaceuticals
41 "The Simpsons" small business owner

159

Across

1 "Two ___ up!"

7 Papa

10 To be sure

11 Four times around the track, maybe

12 Motion detector

13 Since

14 Chemistry, biology and geology

16 Circle parts

19 Shakespeare title word

20 Nasty strain

22 Chews (on)

26 "It's impossible!"

27 One of the Barrymores

28 Heavy, like a muffin

29 Seaside

30 Owns

32 "Brown ___ Girl" (Van Morrison hit)

33 Looking on the bright side of life

37 Weakest chess piece

38 Starch in Chinese cooking

42 Cleveland's lake

43 President Cleveland

44 Barrier for Roger Federer

45 Elvis hit "Return to ___"

Down

1 Sets in the living room

2 "___ Haw"

3 Coffee holder

4 "Little" title role of 2006

5 Voting group

6 Nation that borders Turkey

7 The D of CD

8 Plant with fleshy leaves

9 Dict. entries

11 1999 Jim Carrey movie

15 Defeats by a little bit

16 Enthusiastic

17 Ingredient in paella

18 Prefix in many juice names

21 It comes off an ironing board

23 Hello, at sea

24 "Where ___ you?"

25 Kids take it down hills

31 Belts out a tune

33 Sign on a store

34 Slim (down)

35 Moron

36 Still hurting

39 Relative of the CD

40 Civil War general

41 Go wrong

Across

1 Made "it," in a playground game
7 "How I Met Your Mother" network
10 Very
11 Oversupply
12 Indicate
13 Give 5 stars to, say
14 Woman's name that's also a flower
15 Afternoon snooze
17 Functions
18 Hit the keyboard
19 Arizona city
20 Plural of Mr.
21 "Goodbye, ___ Jean" (opening line of "Candle in the Wind")
23 Learned person
26 In the vicinity
30 Pen
31 Palo ___, Calif.
32 Like this clue's answer
34 Outfit seen in "Black Swan"
35 Injure grievously
36 Humble homes
38 How a slacker sits there
39 Least impressive, to a teenager
40 "What'd I tell you?!"
41 Intimate meetings

Down

1 Boredom
2 Not disposed (to)
3 Spirits that live in bottles
4 Biology subfield, or a 1989 drama starring Matthew Modine
5 Approx.
6 Impersonates
7 Manila envelope features
8 Toast stuff
9 Places
11 TV show set at a hospital in Seattle, or, with one letter changed, a famous biology textbook
16 Thing
20 Mohawk-sporting 1980s icon
22 Singles
23 Gurus
24 Place to play video games
25 Very manly
27 Keeps away from
28 Vouch
29 Wakes from slumber
33 Pepper partner
37 Where to get a shot

161

Across

1 Michelob and others
6 Like secret messages
11 Find a total
12 Up
13 Greek letter after rho
14 Lucky number
15 "Make ___ double!"
16 Number cruncher of April
18 Debt letters
19 Oslo's nat.
20 More number crunchers of April
21 Firecracker that doesn't go off
22 Mom's mom
24 Guarded entrance
25 Based on sound reasoning
27 Common seasoning
29 Earls and such
32 Fla. neighbor
33 "___ no problem!"
34 Letters in many black church names
35 Dull brown hue
36 ___-com (Internet startup)
37 "30 Rock" network
38 Force
40 Stomach issue
42 Sleep loudly
43 Demi or Dudley
44 Levels
45 Discharge

Down

1 Establishing
2 Magazine worker
3 "The Raven" author
4 Bacardi, e.g.
5 Document formatting concern
6 Houses, in Spain
7 Have to pay
8 Country singer who did "You Never Even Called Me by My Name"
9 Barely manage, as a living
10 Remove covering from
17 Ask too many questions about
23 Negating particle
24 Talk casually
26 Halloween getup
27 Person who loves inflicting pain
28 Graduates
30 Glowing campfire remnants
31 Juicy information
33 Keeps the engine in neutral
39 Go wrong
41 Lincoln ___

Across

1 Has the power
4 "___ on a Grecian Urn"
7 He knocked Foreman out in The Rumble in the Jungle
8 Uncle who makes rice
9 English channel?
12 The easy life, moneywise
14 In the style of
15 It is, in Spain
16 Chosen by chance
18 Additionally
20 Curry or Landers
21 Italian sandwiches
23 Takes down the aisle
25 Poehler of "Baby Mama"
26 Inc., in England
28 Nintendo system
29 Pineapple company
31 Past, present and future
33 You may have a spare one
34 "Why did ___ banks? Because I enjoyed it." -- Willie Sutton
35 Larger than it should be
37 Mexican monetary unit
40 Hot dog holder
41 Under
43 Obnoxious person
44 3.12, for Roger Clemens over his career
45 Band that did "Radio Song"
46 Recipe abbr.
47 Secret agent

Down

1 Place to get an espresso
2 "Life is cruel!"
3 Penn State's football team
4 ___-Wan Kenobi
5 They won the 1984 World Series
6 Irish singer of "Only Time"
9 Awful baseball team of film
10 Famous New Wave band, or a type of brownie
11 Video recorder, for short
13 Colombian city known for its drug cartels
17 "I don't think so"
19 Former show of 25-across, for short
21 Tablet
22 Romantic
24 "Pretty sneaky, ___" (line from an old ad for the game Connect Four)
27 The, to Germans
30 Recede, like tidal waters
32 "Uh-unh"
35 Not yet decided, casually
36 Sarcastic "Yeah, sure!"
38 Part of a process
39 What you might say after reading this puzzle's three theme entries aloud
42 Siesta

163

Across

1 Simple earrings
6 Feeling of unease
11 Baseball great Banks
12 Specialty
13 Leona Helmsley's nickname, with "the"
15 1996 Olympics host nation
16 Geneticist's letters
17 Inflated sense of self-worth
18 Extreme ending
19 Mean person, in kid-speak
21 Vegetable used in soups
23 Mineral deposit
24 Quick scissors cut
26 Cotton ___ (Q-tip)
29 2,000 pounds
31 Dishonest way to make money
33 Tony Soprano, for example
37 Ginger ___ (soft drink)
38 Copy
39 Radio host ___ Glass
40 Prius, e.g.
41 Benny Goodman's nickname, with "the"
44 ___ a high note
45 Lack of fighting
46 Takes a breather
47 Acceptances

Down

1 Book after another book
2 Bridge features
3 Like leftovers
4 Six-sided roller
5 Puts in the mail
6 International ___ (diplomat's area)
7 ___ de plume (pen name)
8 Language Sophocles wrote in
9 Play place
10 Choir voice
14 "I'm ___ you!" ("You don't fool me!")
20 The latest
22 First aid ___
25 Elixirs
27 Small trees
28 You don't want to lose this during a bike race
30 Soft ball brand
32 Combines two corporations
33 Creator
34 Express a point of view
35 Is flexible
36 Like some singing voices
42 Obtained
43 Little, in Scotland

Across

1 Aquarium fish
6 People you model yourself after
11 ___ 5200 (1980s console)
12 Plural seen in geometry textbooks
13 Stuff to put on your sandwich if you find strips or bits too crunchy?
15 ___ put (Olympics event)
16 Word after Days or Quality
17 One of the Germans?
19 Sandwich that's the theme of this puzzle
22 California city's nickname
25 Nothing special
26 Demand that your sandwich speak to a higher power?
28 March day
29 Eastwood and Black
30 Brady who throws bombs
31 TV's Dr. ___
32 Flowers around your neck, in Hawaii
33 Flower around your feet, in Hawaii (run!!)
37 The pride felt by your sandwich, when eaten by the Best Man's counterpart?
41 Expect
42 Seek help from
43 Into chess and crosswords, perhaps
44 Horse, in poetry

Down

1 Talks and talks
2 Salt Lake's place
3 Designer Rabanne
4 Occupy Wall Street events
5 Counterweight to yang
6 Golf bag items
7 When the sun comes up
8 Out of the ordinary
9 Say it's so when you know it's not
10 Respected fellow
14 His nose knows...when he's lying
18 Hosp area.
19 First word of two Springsteen album titles
20 It measures logical reasoning and verbal ability: abbr.
21 Christmas gifts, often
22 Zip to and fro
23 Try again
24 Thingamajig
25 Overflow
27 Inventor Whitney
31 "Refugee" singer Tom
32 Put (down)
34 British royal
35 Cast a ballot
36 Its first letter stands for "Alex"
37 Get darker
38 Be in hock to
39 Damage
40 "Another 48 ___" (Eddie Murphy movie)

Across

1 Scented stuff, like Liz Taylor's "White Diamonds"
8 Ignited
11 Mrs. Franklin Roosevelt
12 High card
13 Going around the edge of, as golf ball around the hole
14 Peace: Lat.
15 "___ be a pleasure!"
16 Fired off an e-mail
17 Spoken
20 Grown-ups
22 Slick
23 "So's ___ old man!"
24 Late labor leader Jimmy
26 Keep away from
30 Big record label
32 Former flames
33 Flashy disc on a dancer's costume
36 Loud shout, or a website where you can rate restaurants
37 "Dang it!"
38 Professor's helpers, for short
40 Fish eggs
41 Cigarette stuff
45 30-second spots
46 365 days
47 Kitty or puppy
48 "Ozzie and Harriet" family

Down

1 Each
2 Cotton gin inventor ___ Whitney
3 "Stand" band who broke up in 2011
4 Game show once hosted by Louie Anderson
5 Inch, foot or yard
6 Beginning of the workweek
7 Work measurement
8 Corsage's place
9 "It's impossible!"
10 Smartphone messages
16 Phrase heard on 4-down
17 "That's amazing!"
18 Brazilian city, or a 2011 animated movie set there
19 TV alien who ate cats
21 Billy ___ Williams
25 "Who ___ kidding?"
27 Lumberjack's tool
28 State next to Md.
29 Creepy claim
31 Chant
33 Word before paper or metal
34 Eat away
35 Journey with a point
39 Cain's brother
41 2,000 pounds
42 Company boss
43 Soda container
44 Hosp. areas for surgeons

Across

1 Explosion sound
5 Oil-rich nation invaded by Iraq in 1990
11 Got off, like a horse
12 Ending words of a threat
13 Song with the line "It's Christmastime in the city"
15 "___ had it!"
16 Thompson of "Caroline in the City"
17 Found a chair
18 Like tennis star Novak Djokovic
20 "Stop telling me these things!"
21 Sprinted
22 Street urchin
23 Patron saint of France
26 Poet ___ Bysshe Shelley
27 Kind of school: abbr.
28 Irish or North
29 Came into contact with
30 Bring closer
34 Tchaikovsky's "Overture ___ Major"
35 A deer, a female deer
36 Apple or cherry
37 There are five in "The Twelve Days of Christmas"
40 Black, white and orange bird
41 "That's cool!"
42 Showtime series about a psychopath
43 Elements and Cubes and such

Down

1 Foundation
2 Item in a Greek salad
3 Edmonton hockey player
4 "16 and Pregnant" channel
5 Language spoken in Seoul
6 Of the city
7 Small, as hours of the morning
8 Very skilled athlete
9 ___ Republic of Pakistan
10 Speak before a jury
14 Inventor Howe
19 Edge of a hat
22 Put on
23 Minor deity
24 1968 hit for the Turtles
25 One way to watch movies
26 ___ Pan (peanut butter brand)
28 Pothead
30 "Rolling in the Deep" singer
31 Breathlessness while sleeping
32 What a banker smokes
33 Students take them
38 Part of a lowercase j
39 Business letters

167

Across

1 Academy Award
6 Stopped, like a deer in the headlights
11 Polo designer Lauren
12 Corsage's place
13 "In a perfect world..."
14 Highfalutin' art form
15 Fuel
16 Dance style
18 Letters between M and Q
19 Extreme anger
20 Money for the server
21 "What can I do for you?"
22 No votes
24 Get rid of, as a dictator
26 Owned by you and me
28 Actress Joanne of "All the King's Men"
29 Drunken state
32 Approximately
35 Golf course score
36 Japanese electronics giant (hidden in PINE CONE)
38 Cool
39 Dry ___ (it makes "smoke" in theater productions)
40 Hassle
41 Big bird
42 ___ flush
44 Hits with an open hand
46 Make changes
47 Country great Haggard
48 Endures
49 Hall & ___ (1980s pop duo)

Down

1 Source
2 Big African desert
3 Surprise announcement?
4 iPhone program
5 Butler in "Gone With the Wind"
6 Didn't do well at all, as a movie
7 Talk casually
8 1987 #1 hit for Madonna
9 Terrible scores
10 Go by
17 Assist
23 Eat poshly
25 In favor of
27 McDonald and Reagan
29 Nice football pass
30 Washington state city
31 Communist
33 Easy as pie
34 Masterworks
37 Women's magazine noted for sex quizzes, for short
43 Small worker
45 Broadway actress Salonga

168

Across

1 Clothes, in old slang
5 Act appropriately
11 Breakfast-all-day chain, for short
12 "The Hurt Locker" beat it for Best Picture
13 Christian of fashion
14 New York Indian tribe
15 Singing in Switzerland
17 Get the vapors and fall down
18 You make it in the morning
21 One's house, humorously
23 Frighten
25 Middle of an apple
26 Dog that Garfield's not a huge fan of
27 "Throw ___ from the Train" (Billy Crystal/Danny DeVito movie)
29 Logically reason
30 ___ out a living
31 "The Republic" philosopher
33 DiCaprio of "Inception"
36 My friend, in France
39 Blue-green shade
40 How soda sometimes comes
41 Work on one's muscles
42 Baltimore NFL team
43 Takes to court

Down

1 Neat
2 Indiana neighbor
3 Self-congratulatory statement
4 Police officer's demand when frisking someone
5 Container for water
6 Goings-on
7 Chill out
8 Snacked on
9 Carpet cleaning tool, for short
10 Period of rule
16 Make something up
18 Unhealthy
19 Port in Pennsylvania
20 Animal often hit by cars
21 Company patronized by Wile E. Coyote
22 Barnes & Noble purchase
24 Alternative to eyeglasses
28 Tarzan, e.g.
29 Scottish form of the name John
32 Butcher's cuts
33 Shoe string
34 Comedian ___ Cook
35 Bills often put into vending machines
36 Russian space station
37 ___ whim
38 Part of USNA

169

Across

1 Nuts and ___

6 River-blocking structure

9 Neighbor of a Nevadan or a Coloradan

11 Seep

12 Township in South Africa

13 Former Russian ruler

14 Yo-yos, tops, kites, etc.

15 "Remington ___" (1980s show)

17 "___'s Gold" (1997 movie about a beekeeper)

18 Becomes smaller, as the moon

19 Sexual deviant, in slang

20 Emerges victorious in, as a game

21 Bob of sausage fame

23 Coleman of "Boardwalk Empire"

26 Historical periods

30 100% necessary

31 Zero, in tennis

32 Hardest to locate

34 Garden of ___

35 Poet Pound

36 People who don't throw their money away

38 Cow shouts

39 "Be that as it may..."

40 Letters after em

41 Computer key

Down

1 Destroy, as a crime ring

2 Peter of "Goodbye, Mr. Chips"

3 Attorney

4 Waters of the world, poetically

5 Took a chair

6 Baker's amounts

7 Common shrub

8 Tiniest

10 Rejections

11 2001 George Clooney movie

16 Bed size

20 Path

22 Doggie docs

23 1985 Pointer Sisters hit

24 Book buyer's favorite river

25 Beasts of burden

27 Rat or mouse

28 Hostile (to)

29 Motion detector

33 Mao ___-tung

37 Many a Monopoly property: abbr.

170

Across

1 Brings in, like a crook
5 Sopping wet
11 Latin word heard in biology class
12 He works in a mask
13 One of the waitresses on "Alice"
14 Tooth-related
15 Pretends
16 A million to ___ odds
17 "Hamlet" author: abbr.
19 Car
23 Get less drunk
26 Place for a cat, often
27 Reviewing Roger
28 Put up, like a building
30 "The Raven" author
31 U2's "Where the ___ Have No Name"
33 John of TV and new age music
35 Big airports
36 Keep a watch on
38 Crackable dozen
41 Part of FBI
44 Apple's middle
45 Many Pacific islands
46 Cat's scratcher
47 Moses parted it
48 Works with sums

Down

1 Sight in the night sky
2 With, in Quebec
3 Company that makes lip balm from honey
4 Atom ___ (physicist's equipment)
5 Logic puzzle in the paper
6 Sign of the future
7 Snoring problem
8 First aid supplies, collectively
9 Laundry detergent brand
10 Dolores ___ Rio
18 Sculpting, painting, et al.
20 1997 Peter Fonda movie about a man who works with honey-makers
21 Diplomat's skill
22 Chooses
23 Mo. number 9
24 Instrument featured in "Peter and the Wolf"
25 Country that borders Ecuador
29 "Friday" singer ___ Black
32 America
34 High shoes
37 One of the Ivy League schools
39 Alumnus, for short
40 Keeps 'em in stitches?
41 Setting for many jokes
42 Western tribe a state is named after
43 Fisherman's pole

Across

1 Stole

7 Bacon source

10 Mother ___ (she helped the poor in Calcutta)

11 State that borders Minnesota and Illinois

12 Unpleasant smell

13 Plenty

14 Where to find valuable nuggets

16 "Peace ___ time"

19 And so forth

20 "Be quiet!"

21 Gets rid of, as extra weight

24 Garden of ___

25 Yellowish-brown shade

26 Swedish cars

28 "Tom Sawyer" author

29 Simple bed

30 Angel's instruments

31 Merry-go-round

34 Run ___ (go crazy)

35 Get there

39 Hit or ___ (unpredictable)

40 Fix, as a male cat

41 Bradley and McMahon

42 Informative pieces

Down

1 Roads: abbr.

2 Soaked

3 Extreme wrath

4 Publisher with a cute animal as its logo

5 Accompany

6 "Charlie and the Chocolate Factory" author

7 Black and white vehicle

8 Victorious shout

9 Way through a fence

11 Beatles hit with nonsense lyrics

15 ___ Moines, Ia.

16 Italian ___ (summertime desserts)

17 Nothing at all

18 It's SWIPED in this puzzle

22 Faucet problem

23 NBA team from Phoenix

27 Man's name formed from three consecutive letters of the alphabet

28 "Where ___ a will..."

31 Showed up

32 In the center of

33 Not nuts

36 Call ___ day

37 "Oy ___!"

38 Where some nurses work: abbr.

Across

1 Phony

5 ___-toothed tiger

10 Got better, as cheddar

11 Make oneself look nice

12 Passes a law against

13 Rice dish made with saffron

14 Q followers

15 Mr. Onassis

16 Steve Jobs computer

17 Terre Haute sch.

18 100 yrs.

19 Mel of baseball fame

20 Insect with transparent wings

22 Take ___ time

23 Evict

25 Woody's last name, on "Cheers"

27 Hospital staff members

30 Last part

31 My, in Marseilles

32 Explosive letters in Angry Birds

33 Polished off

34 East: Ger.

35 In the past

36 Some summer births, astrologically

38 Vegetable fried in the South

39 Fire remnant

40 Defeated

41 Last name that means
   "kings" in Spanish

42 Schools of thought

Down

1 Silk or polyester

2 Sampras rival

3 First leg of the Triple Crown

4 Mag workers

5 County where 13-across originated

6 "___ you kidding me?"

7 Last leg of the Triple Crown

8 Tell, like a story

9 Makes law

13 Middle leg of the Triple Crown

15 Rock band named for an electrician's term

21 Assistance

22 Your and my

24 Send packing

25 Jerry Mathers TV role

26 Not late

28 How memory traces are stored (anagram of MANGER)

29 Worn furs

31 Othello and others

37 "That's cool!"

38 ___-Wan Kenobi ("Star Wars" role)

173

Across

1 "Curb Your Enthusiasm" star Larry
6 Greeted from a distance
11 Part of a martini
12 Mentally quick
13 Harder to locate
14 Dr. Seuss title character concerned about the environment
15 Additive seen less and less on Chinese menus
16 Sandwich named for its three main components
18 "Beat it, ya varmint!"
19 Enjoy the Alps, perhaps
20 Nickname of Boston Red Sox great Carl
21 Chemistry suffix
22 Word after red, army or fire
24 Bill with Hamilton on it, in slang
26 Person with secret knowledge
28 Secure, as a seat belt
30 Marry
32 Tool for punching holes in leather
33 Lightning ___ (it's seen on top of a skyscraper)
35 Marlboro or Camel, for short
37 Half a dance
38 Greek letter
39 Future members of a species, in biology class
40 Faint coloring
42 ___ throat
44 Long-gone, as times
45 Core group
46 Put back to zero
47 Kicks out

Down

1 Students' buildings
2 Largest U.S. state in area
3 St. Croix and St. Thomas are part of it
4 "___ been meaning to tell you..."
5 Kentucky ___ (horse race)
6 Danced to Strauss, perhaps
7 In days of yore
8 Sir Richard Branson started it
9 "Seinfeld" role
10 Showtime series set in Miami
17 Hispanics
23 Explosive letters
25 Word before Mexico, Jersey or Hampshire
27 Garden of Eden tempter
28 Part of the equation
29 Indefinite period of time
31 Distract
34 1970s musical genre
36 Looks on in wonder
41 "That's amazing!"
43 Another Greek letter

Across

1 Flip
5 Enlarge, like a photo
11 2012 rival of Ron and Mitt
12 Thelma's movie buddy
13 Parker of "South Park"
14 False
15 "What ___ did he say?"
17 Put on
18 Groups of experts
20 There are many in the Pacific Ocean: abbr.
21 "Nicely done!"
22 Aid arsonists
24 Two-___ paper towels
25 ___ Lankans
26 Tyrrhenian or Tasman
29 Sneaker or loafer
30 Troublemaker
31 Section
34 Kleenex
36 Vizquel at shortstop
37 Owl howl
38 "Seriously!"
40 1981 Best Picture nominee directed by Warren Beatty
43 Person behind the wheel
44 Threesome
45 Lucky rolls
46 Slithery snakes

Down

1 Palindromic explosive
2 The Who song "Love Reign ___ Me"
3 With 26-down, "Saturday Night Live" duo consisting of Nora Dunn and Jan Hooks (with "The")
4 Verve
5 "Saturday Night Live" duo consisting of Dan Aykroyd and John Belushi (with "The")
6 Actor Chaney
7 Be smarter than
8 Sends, like money
9 Normal
10 Jury members
16 /
18 Palindromic music category
19 Every last bit
23 Farm refrain
26 See 3-down
27 Meat eaten by Aussies
28 Donkey Kong, for example
29 Tried very hard
31 Golf course water hazards
32 "That's ___!" (Dean Martin hit)
33 Former Indian prime minister Gandhi
35 Kinda
39 He's a doll
41 Swift swim
42 "Help!!"

175

Across

1 Scandinavian automobiles

6 Become apparent, as a new reality

11 Group of eight

12 Elephant tusk material

13 Make up (for)

14 Violet shade named for a flower

15 Frozen food section staple

17 "Gorillas in the ___"

18 ___ down (ate quickly)

22 "Huh?"

26 Emmy or Oscar

27 Sporty Mazda

28 ___ Genesis (video game company)

29 Student's notebook

30 Where many pandas live

32 Cheese that's an ingredient in 15-across

38 Monte ___ (European gambling mecca)

39 Note sent in Outlook Express, e.g.

40 Mary-Kate or Ashley

41 To some small degree

42 Rock with a crystal inside

43 Has the nerve

Down

1 ___ opera (daytime show)

2 Opening of a play

3 From ___ (the gamut)

4 Mercedes-___

5 How some shrimp are prepared

6 Grain storage structures

7 Creepy movie villain, often

8 Payment for a road

9 Money for the future

10 Largest city in the USA

16 Get ___ of (eliminate)

18 Used to be

19 Have debts to

20 Fall behind

21 Not in any way calm and composed

23 Consumed

24 Devoured

25 ___ and feather

27 Didn't understand properly, as an article

29 Constricting snake

31 Layer in environmental news

32 Man or boy

33 About

34 Watson of the Harry Potter movies

35 Secret den

36 Low-calorie, in product names

37 Some brews

38 Feel like a ___ in the machine

Across

1 Possessed
4 Glass
7 Health resort
10 Individual
11 Country south of Can.
12 Lay out in the sun
13 Fall celebration with lots of beer and a foreign month in its name
16 Worked the fields
17 Solemn promise
18 Male and female
19 Big bone in the leg
20 Celebrity
22 Golden ___ (great time)
23 Not negative: abbr.
26 Ending for Japan or Sudan
27 "Oedipus ___"
28 Picnic crawler
29 "Pardon me..."
31 Sealing stuff
33 Gets ready for a trip
37 Novelist Ferber
38 Mountain where Noah's Ark landed
39 Spring celebration with lots of beer and a foreign month in its name
41 Letters in many black church names
42 Loud laughs
43 Band's vehicle, often
44 Color on China's flag
45 New age chants
46 Squeeze (out a living)

Down

1 Basketball, in slang
2 Joint on the foot
3 Betty Ford Clinic treatment
4 Geometric-sounding meat
5 Not new, like a car
6 Expected score, on a golf course
7 Big passenger boat, back in the day
8 Cow's meadow
9 Louis Pasteur developed a vaccine for it
14 Has to pay
15 Enemy
19 Media as the cornerstone of a democracy
21 ___ Wednesday
23 Racetrack non-participant
24 How cars with good brakes are said to stop
25 In a state of shock
30 Palindromic title for a woman
32 Lake: Fr.
34 Desire strongly
35 Palindromic boat
36 "JFK" director Oliver
38 Eve's dude
40 Palindromic expression of surprise

Across

1 Long story
5 Handy person to have at an unpleasant social event
11 "No ___!"
12 Make possible
13 Peanut and sesame
14 Floating aimlessly
15 President between Roosevelt and Wilson
16 Schnauzer or Rottweiler
17 Instance
19 Scary creature
23 Mrs. Bill Gates
26 Young boy
27 The former Mrs. Donald Trump
28 Light up
30 "Napoleon Dynamite" role
31 Exact revenge
33 Different
35 Single
36 Bread spread
38 Snakes on the Nile
41 "Where are you?" reply
44 Board game with a lead pipe and a rope
45 Part of a tea set
46 Take home, as money
47 Greek letters
48 Went a mile a minute, maybe

Down

1 Get a look at
2 Song in an opera
3 Posh expressions of approval, done with two hands
4 Choose not to vote (or consume alcohol)
5 Formed, like drops of sweat
6 Microsoft Word command
7 North Dakota city, or a 1996 movie
8 Its HQ is the J. Edgar Hoover Building
9 ___ on the Shelf (Christmas figure)
10 Not working any longer: abbr.
18 Unanticipated problem
20 Posh expression of outrage, performed with one hand
21 Autumn tool
22 Where Eve was tempted
23 Wallace or Judge
24 Agatha Christie's "___ Under the Sun"
25 Regarding
29 Dangers
32 Possessive on bottles of glue
34 CD player button
37 Geometry class measurement
39 Unadulterated
40 E-mail program button
41 Suffix with guitar or clarinet
42 "I don't think so"
43 Shade

178

Across

1 Over and done with
5 In the distance
11 World's Fair
12 Spain and Portugal's peninsula
13 Art class material
14 Puts off
15 "Next..."
17 And others
18 "Hey you!"
22 Minor tussle
24 Sword you'll see in London 2012
25 "It all makes sense now!"
26 Great anger
27 Apples
29 "Under the ___ Sun" (2003 drama)
32 Gush (forth)
33 Put a few chips in the pot
34 Very happy state
38 Car for a coffin
41 Show shock
42 Twist or Stone
43 Slurpee rival
44 Church or town leaders
45 ___ out a draw (narrowly avoids defeat, in chess)

Down

1 Chest muscles, for short
2 Car bar
3 Cold War competition
4 Prius people
5 Instrument for the Cajuns
6 Cain killed him
7 Enter again, as data
8 Word after lead or iron
9 Douglas ___ (kind of tree)
10 Musical scale notes
16 Doze
19 Where the cumin and cardamom go
20 Word repeated after "Que," in a song
21 New driver, perhaps
22 ___ Club (Costco rival)
23 Fellow
28 Turn the wheel quickly
29 Falls (off)
30 Durham sch.
31 Cigar, in slang
35 Manipulative person
36 "Interesting..."
37 Monkey cousins
38 Tool with a long handle
39 Letter after kay
40 Assist

179

Across

1 Corporations: abbr.
4 Chat
7 Gallery pieces
8 Exist
9 Took the bench
12 Pastry brand
14 "Terrible" age
15 Meter or millimeter
16 Biblical peak
18 Vice president under Nixon
20 Hazy history
21 Section of a race
22 Hawaiian ___
25 More than a job
27 Unnamed guy
29 Telly org.
32 Ready for customers
33 Jones of "Chasing Pirates"
35 Christmas piece
38 Wife of Zeus
39 ___ Vegas Sun
40 Some potatoes
42 "___-Devil"
43 Gulf Coast st.
44 Woman's name that means "life"
45 Salary
46 Finish up

Down

1 Not formal
2 Color in Holland's flag
3 Food you can pull apart
4 Guy's pal
5 Part
6 Bar glass
9 6 on the Beaufort Scale
10 Tony, e.g.
11 Lugs (around)
13 Polished off
17 Jackson or Rickman
19 Untamed
23 ___-mo
24 Claim on a property
26 Tolstoy title word
27 Face parts
28 Phil mentored her
30 "___ Fink"
31 Went after
34 Surprised sounds
36 Catch
37 Pacific dance
41 For instance

Across

1 The trees, the birds, etc.
7 Beer, casually
11 Online bookstore
12 Largest of seven
13 Bold
14 Car with a roll bar
15 Common insect
16 Jessica of "Dark Angel"
18 Final
20 Being annoying
24 Effortlessness
26 Scooby-___ (dog detective)
27 Breakfast food named for
   a European country
31 Zeus or Poseidon
32 Ambulance staffers, for short
33 "Psst!"
35 Sudden desire
39 One-___ (freak events)
41 Above, in poetry
42 Courtroom dozen
45 Jodie of "The Silence of the Lambs"
47 100-year-old cookie
48 Inconvenience
49 Finishes up
50 Got close to

Down

1 Tennis great Rafael ___
2 Refrigerator brand
3 Bakery items
4 Submachine gun type
5 Gossip columnist Barrett
   (hidden in MICRONATION)
6 Breakfast food named for
   a European country
7 Pat of "Wheel of Fortune"
8 Find a purpose for
9 Item included with many
   board games
10 Drain, as strength
17 Quarterback Favre
19 Perfect score, sometimes
21 Neighbor of Wash. and Mont.
22 Rejections
23 Took possession of
25 Words before hearts, diamonds, clubs or spades
27 Letters between E and I
28 Fish eggs
29 ___'s ice cream
30 Columbus campus, for short
34 "Walking the dog" toys
36 Palindromic part of an engine
37 Silly birds
38 Went wrong
40 Neither none nor all
42 Actor Mantegna
43 Big coffee holder
44 Color in Russia's flag
46 Hotel amenity

181

Across

1 Low point
4 Tablet
7 Baltic or Bering
8 Sports ___ (athletic gear for women)
9 Go down a black diamond, e.g.
12 Nightclub type
14 Magician's rabbit's home
15 Gemstone that can be almost any color
16 Mrs., in Mexico
18 Basmati and jasmine
20 October birthstone
21 Drink in a pot
22 Is OK with
25 Stuffed pasta
27 Hard to believe
29 The Knicks, the Celtics, et al.
32 Foot or meter
33 Heavenly harpist
35 Andre who won Wimbledon in 1992
38 The Bruins' sch.
39 Broccoli or spinach, for short
40 No gods
42 Prior to
43 Be indebted
44 Seoul's country: abbr.
45 Path through the mountains
46 Airline until 2001

Down

1 Accompany
2 Type of cap
3 Vehicle you can push your
  infant in, on the sidewalk
4 Hipster beer, for short
5 Greek god of war
6 Rendezvous

9 Vehicle you can push your infant
  in, in the grocery store
10 Measure of purity, for gold
11 Slanted type, casually
13 Fire
17 Playwright Coward
19 Rescue
23 Espionage org.
24 Pepsi, for one
26 Dance, music, etc.
27 Smooth
28 Felix's last name, on "The Odd Couple"
30 Nobel Prize-winning novelist Saul ___
31 Cold state
34 Filbert or cashew
36 Pollution problem
37 Corny state
41 Agent, briefly

Across

1 Small, cutesy-style
4 Homer Simpson's dad
7 ___ whim
8 "___ appetit!"
9 The ___ Four (Beatles nickname)
12 Good name for a cook?
13 Referee's mistake
15 Laser printer powders
17 Small piece of land
18 ___ 500 (annual auto race)
19 Lake on the border of California and Nevada
20 Scare the heck out of
23 "___ be my pleasure!"
24 "Give me an answer right now!"
26 1200, in Roman numerals
28 Defeat easily
31 Website with an exclamation point
33 Actress Fisher
34 Food, in slang
35 Started making people sweat
37 Straddling
39 Suffix for sugars, in chemistry
40 Billy ___ Williams
41 One of Santa's little helpers
42 Not 'neath
43 30-second spots on TV
44 Attempt

Down

1 Went ballistic
2 Chant
3 Where dirty clothes are thrown
4 Short form, for short
5 Squeezing snakes
6 Last part
9 Where stylish clothes are worn
10 Set aside
11 React to a cut
14 FBI's sister agency
16 "Jane ___"
19 Newbie
21 What a colon means, in a ratio
22 In favor of
25 Night: Fr.
26 "Goodness gracious!"
27 Chili con ___
29 Last pitcher in a baseball game
30 Cafeteria
32 Letters indicating price flexibility
35 Metal a krugerrand is made of
36 One-___ (lucky shots)
38 Vegetable that bothered a princess

183

Across

1 Director's shout
4 Snake that killed Cleopatra
7 "___ understand it..."
8 Baby's syllable
9 Large, like a check
12 Get everyone back together
14 Very unfriendly
15 Court great Arthur
16 Get your beauty sleep
18 "___ Frutti" (Little Richard hit)
20 Spreadable delicacy
21 Hotel amenity
22 Head cavities
25 "Smooth" guitarist
27 House agent
29 Laundry detergent brand
32 "M*A*S*H" man
33 Put in the fridge
35 ___ fin (shark's giveaway)
38 Not being productive
39 Hank Azaria voices him
   on "The Simpsons"
40 Mercury of Queen
42 "Automatic for the People" band
43 Orbison who sang "Only the Lonely"
44 Was in first place
45 First on the list
46 Newspaper people, for short

Down

1 Purity measurements
2 Exhausts
3 Hermetically sealed
4 Long ___ (way back when)
5 Like some grapes
6 Benedict XVI or John Paul II
9 In excellent shape
10 Less than 90 degrees, as an angle
11 Uses a keyboard
13 Not working any more: abbr.
17 Went around and around
19 "___ that the truth?"
23 Simpson Trial judge
24 Drug informant, disparagingly
26 "Such a pity!"
27 Plane-finding palindrome
28 Leave town in a gown, maybe
30 United
31 Runs, as a shirt's colors
34 Concealed oneself
36 ___-Caribbean music
37 "Dianetics" author Hubbard
41 It may be blue

Across

1 More than hate
6 Beer ingredient
10 Sporty wheels
11 Give off
12 Drinks at Kentucky Derby parties
14 Canadian creature
15 Channel you can watch Jeremy Lin highlights on
16 Sweet serve
17 Japanese grappling
21 Conductor's title
25 "I don't think so"
26 Make smile
27 Rival of Djokovic and Federer
29 Each
30 Internet startups
32 Too-good type
34 "Stop talking in the theater!"
35 Connecticut school
37 Actor Tayback of "Alice"
40 Tropical drink
43 Fleshy plant
44 More than now and again
45 The latest
46 Give a hand to

Down

1 Company that sells anti-Road Runner devices
2 Prepare pasta
3 Gorgeous guy
4 Select
5 Said no to
6 Beatles album with an exclamation point
7 Signs of what's to come
8 Palindromic Dickens kid
9 John and Paul: abbr.
13 Loser, in anti-drug ads
16 Complete jerk
18 Microsoft Word command when you make a mistake
19 Sir's counterpart
20 Severe-looking birds
21 Google ___
22 "So true!"
23 Currency named for a continent
24 Working
28 German shout
31 Capital city where you can spend 23-down
33 At this point
36 A long time
37 Don Corleone of "The Godfather"
38 Clinches, as a victory
39 Word on pennies
40 Dude
41 Bar order
42 Alien's spaceship, maybe

185

Across

1 "Quit buzzing around me!"
5 Charlie of "Hot Shots!"
10 Game show host Ben
11 Positive attitude
12 Intimate restaurant reservation
14 Misstep
15 Cut (off)
16 Bolted
17 Many a Monopoly property: abbr.
18 "Who ___ you?"
19 Previously
20 Making kitten sounds
22 Turner and Williams
23 Microwave oven sounds
25 Unwanted e-mails
28 Strikes lightly, as a window pane
32 Forty winks
33 Pack animal
34 "Beautiful work!"
35 Chemistry suffix
36 Paul, John and George, but not Ringo: abbr.
37 Tyler who's also a Roman numeral
38 Fox show with Neve Campbell
41 Host
42 More experienced in life
43 Intimidate
44 Flag lady

Down

1 Keep food from
2 Tel Aviv tongue
3 Grapeseed or sesame
4 Like some country bridges
5 Listerine competitor
6 Laughter syllable
7 Main course
8 Playwright Albee
9 Without an owner
10 Prepare vegetables in a healthy way
13 Doesn't remember that one must
21 Company that created the chess program Deep Blue
22 Recipe amt.
24 Impersonate successfully
25 Beat at the last second, on eBay
26 Country with a canal
27 First glance
29 Stripes' counterparts, in pool
30 Mediterranean bites
31 "Over my dead body!"
33 Thus far
39 One million divided by one hundred thousand
40 Good name for a plumber?

186

Across

1 Wetland area
6 Beloved cartoon elephant
11 Ann ___, Mich.
12 Whack-___ (arcade game)
13 Symbol of wealth
15 Eye problem
16 Put a stop to
17 In a sneaky way
19 Explode
22 "Indeedy"
25 Soft drink that's also an R.E.M. song
28 Get down on one's knees
29 Like this crossword puzzle
30 1970s-80s show about motorcycle cops
32 Hello, in Arabic
35 Desperate cry
39 Soldier's award
41 Love to pieces
42 Part of a play
43 Cooper cars
44 Implanted tube

Down

1 Talk back to
2 Official order
3 In a skilled way
4 Stops dwelling on the past
5 Not post-
6 ___ metabolism
7 Sufficiently
8 Italy's shape
9 Fleshy plant
10 Tear to pieces
14 What it never is for the three colors in this puzzle's long entries, since they don't have any common ones

18 Campfire piece
19 Amorphous amount
20 Calif. neighbor
21 Work at a grocery store, sometimes
22 "This is goood!"
23 Find work for
24 The third degree?
26 Capitalized letters in 30-across's title
27 Aretha Franklin's signature song
30 Italian island that gave its name to pants
31 Nathan and Alan
32 E-mail you don't want
33 German automaker
34 Scientology founder Hubbard
36 No longer with us
37 Andrews of ESPN
38 Battling each other
40 Holds

Across

1 Kyoto's country
6 Supports
11 Give a grand speech
12 Shining
13 Underwear brand
14 John of farming equipment
15 "Parks and Recreation" network
16 Secondly
18 "Honest" president
19 Yoga studio class
20 Wal-Mart founder Walton
21 Filbert or pecan
22 Gabs non-stop
24 Offers a counterargument against
26 Q-tip's target
28 Bite, but not hard
29 Restaurant furniture
32 "___ Thing You Do!"
35 Pitching number with a decimal
36 Perfect score, sometimes
38 "Rosemary's Baby" novelist Levin
39 Total: abbr.
40 Chopping tool
41 Spinning fun
42 LaBelle or LuPone
44 Misbehave
46 Word in theater names
47 The ones I'm holding
48 Bakery buys
49 Took on

Down

1 Cash in a record store
2 Saudi ___
3 It's ladled onto a griddle
4 Chowed down on
5 High homes
6 Ominous sign
7 Years you've been around
8 Fourth out of nine, in baseball
9 Gymnastics great Olga ___
10 Dentists warn against them
17 Spanish-American or Korean
23 Actor Mineo
25 Small piece
27 Holds onto
29 China Jasmine holder
30 Spain's navy, back in the day
31 Touchy subject?
33 Stimulate
34 Prepared a keg
37 Under, in poems
43 Palindromic kid
45 Letter between phi and psi

Across

1 Shook hands with
4 City vehicle
7 Palindromic name
8 Greek H
9 "___-Tac-Dough" (Wink Martindale game show)
12 It may include a photo
14 www.rice.___
15 Little devils
16 Toolbox item
18 Springs
20 Apple tablet
21 Cat-eater of TV
22 Dutch beers
25 "Miss Being Mrs." singer Lynn
27 Washington city
29 Basketball hoop
32 Money in Madrid
33 Store number
35 They have one more wheel than bikes
38 Alligator shirt brand
39 Man's name that's also a series of intellectual lectures
40 What you cross flying from America to England
42 "___ et labora"
43 Mooing creature
44 Zero, to soccer players
45 Silly laugh sound
46 Expert

Down

1 Capital of the Philippines
2 Tooth cover
3 City that's home to the NFL's Buccaneers
4 Put money on it
5 State often mentioned in the musical "The Book of Mormon"
6 Grand story
9 City just east of Phoenix
10 Perfect
11 Miss Muffet ate them with whey
13 Mentalist's claim
17 Catcher's ___
19 ___ Lee of baked goods
23 Dudes
24 "___ lively!"
26 "Alright, you win!"
27 ___ music (compose a score for)
28 Less tainted
30 Classic, as an image
31 Interfere
34 Grave letters
36 Work with acid
37 It's just over a foot long?
41 Flock female

Across

1 School session
6 Velveeta makers
11 Lacked options
12 Lousy car
13 Jordan's capital
14 "Your Movie Sucks" author Roger
15 Online magazine named for a fictional newspaper in an Evelyn Waugh novel (with "The")
17 Find offensive
18 Burn
20 Couldn't live without
24 Big ISP
25 Classic S.E. Hinton book
26 Palindromic biblical figure
27 Greatest hits
29 Way to make a quick buck
30 Cougar or coati
32 Magazine named for a novel by Thackeray
36 Blue ___ Mountains
37 Wilkes-___ (Pennsylvania city)
38 Jogging track figures
39 Sections
40 "Glengarry Glen Ross" playwright
41 Failed to

Down

1 African nation that's also a man's name
2 Dalai ___
3 Navy bosses
4 Less fresh
5 Some HDTVs
6 Sneezer's need
7 Money back
8 Site of Iowa's big straw poll
9 Word in many city names
10 Blasting palindrome
16 Get something valuable (from)
18 Hack's vehicle
19 Tool in a shed
21 Stated with conviction
22 Mrs. Juan Peron
23 Not Rep.
25 Most swanky
28 Long hair problem
29 African trip
31 "Sorry about that!"
32 Long live
33 Partner of 26-across
34 Where Farsi is spoken
35 Take five, say
36 CD-___

190

Across

1 Downright mean
6 Naples noodles
11 More
12 Richest man on the Titanic
13 Get ready to drive
14 Animal with a horn
15 Sierra Mist makers
17 Was winning
18 Republicans, with "The"
20 Studio stand
22 It's for the birds
24 Sets a price
27 Ladies' counterparts
28 Bandleader Shaw
29 Mythical ship
30 Marked down
31 Quick
33 ___ de plume
34 Stick (out)
36 Mark, as cattle
38 Make up (for)
40 Garden hose shapes
43 Painter who's one letter off from another painter
44 ___ child
45 Gets rid of, as old skin
46 "The Bellelli Family" artist

Down

1 Ping-pong table feature
2 "The Shining" prop
3 Help crossing a stream
4 Genuine
5 They won't stop talking
6 Birth city of 46-across
7 Wood used for hockey sticks
8 Not defeated
9 Way of speaking
10 Infielder's nickname
16 For example
18 Lady ___
19 Completed
21 Pair by the hair
23 Small particle
25 Metric weight, casually
26 Give the appearance of being
28 Stomach settler
30 Most common hockey player in crosswords
32 Helps with a heist
34 Rocks out
35 Six-sided state
37 Zippo
39 Mr. Beatty
41 ___ Michele of "Glee"
42 AARP members

191

Across

1 One of the Seven Deadly Sins
6 "___ Magnolias"
11 "Around the World in 80 Days" author
12 First word on the phone
13 Spa brand
14 Chipmunks leader
15 Game requiring no equipment
16 Beaver's structure
18 Word after dry or Italian
19 "Without further ___..."
20 Chats with, online
21 Man, to a store clerk
22 Once in a blue moon
24 Pretends
25 "Wonderful!!!"
26 "Boardwalk Empire" channel
27 Hit flies
29 Romantic request
32 Part of a cornstalk
33 Weep uncontrollably
34 Government money
35 Thieve
36 Its HQ is in Langley, Va.
37 Preceding
38 Hawaii-based airline from 1946-2008
40 Teal or taupe
42 ___ Pan peanut butter
43 Slave
44 Contest submission
45 Pitching wedges, e.g.

Down

1 Hit James Cameron movie
2 State in the Great Basin
3 He hit #1 in 1986 with "Shake You Down"
4 Last stop
5 Without hesitation
6 Bogus proceedings
7 ___ Avivans (some Israelis)
8 Singer with the hits "Alison" and "Everyday I Write the Book"
9 Bring forth
10 They shun company
17 Jimmy Carter's daughter
23 Devour
24 "Rock-hard" muscles
26 Japanese grill
27 Minor tussle
28 Like some itchy sweaters
29 Pond fish
30 Leave on an island
31 Uses, as influence
33 Frightening
39 Not him
41 Above, in poems

192

Across

1 Missing to the right or left, as a field goal
5 Start of the weekend, if you play it right
11 Object
12 Indicate
13 Tycoon of the 1800s
15 Go in
16 Brady and Hooks
17 The theatrical arts
20 Makes believe
23 Part of a BLT
27 Ghost's shout
28 One of a cat's four
29 Esquire's field of study
30 Black and white vehicle
32 Coal's place
33 In reserve
35 Wheel from Holland
38 "Goodbye, Genevieve!"
42 Kids shoot them at each other
45 At first, second or third
46 Words in a movie
47 Went across a frozen pond
48 Part of Virgo or Aries

Down

1 TV show set in Baltimore, with "The"
2 Lay ___ the line (gamble)
3 Red ink
4 Puts (inside)
5 Four before LBJ
6 Civil War fighter, for short
7 Stuck
8 Explorer of kids' TV
9 Oodles
10 Strong desires
14 Go awry
18 They made Missile Command
19 Do the lawn
20 1-2-3 of 26
21 Dove's sound
22 Defeat
24 He stung like a bee
25 Sit out by the pool
26 Have bills
28 Give a bad review to
31 Fighting
32 Gold, silver and bronze
34 Transportation in the city
35 Cupid, to the Greeks
36 Showy basketball play
37 Swedish quartet
39 ___ to win it
40 Novelist Ferber
41 Computer owner
43 Ending for Canton or Nepal
44 Color in Japan's flag

193

Across

1 Ginger ___
4 Tire measurement, for short
7 Kilmer of "The Doors"
8 Battery size
9 Fri. preceder
12 With skill
14 Drenched
15 Tape for later, in a way
16 Old Ford
18 One-named "Someone Like You" singer
20 Fashion magazine with a French name
21 Took off
22 Miss greatly
25 Everything else
27 Person with sinister plans
29 "Curb Your Enthusiasm" channel
32 "So funny!"
33 "FOR SALE BY ___"
35 Not knowing right from wrong, like a baby
38 "Howzit goin'?"
39 Not old, in Berlin
40 Square, rectangle or triangle
42 S. ___ (Seoul's country: abbr.)
43 Have to repay
44 Squeeze
45 Favored one
46 Three, to Italians

Down

1 Online representation
2 Pretentious
3 Time just before the deadline
4 Fink
5 Part of the hand that can be read
6 Mustard alternative
9 Shakespeare play named for when it was first performed
10 "I've answered the phone, now who are you?"
11 Say under one's breath
13 Sen. or Rep.
17 M.B.A. and Ph.D.
19 Kind of sch.
23 You can dig it!
24 Roman emperor after Claudius
26 Catch word of
27 Hit a golf ball wrong, sometimes
28 Brief, uncredited appearance
30 ___ own best friend
31 Sweet food, or its color
34 "How come?"
36 Each
37 Rob of "Parks and Recreation"
41 Permit

Across

1 Channel once known for playing songs
4 "Arlington Road" org.
7 Quick punch
10 Great anger
11 Rand who wrote "The Fountainhead"
12 Novak Djokovic blast
13 "Understand?"
14 One-seventh of the rainbow
15 "The Motorcycle Diaries" guy
16 Vegetable often served fried
18 Squabble
20 Fit for a queen
22 Get madder and madder
25 Turkey is part of it
29 With 30-across, cutesy Japanese brand of accessories
30 See 29-across
31 "What ___ can I say?"
32 Leave puzzled
33 Backbone
35 Quick preview of an upcoming show
38 Sunup
42 Captain Morgan or Bacardi
43 Throw in there
45 Tina of "30 Rock"
46 Exist
47 "The Good Shepherd" org.
48 What people generally think of you, for short
49 "A ___ on both your houses!"
50 "Psst!"
51 Unusual

Down

1 Japanese soup
2 "Star ___" (Shatner show)
3 Turn
4 Much
5 With 32-down, musical about a rock star getting drafted
6 Country where the game of chess originated
7 Word after pepper or Monterey
8 Need an ibuprofen
9 Schlitz or St. Pauli Girl
17 Without cunning
19 Stated
21 "Now I get it!"
22 "Ain't ___ Sweet"
23 Sushi fish
24 Golfer who won the U.S. Open in 1994 and 1997
26 Disco ___ ("The Simpsons" character)
27 Of a thing
28 Approval at sea
30 Half a math game
32 See 5-down
34 Fruit with fuzz
35 Leave no escape
36 Monetary unit in Munich
37 Card that rivals MC
39 Frizzy hairdo
40 Unwelcome garden "guest"
41 Force often seen in TV shows, for short
44 24 hours

195

Across

1 "The Stranger" author
6 Prickly plants
11 Oak-to-be
12 Indian, for one
13 Sworn-upon book
14 Lends a hand
15 Mean Amin
16 Ending for Gator or Power
18 Hawaiian circle
19 Zero, in some scores
20 Relatives
21 "___ Doubtfire"
22 Movie parts
24 "Surely you ___!"
25 Salieri's portrayer, in "Amadeus"
27 Country singer McCann
29 SAT section
32 Santa ___
33 D.C. type
34 Nutritionist's amt.
35 Soldier in gray
36 Brainy-looking bird
37 Art, to Tacitus
38 Bob of sausage fame
40 "Be quiet!"
42 Band tapes
43 Brand for a headache
44 Take to the stump
45 Shocked with a device

Down

1 Campground shelters
2 Like lemon juice
3 Gulf Coast city
4 Web addy
5 Shoe for playing b-ball
6 Leonard of "Hallelujah"
7 Serve right on the T, often
8 Microbiological barriers
9 Diminishes
10 Put one's foot down
17 Wash one's hands of
23 Org. for shooters and dunkers
24 Tip's place, often
26 Wild one
27 Texas city
28 Game similar to If You Had To
30 Disk's place
31 Went the distance
33 Sheriff's boys
39 "We are ___ amused"
41 In the style of

Across

1 Kidney-related
6 "Cola Wars" side
11 Concert site
12 Deodorant brand
13 One of Bob Marley's sons, or a cartoon character with a big head
14 Periods of unrest
15 Enthusiasm
16 Puerto ___
17 San Angelo's state
19 Dangerous driving weather
22 Organized the sock drawer
24 Vietnamese soup
25 Actress Tyler (also the Roman numeral for 54)
26 Little bit (of a drink)
28 12 months old
29 Poem often about a person
30 TV watchdog
32 Japan's money
33 Vietnam's capital
34 Unaccounted for
36 Brigham Young University is there
39 Ocean ___ (big boat)
41 Nimble
42 They had a South American empire
43 Relish
44 Last name that sounds like it hurts
45 Aim the car

Down

1 Give someone a hard time
2 Great Lakes port
3 Gloomy Gus's girlfriend?
4 Fisherman
5 Set (down)
6 The Louvre's city
7 Idle chattering in Monty Python sketches?
8 Smoking gun, e.g.
9 Use a sofa
10 They may include photos
16 Not mainstream
18 Marks a ballot, perhaps
20 "Whoops!"
21 Ending for theater or church
22 Trick
23 Helper
27 Bic or Mont Blanc
31 Snickers bar ingredient
33 Old West "vehicle"
35 Be a good mama cat to your kittens
37 Plant with fleshy leaves
38 Mr., to Germans
39 One of two on the face
40 ___ way (kind of)
41 Rude type

197

Across

1 Another name for the sun
4 "The Cask of Amontillado" author
7 Despite, in odes
8 100%
9 Bunting tool
12 Former North Carolina senator John
14 Part of some e-mail addresses
15 Peggy and Spike
16 Submit, as a contest entry
18 Rope for cattle
20 Section
21 Elementary school class
22 Not merely angry
25 New York city
27 Astronaut Gus
29 ___-jongg
32 Traveled on
33 Farfalle or gemelli
35 Makes sense
38 Reynolds or Lancaster
39 Two after FDR
40 Big piece of ice
42 Damascus's nation: abbr.
43 It's made of flowers in Hawaii, traditionally
44 Half an African fly
45 Starch eaten in West Africa
46 Runway guess, for short

Down

1 Belgian beer brand
2 "My word!"
3 Contract winner, often
4 It may be 4, for those who shout "Fore!"
5 Former GM make

6 Different
9 Furniture store buy
10 Goodbye, in Grenoble
11 Sushi fish
13 Fool
17 Get good, as with a tackle in football
19 Trade-___ (pros and cons)
23 Disc in the sky
24 Way on or off the interstate
26 Finds a job for
27 Former students
28 Late actor McDowall
30 Not moving
31 Loathing
34 Jackson 5 hit
36 Unpleasant, as a confrontation
37 "Not guilty," for one
41 Rival of Aquafresh

Across

1 Baby's breakfast blocker
4 ___ favor (please, in Spanish)
7 Oliver Stone movie about a presidential assassination
10 Straggler's question
12 Bush Administration spokesman Fleischer
13 13
15 Put out, as effort
16 Seeped (out)
17 How a pig may be roasted
19 Military forces
22 Recipe instruction
24 Arthur of "The Golden Girls"
25 Upstate N.Y. college
27 Thurman of "Be Cool"
28 Candy ___
30 Where pigs may be kept
32 Beautiful sounding, as poetry
34 Fess up, as to a crime
35 1970s icon Cheryl ___
39 Student not loved by other students
41 Dude
42 Nail polish remover component
43 Tricky
44 Female in the forest
45 Work with a needle

Down

1 Movie pig
2 Theater with a big screen
3 Two-wheeled vehicle
4 Law firm big shot
5 Periods after a tie, in sports: abbr.
6 Second chances, casually
7 Make things interesting
8 When to enjoy your hobbies
9 Gentle
11 French man's name that means "the king"
14 "I dropped something!"
18 Jelly served with pate
19 "Castle" network
20 Genuine article
21 Lots, and I mean LOTS!
23 Took off
26 Hanging out up high, like a cat
29 Ex-NHL player ___ Lindros
31 Top party invitees
33 "___ to Be You"
34 Bank features
36 Grand story (anagram of POSE)
37 Hackman of "Unforgiven"
38 Meal eaten with a spoon
40 Prefix for green people

199

Across

1 Fitting

7 Indicate agreement

10 Los Angeles suburb mentioned in Tom Petty's "Free Fallin'"

11 Window section

12 Brushes aside

13 Incorporates

14 Football penalty

16 Took a bus or a train

19 Band piece

20 Head honcho

21 Enjoying

25 Shoulder muscles

27 No housecat

28 Sharpshooter

30 Novelist Roberts

31 "What I think is..." for short

32 High school dance

33 Quesadilla component

37 Major

38 Throw trash on the ground

42 Eye hair

43 "More songs, please!"

44 Arctic animal

45 Warm up, like yesterday's dinner

Down

1 7, on some phones

2 Unit, in weightlifting

3 Columbus sch.

4 Singer's asset

5 Bart's teacher

6 Imp

7 Space race org.

8 Take ___ time (don't hurry)

9 Office furniture

11 October excursion site

15 Send off

16 Warren Beatty movie

17 Beasts of burden

18 Place for pastrami

22 "Young Frankenstein" role

23 Fiddler of Rome

24 Ending for milli- or centi-

26 Kind of

29 ___ coaster

33 Start for commute or vision

34 National gemstone of Australia

35 World conqueror's board game

36 Grocery store hassle

39 One of ten on the body

40 Period of the past

41 Not working any longer: abbr.

200

Across

1 "Revolver" or "Rubber Soul"
6 "That's hogwash!"
9 Send into orbit
11 "Nicely done!"
12 Now and then
14 Actress Thurman
15 Like workers on a pension: abbr.
16 "The Rumble in the Jungle" victor
17 Winery container
18 Agatha Christie's "What ___ McGillicuddy Saw!"
19 She saves the day
21 Came out on top
22 Medieval alcoholic drink
23 French leader burned at the stake
26 Not sure what to do
27 A long way
28 Bodybuilders lift them
30 Have a little of
33 Hard water
34 Museum stuff
35 Yoko who sang "Every Man Has a Woman Who Loves Him"
36 ___-sequitur
37 Mixers
39 Obtained
40 New York's ___ Stadium
41 Ernie of golf fame
42 Takes it easy

Down

1 It wakes you up
2 Not now
3 Ashtray things
4 Two less than tri-
5 Ed who was on "The Tonight Show"
6 Maiden name of Jacqueline Kennedy and Marge Simpson
7 Book of facts
8 Like some arguments
10 "The face that launched a thousand ships"
13 Polite address for a man
20 Sharif of "Funny Girl"
21 Designer Vera
23 Snoopy's alter ego, in "Peanuts"
24 Aligns
25 Tracy Chapman hit of 1988
26 Little feeling, as of pain or guilt
29 Is in possession of
30 Makes very wet
31 Good spot for a harbor
32 Plays to the camera
38 Chemistry suffix

Across

1 Hesitant sounds
4 "If I ___ a Hammer"
7 Not yet specified, as a date
10 "___ & Order"
11 Numero ___ (the best)
12 Picasso's field
13 "___ Jones's Diary"
15 ___-Man (1980s video game)
16 Big bird
17 Puerto ___ (Caribbean island)
18 Curds and ___ (what Little Miss Muffet ate)
19 Kindle purchases
21 Tap, in the kitchen
22 Phrase justifying revenge
26 Year between sophomore and senior
27 Brand of Mexican food
28 Put gas in your car
32 Celebrity
33 Capital of the Bahamas
35 Animal of the Yukon
36 Not strict
37 ___-wee Herman
38 "See ya!"
39 ___ de Janeiro (2016 Olympics host city)
40 What 26-acrosses attend: abbr.
41 Hanukkah celebrator
42 ___ Diego

Down

1 Arm bender
2 Very tough, as criticism
3 Run a credit card through the machine
4 Enormous
5 Phrase justifying revenge
6 Part of a lowercase i or j
7 Pudding flavor
8 NCAA tournament listing
9 With no profit made
14 Parched
17 Easy victory
20 Saloon
22 Teenage Mutant Ninja ___
23 Nutritionist's amounts
24 Layer, as of a wedding cake
25 Dangerous driving weather
26 "Catch-22" author Heller
28 Greek letter
29 Employers
30 Madness
31 Wear, as clothing
34 From the top
36 President after JFK

202

Across

1 June gift tag words
6 Of Benedict XVI or John Paul II
11 Gloss over, like a syllable
12 Calabria's country
13 Jeans jacket material
14 More recent
15 On the way out
17 "Now do you understand?"
18 "The ___ Must Be Crazy"
20 Choose (with "for")
22 Hullabaloo
23 ___ thing or two about (has some skill in)
26 Egyptian peninsula
28 They're painted at salons
30 Drink in December
32 Little bit, as of brandy
33 Self-importance
34 Punk's ___ Pop
35 Ginormous
38 Some cigarettes
40 State bordering Canada
42 Hubristic woman of Greek myth
45 12
46 Boat that anagrams to "ocean"
47 Casual language
48 Mystery writer's award

Down

1 Turner or Williams
2 "Bravo!"
3 Doorbell sound
4 "Hasta luego"
5 Moore or Lovato
6 Table tennis
7 Stuffed in one's piehole
8 Cat's four
9 Protected from the wind
10 Ancient stringed instrument
16 ___-compete agreement
18 Food for a Ford
19 Garfield's dog foil
21 Airline until 2001
23 Movie ape
24 Like some accents
25 Sacha Baron Cohen character
27 Get along in years
29 Secret agent
31 "Tic-Tac-Dough" line
34 Homer epic
35 eBay attempts
36 "American ___"
37 The Middle East's ___ Strip
39 Not repeatedly
41 Egg layer
43 Big snake
44 Ending for musket or mountain

Across

1 Atlas page
4 Fox rival
7 Pop-ups, often
10 "Son ___ gun!"
11 Zodiac sign
12 Compete
13 He shot an apple off his son's head
16 Toledo's lake
17 Dull
18 "You're welcome," to Juan
21 Adorable
22 Designer Wang
24 Ending for mountain or musket
25 Longtime CEO of Apple
28 Farrow of acting or Hamm of soccer
29 "Chestnuts roasting ___ open fire..."
30 Pound or Klein
32 HBO show about a sports agent
36 Money owed
38 Not fooled by
39 An apple famously hit him on the head -- gravity!
42 Baby bear
43 Homer Simpson's dad
44 Ending for some e-mail addresses
45 Secret agent
46 Bad: Fr.
47 "Fantastic Mr. Fox" director Anderson

Down

1 Did the lawn
2 "Hearts ___" (John Ritter sitcom)
3 Sarah from Alaska
4 Boxing great
5 Arthur of "The Golden Girls"
6 Barbershop buy
7 Alphabet City street
8 Gets bigger, as a pupil of the eye
9 Buyer's counterpart
14 Skedaddle
15 Part of XXX or OOO
19 "Whip It" band
20 Stadium
23 Slightly open
25 Assesses
26 Toni Morrison novel
27 Not too hot, like a burner
28 Ambulance workers
31 One day ___ time
33 Being dragged behind
34 Shop
35 "Glee" numbers
37 E-mail from Nigeria, perhaps
40 Jeremy Lin's group, for short
41 Fish that's a general backwards

Across

1 A game or a cereal
5 Post, as on a corkboard
10 Vegetable often served fried
11 "That ___ of the craziest things I've ever heard"
12 Miller or Molson
13 Require a kleenex
14 MIT subject
16 ___ machine (commonly heard but redundant phrase)
17 Simple shelter
19 Tree common in Canada
21 Volcanic stuff
22 Palindromic woman's name
23 Jaguar or puma
26 That gal's
27 Church title, for short
28 Whatever number of
29 There was much of it for Shakespeare
30 Mr. Manning
31 One of 435 in D.C.
32 ___ the way of (impeded)
34 Be behind on bills
35 Meat source in Finland
36 Young of "Old Man"
38 Aspen pastime
40 Pill holder
43 Burn perfume, in religious ceremonies
44 Not pro-
45 That is
46 Bread in an Indian restaurant

Down

1 Alternative to a passing shot
2 Gen. Eisenhower
3 It's 15 feet from the hoop, in basketball
4 Deserve
5 Cherry or apple
6 Computin' Newton
7 2005 and 2009 NCAA basketball champs
8 Latin word on U.S. coins
9 ___ rally (high school event)
13 Basketball violation
15 Intimidating looks
17 "Hilarious!"
18 Owned before by someone else
20 Gully
24 From square one
25 Solve a crossword, sometimes
33 "___ Before Dying"
35 ___ out (just managed)
37 John, in Moscow
38 ___-fi movies
39 Basketball or tennis equipment
41 ___ crossroads
42 NBA star Jeremy ___, hidden in this puzzle's three long entries

205

Across

1 Washed (down)
6 Remove from memory
11 It's sometimes sprained
12 Female horses
13 Ask a tough trivia question
14 Ancient Peruvians
15 Chum
16 Smart bird
18 Birmingham's state: abbr.
19 Full of fanfare
21 One-seventh of a week
22 2016 Olympics city, for short
23 Food cans, to Brits
24 How things stand in general
27 Creature the Chesapeake Bay is known for
28 Court
29 "___ dead, Jim" ("Star Trek" line)
30 Lunges
34 ___ Wednesday
35 Fine and dandy
36 Head piece
37 Bend (down)
39 Close call
41 Keep away from
42 Violin stroke
43 Put off
44 Histories

Down

1 Metal plates on doors
2 How beer may be served
3 Top part of a skeleton
4 Tree type
5 Bank transaction
6 Poet Dickinson
7 Oversaw
8 2000s CBS show "Joan of ___"
9 Material like an adhesive
10 Ralph Waldo Emerson pieces
17 VIPs, collectively
20 Riyadh resident
23 Old word for you
24 Hit the mat
25 Negotiate, like details
26 Builds, as an appetite
27 Took off after
30 Tail (off)
31 Unions don't like them
32 Card like the Hanged Man
33 Gushes
38 Kind of poem
40 Tax expert, for short

Across

1 Metered vehicles
5 Work on the bomb squad
11 Passing notice, for short
12 Pencil end
13 Serve-and-volleyer Sampras
14 Pinpoint
15 Put a halt to
16 Exploit
17 Fabricated story
19 Stumble
23 Husbands and wives
26 Milieu for the Boston Bruins
27 Like John Tyler, among presidents
28 Mexican restaurant order
30 Bruno Mars song "Just the Way You ___"
31 Silver or selenium
33 Believes, as an excuse
35 Watson or Samms
36 Quick greetings
38 Verbal
41 They may say "kiss the cook"
44 Brief letter
45 Elvis Presley hit "In the ___"
46 Part of, as a conspiracy
47 Like some favorites
48 Intentions

Down

1 Officers
2 Assist in criminal activity
3 Chewy candy
4 Leave for a while
5 Extra special
6 Greek god
7 Aspect
8 (The) Union
9 Fully prepared
10 Prior to, in verse
18 He lost to Nastase in the 1972 U.S. Open final
20 "The San Francisco Treat"
21 Desktop image
22 Bug that bugs you
23 Guess
24 Lima's land
25 Rose stalk
29 Colorless gas
32 Piano teacher's hour
34 Word after flu or tetanus
37 "___ the Woods"
39 Tiny particle
40 Eye part
41 In time gone by
42 College prof.'s degree
43 Valentine's Day color

207

Across

1 Parodied
7 Loud landing sound
11 "Conceding that..."
12 Smart and seasoned
13 Drink with an umbrella
14 Sign on a store
15 Bed & breakfasts
16 Letters on some art show works
18 Healthy cereal
21 Four of 52
25 Scenes of competition
27 How to work on your keyboard
29 "All ___!"
30 Win over
31 Pate jelly
32 "The bad cholesterol"
33 Vergil verses, e.g.
37 Agree
40 Mountain climber's tool
42 Complete
43 Irritates repeatedly
44 Peeping pair
45 Tacky art

Down

1 Sorta
2 ___ Williams (co-founder of Blogger and Twitter)
3 Not "ja"
4 Blows up, casually
5 Former USSR rival
6 How to work with your mouse
7 Some dance moves
8 Cool
9 Find a purpose for
10 Lion's house
17 Industrialist Henry
19 From the top
20 City across the continent from NY, NY
21 "Eureka!"
22 Largest island on the Caribbean
23 Genesis man
24 Office items
26 The heavens
28 Like the climate in Tucson
33 Fuel in Ireland
34 Big galoots
35 Honcho
36 Blend together
37 Barack's #2
38 Vine that climbs
39 Scary stinger
41 ___ Omega (major sorority)

208

Across

1 Comes down with
4 "Where ___ we?"
7 Giants great Mel
8 Word with chicken or small
9 "Don't tase me, ___"
12 Summarized
14 Will Smith's music
15 Prefix with suction
16 "I'm serious!"
18 Drained, as energy
20 Related (to)
21 It is, in Ibiza
22 Traveled
23 Throw in
25 John King's channel
27 Aid group, often: abbr.
28 2012 rival of Ron, Mitt and Newt
30 Opening word of a letter
32 Guy
33 Hold against
36 Football coach Amos ___ Stagg
38 Frozen drink brand
39 12th of 12: abbr.
40 Thornton Wilder play
42 Biblical floater
43 "First of all..."
44 Blushing
45 Highly successful kickoff
   returns: abbr.
46 Medicos, for short

Down

1 Wild cries
2 Heart parts
3 It's right twice a day
4 Copy
5 How 9-down goes, but 3-down doesn't
6 Former Major League Baseball player in Canada
9 It keeps playing over and over
10 Doing a fall job
11 Not completely turned off by
13 Defeats
17 Part of the face
19 And so forth
23 Spain's navy, once
24 User of an old phone
26 French word in the society pages
29 Mr. Kesey
31 "___ happens..."
34 More fresh
35 Watches the bar
37 ___ suit
41 Hi-___ graphics

209

Across

1 Some sneakers
6 Elephant's ivory
11 Get rid of, as information on a disk
12 "The game is ___!"
13 Nursery rhyme bird
15 Mono-
16 Earn after expenses
17 Most common word in written English
18 ___ Tin Tin
19 One of four in a deck of cards
20 That girl
21 Battle wound
23 California dunkers
25 Awesome, in slang
27 ____'s holiday (doing on vacation what you do for work)
30 Not in any danger
34 Ending for persist or consist
35 Like a lot
37 Courteney on "Friends"
38 Doc's org.
39 Hotel's cousin
40 Exist
41 "Lookie here!"
44 Just perfect
45 Person's "equator"
46 Examinations
47 Hits flies

Down

1 Big bones
2 Not what you'd expect
3 Sonia Sotomayor, e.g.
4 End of a cigarette
5 Beatles song "I've Just ___ Face"
6 Gang up on
7 Saucer in the sky
8 Make better
9 Permitted
10 Heads of cattle
14 In a relaxed position
22 Dashboard abbr.
24 Sends to the canvas
26 Some tires
27 "Get outta here!"
28 Like a messy person's bed
29 Vampire killers
31 National park in Maine
32 Woods
33 Puts forth, as effort
36 Chews (on)
42 "Have some food!"
43 "I don't think so"

210

Across

1 Mitchell who sang "Big Yellow Taxi"
5 Big ___ (WWI weapon's nickname)
11 Help in a crime
12 Describe, as a plan
13 Neighbor of Illinois
14 Retaliate for
15 "___ Miserables"
16 Cards quartet
17 Water ___ (Monopoly property)
19 High limb?
22 Burn badly
24 Feeling sad
25 Strikes other people (as)
27 They have George Washington on them
28 Complains constantly
29 Toes count
30 Enjoy the rink
31 Jason or Captain William
32 Permanent body art, casually
35 Person without melanin
38 Words ___ Friends (Facebook game)
39 Playground fun for two
40 Watson who played Hermione Granger
41 Becomes fully recognized, as a new reality
42 Word in Oscar categories

Down

1 Monopoly space with bars on it
2 First ___ (orchestra chair)
3 Connie Chung and Lesley Stahl
4 "Give ___ rest!"
5 2001 movie set in Somalia
6 Part of the roof
7 Marble and seedless
8 2,000 pounds
9 Bear ___ (big greeting)
10 Noshed on
16 Semicircular lines
18 Mined minerals
19 Break from socializing
20 Trick
21 Untidy scene
22 Glaswegian or Edinburgher
23 Ice cream scoop's home
24 Englishman, casually
26 African nation, or a man's name
30 Egypt's ___ Peninsula
31 Smooch
33 They give out cash
34 Not this
35 Load-carrying creature
36 "Do the Right Thing" director Spike
37 Put money (on something)
38 Spider's weaving

211

Across

1 The Divine ___ (Bette Midler nickname)

6 Tin or tungsten

11 Bring together

12 Run off and get hitched

13 Golf course warnings

14 Bring up, as an issue

15 Taste in a store

17 Simpson, Bonet and Vanderpump

18 Website named for the part of California where it was founded

21 Afternoon snooze

25 "2 funny!"

26 18-across attempt

27 Big beer container

28 Parking lot slots

30 "See ya," in Siena

31 Evoking nostalgia

33 Magazine devoted to keeping life uncluttered

38 Prefix with tasking or talented

39 Say something

40 Mary-Kate or Merlin

41 Creepy

42 John of tractors

43 Unfair putdowns

Down

1 Botch

2 "___ out?" (question to a pet at the door)

3 Be the father, in the Bible

4 ___ Dan ("Deacon Blues" band)

5 Soccer superstar Lionel ___

6 Sea beauty

7 Pass, like time

8 Work hard

9 Church section

10 Blue jeans brand

16 Basketball statistic

18 Ernie of golf

19 Offshoot of jazz

20 Pie ___ mode

22 Go down a black diamond run, e.g.

23 Drink that may be unsweetened

24 In the past

26 Most direct route

29 Meteor indentation

30 Force

32 Gets out of bed

33 Govern

34 Different

35 Country where Machu Picchu is

36 Lion's home

37 ___ out a win (barely defeats)

38 "The ___ Squad"

Across

1 Harvard rival
4 Lousy
7 Hockey great Bobby
8 Ginger ___
9 English channel?
12 Hawaiian food
13 Tending to swing back and forth, as with moods
15 No friend
17 "The Republic" philosopher
18 ___ double take (looked again)
19 Haunting sound
20 Like some triangles
24 "One Flew Over the Cuckoo's Nest" author Kesey
25 Africa's most populous country
27 Cleansed (of)
29 Puzzle great Martin ___
32 ___ and crafts
34 ___ Garrett ("The Facts of Life" character played by Charlotte Rae)
35 Jumps verbally (on)
37 Biting your fingernails, e.g.
38 The same as
40 Big T-shirt size: abbr.
41 Six-sided roller
42 Little battery
43 College Park school, home of the Terrapins: abbr.
44 Chicken ___ (childhood illness)
45 Van Gogh cut his off

Down

1 Bikes that need fuel...or not
2 Not what you'd think
3 Having stood the test of time
4 Cradle sleeper
5 Boxer who often sparred verbally with Howard Cosell
6 Johnny of "Pirates of the Caribbean"
9 Badly bruised
10 Enjoy the tub
11 Sing like Sinatra
14 "Bravo!"
16 African country where Timbuktu is
21 Chick's first home
22 Teacher's org.
23 Go awry
26 Conception
27 Went quickly
28 Baghdadi, e.g.
30 Puzzle
31 Not fit for kids, as a movie
33 Where to procure a pedicure
36 Smack
37 Big put-on
39 "The ___ of Pooh"

213

Across

1 Military bases: abbr.
4 Boat with torpedoes
7 H.S. figure
10 Talk constantly
11 Solid ___ rock
12 Parks & ___
13 Novelist played by Julie Dench in a 2001 movie
16 Camping org.
17 Fall tool
18 "Alright, Still" singer
22 Fuss
23 Baltic or Barents
24 Rice dish
27 Unfair attack on someone's character
31 Wharton deg.
33 Portraits and such
34 Cousin of Bo & Luke
37 D.C. leader
39 Kung ___ chicken
40 Political matriarch
45 Country music's ___ Ridge Boys
46 Printer cartridge contents
47 It's not me
48 "The Ghost and ___ Muir"
49 Obnoxious person
50 Mental power, it's said

Down

1 "Just so it's known..."
2 Sticky stuff
3 Enjoy the Alps, maybe
4 Pacific island nation
5 Often-ordered drinks...
6 ...and where they're ordered
7 React to a pun
8 Use your beak
9 Dull soreness
14 Kite site
15 Have night vision?

18 ___ of luxury
19 Mean Amin
20 "Hilarious," to texters
21 "___ Miserables"
25 Blow away
26 "Arlington Road" org.
28 Water: Fr.
29 Steven Spielberg title word
30 Hwy.
32 Deciduous trees
34 Classroom furniture
35 N.Y. squad, familiarly
36 Quixote or Cornelius
37 Teen dance
38 Crowd's sound
41 Rio and Sedona maker
42 Reversible body part, as it were
43 Two, to Tulum residents
44 "Uh-huh!"

Across

1 "Spare" body part
4 No spring chicken
7 Child's shout
10 1970s band that did "Don't Bring Me Down"
11 Joke around
12 Cry of discovery
13 Why some people do crazy things
15 Yang's counterpart, to the Chinese
16 Viper or boa constrictor
17 Microsoft game console
18 Underworld river, to the ancient Greeks
19 One and only
21 Sailor's "sure thing!"
22 Went without food on purpose
25 Negative answers
26 Pan for stir-fry
27 Mineral deposit
28 Where badly-bowled bowling balls go
30 Apple computer
31 To the right, in an atlas
32 Just "meh"
33 Groucho or Harpo
35 Phantom's art form, in a musical's title
37 Assistance
38 Quickly and slowly, for two
40 Palindromic woman's name
41 Equipment for the Red Sox
42 "Outstanding!"
43 Fifth month
44 The S in iOS
45 Soaked

Down

1 Basketball game figure with a whistle, for short
2 Sentence spoken over a spotty cell phone connection
3 Very naive, in a phrase
4 "Alright, I give up!"
5 Doesn't plan with an eye to the future
6 President between HST and JFK
7 1971 Jackson 5 hit
8 Dayton's state
9 No-tail cat
14 Not strict, like rule enforcement
17 Big T-shirt sizes: abbr.
18 Belted out a tune
20 Tree whose wood is used for furniture
23 Like some pen ink
24 Art ___ (design style seen in South Beach)
26 "Rushmore" director Anderson
29 Bread for the feds
32 "It's right over there!"
33 Sir's female counterpart
34 Verdi opera set in Egypt
36 Some soldiers: abbr.
38 "Six-pack" on the stomach
39 6-3 or 7-6, in tennis

215

Across

1 Shocks with a device
6 Repeated behavior
11 Limber, like a yoga instructor
12 ___ Spring (brand of soap)
13 Angelina of "Changeling"
14 Estelle of "The Golden Girls"
15 ___ crust (outer layer of our planet)
17 Author ___ Christian Andersen
19 Fighting (with)
23 Not home
24 "___ see it..."
25 Before, in poetry
26 Kind of verse
27 Flower delivery letters
28 They get you into a concert, casually
29 Douglas ___ (kind of tree)
30 Even score
31 Plumb of "The Brady Bunch"
32 Part of a flower
34 War god, to Ancient Greeks
35 Imploring
37 Rock ___ ("Tommy," for example)
40 Golf great Sam
43 Like a good dog
44 Russian Revolution leader
45 Live
46 Spare

Down

1 ___ Mahal
2 In the past
3 When Charlie Chaplin began his career
4 Sewing machine inventor Howe
5 Mystic
6 When sandcastles disappear
7 "You ___ right!"
8 Small amount
9 Suffix with clarinet or harpsichord
10 "Honor ___ father"
16 Wine bar event
17 ___ it (walks)
18 IRS intrusion
20 What each of this puzzle's three theme entries ends in a brand of
21 Get behind the wheel
22 Male and female
24 "In the end..."
33 Wall painting
34 Claim as one's own, as land
36 ___ of Wight (it's off the coast of England)
37 Time-tested
38 Punching sound
39 Palindromic body part
41 It's all around you
42 ___ test ("Law & Order" evidence)

Across

1. It makes a guitar louder
4. Relaxed sighs
7. Jeep or Jetta
8. Big cat in the sky
9. Logo abbrs.
12. Reflexive pronoun
14. Edgy
15. Babe or Baby follower
16. "You and what army?"
18. Archibald and Thurmond of the NBA Hall of Fame
20. Inter ___
21. Shrewd
22. Foyer feature
25. Ready to drink, like a beer
27. Fine
29. Tree that sounds like a sheep
32. They can eject managers
33. Be bright
35. Ups the stakes
38. Cuzco builder
39. Greed is one
40. Chewy candy
42. Yukon creature
43. English 101 word
44. Ending for ranch or Canyon
45. Title TV psychopath, casually
46. Place to study

Down

1. Oaks of the future
2. Owner's guidebook
3. 1986 Molly Ringwald movie
4. Lager's cousin
5. Steering wheel
6. Living room piece
9. 1986 Chris de Burgh song that hit #3
10. Imitate
11. Vocalize
13. Pronoun for a boat
17. Malone or Marx
19. Poet/songwriter Silverstein
23. Part of a play
24. Tops and balls and such
26. Mama of music
27. "European carryall," in a "Seinfeld" episode
28. Clicked communication
30. "Play more!"
31. One of six in Clue
34. Wasn't out in the open
36. "My goodness!"
37. "Absotively posilutely!"
41. Tex-___ food

Across

1 Fall back
4 Spearheaded
7 Ruin
8 Facial business
9 Cooking spray brand
12 "Give that to me now!"
14 Mono-
15 It may be eaten with chicken tikka masala
16 Milk container
18 Grant
20 Springfield bus driver
21 Atlas page
22 Not later
25 Inexact but large number
27 Chronologically ambiguous
29 Locating device
32 Indicates "yes"
33 Evil figure
35 Lifts
38 Karate studio
39 Lodge
40 Shiraz seller
42 Identify
43 Actress Lupino
44 Ambulance worker, for short
45 Recent
46 German's "the"

Down

1 "8 Mile" actor
2 Curved fruit
3 Starchy dessert
4 "Acid"
5 Legendary
6 Info
9 Tucking in
10 Make ___ of (mentally highlight)
11 Unimportant
13 Brian of "Here Come the Warm Jets"
17 Part in a play
19 Shed some tears
23 Scarfed down
24 Warren Beatty film of 1981
26 Church service
27 Nerdy
28 Not a soul
30 Word before party or top
31 Is audibly derisive
34 Ending for lime or lemon
36 Bed size
37 Accompanying dish
41 "I don't think so"

Across

1 "Green ___"
6 RC and Pepsi
11 Country that shares a long border with Argentina
12 Queen of ___ (Biblical figure)
13 Bird that's also a golf achievement
14 Terrible
15 Slightest bit
17 Ending for kitchen or luncheon
18 Musical with meowing
20 Pack animal
22 "What didja say?"
23 Nice steak
26 It's low for a Cy Young winner
27 Obnoxious person
28 Cranberries hit "___ to My Family"
29 Entered quickly, like a stage
31 Peg for drivers
32 North Carolina college
33 "My word!"
34 Financial burden
36 Lion cryin'
38 Attorney-___
40 NBA venue
43 Part of Louisiana's capital
44 Takes off
45 Leg benders
46 Techno instrument, for short

Down

1 Highest heart
2 "___-ching!"
3 One possible spin in 16-down
4 Island where names were changed
5 Spotted
6 Former rival of the USA
7 "What're ya gonna do?"
8 Another possible spin in 16-down
9 Share a border with
10 Event with bargains
16 Game that ties you up in knots
18 Singer who won a Best Actress Oscar for "Moonstruck"
19 Atmosphere
21 Roughly
23 Destroyed a destroyer
24 Thought
25 Be unable to live without
30 Power ___
33 When the rooster crows
34 Lacking light
35 Famed English prep school
37 Big galoots
39 Director Craven or Anderson
41 Earn
42 Volcano's output

219

Across

1 Sends phone messages
6 Famous catalog
11 First name in the Bible, alphabetically
12 First Lady before Michelle
13 Sink-unclogging brand
14 Playful water creature
15 Trees whose wood is used to make archery bows
17 Poker table item
18 Throw
20 Cigar stuff
22 Baseball game honcho
23 Of acceptable quality
27 Shakes hands with
29 Feminine personality, in psychology
30 Unease
32 "Fly's undone!"
33 University's web address part
34 NASDAQ rival
35 Lip ___ contest
38 Slant
40 "___ you care to elaborate?"
42 Critical
45 Sound
46 Musical set in Argentina
47 Gets ready, in slang
48 Male and female

Down

1 Tiny bit
2 Hair may hide it
3 Glasses that supposedly let you see through walls
4 Shades
5 The white stuff
6 "Jenny from the Block" singer, for short
7 Finally understand
8 Babe with a bat
9 "Able was I ___ saw Elba"
10 Time ___
16 It's tapped from trees
18 Mountain cat
19 "I could not agree more!"
21 Stick around
23 Not new
24 Sugary cylinders
25 Poehler and Grant
26 Level
28 Neckwear accessory
31 Bath
34 Gullible
35 Make a trade
36 "Follow ___ Bliss" (B-52's song)
37 Lacking clothing
39 St. ___ (skin care brand)
41 Two, to Antonio
43 Put away
44 Scale notes

220

Across

1 Soap ___ (mildew's cousin)
5 "Yeah, right!"
11 California valley known for its wineries
12 Fix, like a kitten
13 Baseball game workers, for short
14 Part of a shirt used by magicians
15 Brainy sort
16 Suffix for Darwin or defeat
17 Enjoy a novella
19 Food sometimes poached
23 Appalachian instruments
26 Eminem's music
27 Pres. Eisenhower
28 Telecom letters
29 Mr. Nahasapeemapetilon
30 DVR button
31 William of "Star Trek"
33 Manufacture
35 Van Morrison's "Brown ___ Girl"
36 CEO, e.g.
38 Poses some questions
41 Spain's navy, back in the day
44 Wooden part of a bed
45 Front end ___ (construction equipment)
46 "I could ___ horse!"
47 Winning or losing run
48 Pollution issue

Down

1 Like a bug in a rug
2 Showed up
3 Kind of home run that's hit high
4 Concealed, like someone's face
5 Kind of home run where the batter needs to run quickly
6 Tillis and Gibson
7 "Oh yeah? What're YOU gonna do about it?"
8 Western tribe for whom Salt Lake City's state is named
9 Gun (the motor)
10 Prior to
18 "It's so sad!"
20 Kind of home run that earns 4 RBI
21 Look on with mouth wide open
22 Incite
23 Law ___ (kind of business)
24 Swedish superstore
25 Stick around
32 Makes fun of on the playground
34 Dodge
37 Concept
39 O.J. Simpson trial figure ___ Kaelin
40 Without a date
41 Pacino and Michaels
42 Become inedible
43 Ruin

221

Across

1 Late superteacher Escalante
6 Site where "snipers" prowl for bargains
10 Trees used to make wooden matches
12 It's stored in the gallbladder
13 Tony Danza sitcom
15 ___-Americans
16 Full of current events, like a website
19 Hint
23 Snacked on
24 Consecutively
26 Rihanna #1 hit of 2010
29 World ___
30 "___ Miserables"
31 "Portland, Oregon" singer Loretta
32 Mindless creature
34 Practice punches
36 Kids' book series
43 Cannes coin
44 Begin a journey
45 Stick around
46 Pores over Poe or Pope

Down

1 Part of the face
2 Tend to one's cigar
3 Wall Street operation, for short
4 Table-like structures in the Southwest
5 Contest submission
6 Low point
7 Life summary
8 Hirt and Hirschfeld
9 "What can I do for you?"
11 ___-cha chicken (Chinese menu dish)
14 Ivory's counterpart
16 Casual rejections
17 RFK's wife
18 Exhausted
20 Brown or Marino
21 Brush brand
22 Shakespeare title character
24 Types to
25 One way to go
27 Three-letter metal
28 Get the feeling
32 Less polished
33 Give a talk
35 Extra notes, at the end of a letter
36 NBA great Unseld
37 Pizza ___
38 Throwing number
39 Rogers on a horse
40 Mauna ___, Hawaii
41 Movie that flops
42 Additional pds.

222

Across

1 Circular dance
5 Take to the ice
10 In ___ (stuck)
11 Wood used for chests
12 John or Jane
13 Yellow food
14 Textbook section
16 Weekend warriors: abbr.
17 Matured
21 Toast spread
23 Approves
25 Street: Fr.
26 Punching legend
27 Frequently, in poetry
28 "Where ___ we?"
29 Singer Shannon
30 For one
31 Soda
32 Car rod
34 Front of an airplane
36 Where records are stored
40 No Oscar winner
43 Low or high
44 Didn't just aah
45 Yard or kilometer
46 Silly bird
47 They may have their own door

Down

1 Put on the wall
2 Spoken
3 Where gossip is spread
4 "I can't believe I ___ much!"
5 Wound forever
6 Neighbor of South Sudan
7 Palindromic woman's name
8 Vacation "souvenir"
9 Time
13 Where gossip is spread
15 Get low
18 Where gossip is spread
19 Mark replacement
20 Highly philosophical
21 Will Smith's wife
22 "Jeopardy!" name
24 ____'s (beer brand)
33 Roof parts
35 Classic exercise
37 Compete at a rodeo
38 Change a few things
39 Goes down
40 Wetland
41 Holstein holler
42 "Now I've got you!"

223

Across

1 Apple drink
6 Picture puzzle
11 Grownup
12 Blow like a volcano
13 Head holders
14 Real nutcase
15 Talks and talks and talks
16 Ted Danson sitcom, or tennis star Boris
17 Born long ago
18 Iguana or pot-bellied pig, to some people
19 Black-and-yellow buzzer
20 Lender who charges too much interest
22 Little labs
23 Made of clay
25 Disgusting, to a kid
27 Address, as a problem
30 Egg ___ (Christmas concoction)
31 Furniture with springs
32 Upper limit, for short
33 Stole from unguarded stores
35 Stronghold
36 Honolulu hello
37 In the area
38 More experienced
39 Great Plains food source
40 Pansy parts
41 Shell out, as cash

Down

1 Words starting a request
2 Dearest principles
3 Kids' game played in a circle
4 Antlered Alaskan animals
5 Some turns on the road: abbr.
6 Put back to zero
7 Country singer Church
8 Variation of 3-down, as played by 4-down?
9 Maintenance
10 Mall tenants
16 Criticized harshly
18 Apiece
21 King: Sp.
22 Photo
24 Magazine with "Spy vs. Spy"
25 Relatives by marriage
26 "Relax!"
28 Gary who wrote the comic strip The Far Side
29 Branch out
31 Chicago's NFL team
34 Not us
35 Toss (a coin)
37 "How I Met Your Mother" network

224

Across

1 Potter's materials
6 Put off, as a decision
11 Jones who sang "Come Away With Me"
12 Soothe, as fears
13 Chip flavor
15 "That's incredible!"
16 Meowing group
17 Palo ___, Calif.
20 Suitable
22 Prefix with classical
23 Be the instigator
27 It's served with fish sticks
29 "It slipped my mind, sorry"
30 Common container
31 Tour group?
32 Gasp for air
33 Slope pair
36 Goat's groan
38 Layer of our planet
43 "Remember the ___!"
44 Complete and total
45 Buy more issues of a magazine
46 Food you've made by solving this puzzle (see the last word of the three theme entries)

Down

1 Fox News rival
2 Mauna ___ (Hawaiian volcano)
3 Curved shape
4 Google alternative
5 "Beat it, fly!"
6 "Zip-A-Dee-Doo-___"
7 Model Carmen ___
8 ___ market
9 To the right, in an atlas
10 Some loaves of bread
14 Internet gathering spots
17 Against
18 It falls in fall
19 Lawnmower brand that means "bull"
21 Time gone by
23 Goes down
24 Big brass instrument
25 Larger-than-life figure
26 Send a message to
28 "Would I steer you wrong?"
32 Opening episode of a miniseries
33 Cook quickly, like tuna
34 Dark green vegetable
35 Persian Gulf nation
37 Katy Perry's "___ of Coffee"
39 In what way?
40 Potato chip brand
41 "___ you!"
42 "___ la la la la..."

225

Across

1 Easy to grasp
6 Novelist Canetti
11 Pacifist Pennsylvanians
12 ___ Jeane Baker (Marilyn Monroe's real name)
13 Starting to be interesting, as a book
15 Rival of Woods and Mickelson
16 Teacher's org.
17 Rapa ___ (Easter Island)
18 52, in Ancient Rome
19 It's south of Eur.
20 Chemistry suffix
21 Beach grains
23 Order from the leader
25 Went wrong
27 Bed cover
29 Plush carpet
33 Weight room unit
34 Central, in combinations
36 Eggs, to a scientist
37 Stomach six-pack
38 Lingered over lunch, e.g.
39 Recycling container
40 TV show about a former chemistry teacher
43 Water in a boat
44 Big hotel room
45 The British ___
46 Try to win, like a contest

Down

1 Food that New York City and Montreal are known for
2 ___ Bedelia (children's book character)
3 Uses, like a chair
4 Ending for real or surreal
5 The Yellow River's country
6 Fencing cry
7 Cabin component
8 Not what you'd think
9 Total
10 ___ Hawkins dance
14 Ancient Egyptian queen
22 Residential neighborhood: abbr.
24 Bouncers ask for them
26 Movies that have already been done
27 Random wreckage
28 Get the customer to spend more
30 J.R.R. Tolkien creature
31 Take to the skies
32 Guy goose
33 Temple figure
35 Heavy, like bread
41 Your number of years
42 Glock or SIG Sauer

226

Across

1 All-encompassing category: abbr.
5 ___ Romeo (Italian car company)
9 Kind of bean
10 "Cosmos" author Sagan
11 Feature of a Las Vegas "bandit"
13 Stocking trouble
14 Compass dir.
15 Driver's license info, for short
17 Letters before lab or test
18 "The ___ Squad"
19 Brad Paisley's "Working ___ Tan"
20 Highest possible card in a flush
21 Had no basis in reality
24 Head of a monastery
25 Subtle quality of some humor
29 Actor DiCaprio
30 Head protrusion
31 "___ I but known..."
33 Every last bit
34 Card game that means "one"
35 In the manner of
36 Stubborn animal
38 Blinking square or line, on a computer screen
40 Fired
41 Boarded
42 Warren Beatty epic
43 McGregor of "Trainspotting"

Down

1 Small fish, or the boat in "Gilligan's Island"
2 "___ Doctor" (Dr. Dre/Eminem song)
3 Train stop: abbr.
4 Chicken dish made with ham and cheese
5 Cooling units, for short
6 Martin of "Ed Wood"
7 Country whose flag you can make from the last word of the three long down entries
8 Pond growth
9 Frost's "Stopping by Woods on a Snowy Evening" is one
12 Highest peak in the Alps
16 Louisiana's capital
22 ___ Paulo, Brazil
23 95 or 66: abbr.
25 Extra special
26 Tossed the dice
27 California mountain, or a drink brand
28 Bar
29 Alexander or Odom
32 "Shoot!"
37 WSJ workers
39 Concert ticket info

Across

1 Up to now
6 Clever
11 Kick out of the country
12 Wrong step
13 Worked on one's physique
14 To the right, maybe
15 Illuminated sign
17 Holder for 3-down
18 Not many
20 Herb with salmon
22 WWII side
24 Car for a while
28 The Macarena, e.g.
30 Material to keep out of the rain
31 Come forth
33 Wise person
34 A long time
36 One of the primary colors
37 Mausoleum
40 Door opener
42 Most Meccans
44 Parts
47 Zahn of news
48 "Superman" actor
49 Actress Page of "Juno"
50 Seuss character

Down

1 6-3 or 6-4, in tennis
2 Kitchenware brand
3 Vintages
4 Mr. Trebek
5 Tried again
6 Irish or Caribbean
7 North Pole resident
8 Opera number
9 Fishing store's supply
10 Odyssey

16 ___ the cows come home
18 Lose strength
19 Big test
21 ___ Gatos, Calif.
23 Game with bingos
25 It won't get you drunk
26 Small lead
27 Oboe player's need
29 One of a dozen
32 "Mice!"
35 Nasty look
37 Record
38 Not written
39 Injure viciously
41 Cookie you can stack
43 ___ Diego Chicken
45 Actress Gardner
46 Gender

228

Across

1 Ideal society
7 Persian or Egyptian Mau
10 Freaks out
11 Hostess product
12 Where thespians perform
13 Middle Eastern country whose capital is Muscat
14 Poetic form
15 Pass, as time
16 Options at a restaurant
19 Used the sofa
21 Lighted sign in a movie theater
22 Round 3-D shape
26 Italian city Christopher Columbus hailed from
28 Choir voice
29 Beautiful to look at
31 Hollywood goodbye
32 To and ___
33 100 to 1, say
34 ___ Bell (fast food chain)
37 "Jersey Shore" channel
39 Greek drink
40 Write a check before receiving a service
44 Pitt of "Burn After Reading"
45 Cologne's continent
46 Listening device?
47 Ease

Down

1 Delivery company called "Brown"
2 Piece of body art, for short
3 ___ roll (doing well)
4 Eat everything in sight
5 Like some tea or coffee
6 Evaluate
7 Perry who sang "Some Enchanted Evening"
8 Melville captain
9 Soprano or Danza
11 Leave your bedmate cold
16 Ryan and White
17 Big boss, for short
18 After "front" or "back," half of a golf course
20 Appropriate
23 Oklahoma city, or an old-school woman's name
24 Path
25 God of romantic love
27 You're breathing it now
30 Force
34 English 101 verb
35 Surrounding atmosphere
36 Russia-ruling Romanov, e.g.
38 Not false
41 Where to send letters: abbr.
42 Mimic
43 Monetary unit in Matsumoto

229

Across

1 Actresses Hennessy and Clayburgh
6 Performs at karaoke night
11 ___ flu
12 Considering everything
13 "Throw ___ From the Train"
14 Persuasive article
15 Share a meal (with)
17 Striped animal
18 1995 movie about a pig
21 Acquired
25 Wedding day words
26 Fish eggs
27 Fold, as a company
31 Cracklin' Oat ___ (cereal brand)
32 Queen of ___ (Biblical character)
34 What you may paint someone with
39 Basketball, in slang
40 First letter, to Greeks
41 Like some challenges
42 Permit past the door
43 Animal known for its laugh
44 French city

Down

1 Door holder
2 Singer Novello
3 Key ___ pie
4 Class for an expecting mother
5 King cobra or black mamba
6 ___ Nevada (mountain range)
7 Pants measurement
8 Org. that sent up the space shuttles
9 Happy
10 Sneaky
16 London-based TV network

18 ___ Mac (McDonald's sandwich)
19 "Without further ___..."
20 Newhart or Dylan
22 Go astray
23 ___ constrictor
24 Japan's currency
28 Annual tennis or golf tournament
29 Drink brand named for a mountain
30 Knight or Turner
31 Grain used in soup
33 Another slang term for 39-across
34 Very thin
35 Italy's capital
36 Plotting
37 Body part under the knee
38 ___ Christian Andersen ("The Ugly Duckling" author)
39 "What did you say?"

230

Across

1 Freezer cubes
4 Feedbag bit
7 Not bottom
10 Quick snooze
11 Sign on a car, maybe
13 Trick play in football
15 Sign of what's to come
16 "The Tell-Tale Heart" author
17 Neither fish ___ fowl
20 Three, in cards
23 Traveling the streets of New York City, perhaps
26 Unified
27 Dangerous conditions for drivers
29 Sandwich named for its three main ingredients
30 Publicity ___ (things done just for attention)
31 "___ any wonder?"
33 "Quiet on the ___!"
34 By way of
36 Tennis champ Arthur
40 Changed one's political positions for convenience
44 Stopped working for good
45 Part of WHO
46 "Hurrah!"
47 Have to pay back
48 Slinky or Rubik's Cube

Down

1 The 411
2 Relaxed
3 Sword used in the Olympics
4 Not working that day
5 "You've Got Mail" company
6 Vacation
7 Become a permanent part of the landscape
8 "Bravo!"
9 Each
12 Get off ___-free (escape punishment)
14 Karenina and Paquin
18 Folk singer Phil
19 Simple water vessels
21 Finishes up
22 "What can I do for you?"
23 Social troubles
24 ___ scene (it's seen at Christmas)
25 One of the three primary colors
27 Crime-fighter gp.
28 How some beer is served
32 Great Plains home for an Indian
35 High hairstyle
37 Leopard's marking
38 He saves the day
39 Pushing the boundaries
40 Cook fish, perhaps
41 Actress Thompson
42 Actor Ayres
43 Kind of poem

231

Across

1 Shoe brand Thom ___

5 Discusses, as a point

11 "Whoops!"

12 Stir up, as emotions

13 "Me and Bobby McGee" singer

15 Give a speech

16 Cousins of adjectives and adverbs

17 Fleming and Ziering

19 Magician's word

22 African nation

26 Denim garment

28 Category

29 Church instruments

30 Spanish river

31 Intentionally setting a fire

35 Shaped like an egg

39 Inexpensive baubles

41 Kind of clock or watch

42 Thunderstorm drops

43 Gives money back to

44 AMEX or NASDAQ rival

Down

1 Lucky charm

2 Burn badly

3 Actress Kendrick

4 Contradictory phrase

5 Leon Uris novel "The ___"

6 Actor Jeremy of "Reversal of Fortune"

7 "___ the mornin' to ya!"

8 "Star Trek" role

9 A ___ "apple"

10 Bills with Hamilton on them

14 Chairs

18 Unemployed person's problem

19 Nighttime wear, for short

20 ___ Speedwagon

21 Listening device?

22 He lost to Nixon in 1972

23 Crook's alter ego

24 Author Deighton

25 "___ Too Late"

27 Bow and ___

30 "Have fun!"

31 Slightly open, like a door

32 Ancient Norse letter

33 Make a sound using two fingers

34 State north of Texas: abbr.

36 Oil of ___

37 Part of the eye

38 Unit of force

40 Latin abbrs.

Across

1 B.B. King's musical genre
6 Word before liberties or disobedience
11 Bald ___ (symbol of America)
12 Basketball stadium
13 They crisscross the landscape
15 Perfect score, sometimes
16 Olive ___
17 "___ the season..."
18 Unusual
19 Some football linemen: abbr.
20 Dollar bill
21 Travel far and wide
23 Cuts in Norway's coastline
25 Used foul language
27 Flag
30 Ron Paul's senator son
34 Extreme anger
35 Devoured
37 Apiece
38 Uncooked
39 Cartoon devil, for short
40 High card
41 They're full of garbage
44 Dutch city, with "the"
45 Campfire stuff
46 Take the wheel
47 Run-down and possibly dangerous

Down

1 Person making a wager
2 Texas city
3 Idi Amin's nation
4 Manning at quarterback
5 Mr. in Mexico
6 Fast-food chain
7 Levin or Gershwin
8 ___ analysis
9 One way to pay someone back
10 Scottish girls
14 Equalizing phrase
22 Popular online portal
24 "___ the ramparts..."
26 What it's like outside
27 Maternity ward events
28 Mountain where Noah's Ark landed
29 Spiritual music genre
31 Indian tribe for whom a helicopter is named
32 Did some smooching
33 Like upscale parties
36 Pound and Klein
42 Take to court
43 Find work for

233

Across

1 Looks over quickly
6 Track and field events
11 Occult deck of cards
12 Legislate
13 Ireland's nickname, with "The"
15 Delivery vehicle
16 Baby's protector
17 Toni Morrison book "___ Baby"
18 Victorian, for one
19 "Law & Order: ___"
20 Jeremy of basketball fame
21 Sniffer
23 Village or church leader
25 "Around the ___ in 80 Days"
27 Became mature
30 Devours
34 "Losing My Religion" band
35 Little kid
37 Drink from a dish
38 One of Tarzan's pals
39 "Awesome!"
40 Drink that comes in a pint
41 Grocery store section
   with Apple Jacks
44 Avid
45 Irritated
46 Horse, in poems
47 Approaches

Down

1 Director Spielberg
2 Classic Chevrolet
3 Stadiums
4 Neither here ___ there
5 Random guesses
6 Drink that will keep you up all night

7 Singer DiFranco
8 Make a two-piece chess move
9 Bakery buy
10 Backs of boats
14 City the Beatles came from
22 "Gross!"
24 President before JFK
26 ___ Bound
27 Kelly and Jones
28 Echo
29 Come to the forefront
31 Juneau's state
32 Higher, as a building
33 Goes over the limit
36 Tom Sawyer's creator
42 Wide shoe size
43 Anger

Across

1 Ready
4 Clothing store, with "The"
7 ___ Wednesday
8 Paid performer
9 Some computers
12 It's put on many injuries
14 Mouse cousin
15 Weak, as an excuse
16 Capital of Montana
18 Work that looks different from different angles
20 Oodles
21 Medium: abbr.
22 Like Halloween houses
25 It makes cubes in the freezer
27 Salaries
29 Greek letter
32 Feeling blue
33 Great grade
35 Instantly
38 Heaven's counterpart
39 Not him
40 Just the facts
42 Like half of all whole numbers
43 Calif., Fla., Ill., etc.
44 ___ Francisco Bay
45 Susan of "The Partridge Family"
46 Finale

Down

1 Seaman
2 Get out of jail free
3 What someone may make you say before they do something for you
4 4.00, for example
5 St. Louis feature
6 Jab
9 What someone may make you say before they do something for you, if they're being really annoying
10 Paddled watercraft
11 Get on your feet
13 Apiece
17 Actress Turner
19 Not us
23 Devoured
24 ___ major (constellation)
26 State next to R.I.
27 State next to Montana
28 Famous
30 ___ of Swat (Babe Ruth's nickname)
31 Corsica, Crete or Capri
34 The third degree?
36 Gunk
37 Simplify
41 Path

Across

1 Money: Ger.
5 One of the U.S. Virgin Islands
11 Lion's home
12 One of the Muses
13 Emerald ___ (Ireland's nickname)
14 Old age
15 Second Greek letter
16 "___ hear!"
17 Just so-so
19 Food in a trough
23 Vienna's country
27 Water: Fr.
28 Song on "Beatles for Sale"
30 In the past
31 Begins a journey
32 Cribbage needs
34 "Help!"
35 Many an NYC dwelling
37 Functions
41 Saudi ___
44 "___ be fun!"
45 Rent out to someone else
46 Moon landing letters
47 Leave the country?
48 Got larger

Down

1 Silver-tongued
2 Soothe, as someone's mind
3 Voice feature
4 Have as a goal someday
5 Florida's nickname, with "The"
6 Musical group of three
7 Singer Joplin
8 "First..."
9 Popular movie or sing
10 No vote, in Congress
18 God of love
20 Brick toy brand
21 Pearl Harbor's island
22 Golf shot measured in feet
23 "Do I have to draw you ___?"
24 Sudden impulse
25 Pollution problem
26 Choir voice
29 Giving out
33 Nice fur
36 The ___ Piper of Hamelin
38 Part of a constellation
39 "What ___ can I say?"
40 Cole ___
41 Ninny
42 Wish you could take back
43 First three of 26

Across

1 Part of a royal flush
4 Bradley and McMahon
7 "Hilarious!"
10 Shout at a Real Madrid game
11 King ___ (ruler of old Egypt)
12 Peyton Manning's brother
13 Singer DiFranco
14 ___ out the victory (barely defeat)
15 Come out on tip
16 Private e-mail address ending?
17 Stephen of "The Crying Game"
18 "___ heard!"
19 Japanese airline
20 Nickname for Edward
21 One of 100 in DC
22 Average
24 Neighbor of Earth
25 Thousand thousand
27 Flat "table" feature of the West
29 Contradictory shout
32 ___-rock (music genre)
33 Hosp. workers
34 Movie frame
35 ___ es Salaam (African city)
36 Turkish title
37 ___ Vegas
38 Brazilian city, briefly
39 Home full of mud
40 Beer variety
41 Business off the highway
42 Lean-___ (camping structures)
43 ___ Tin Tin
44 B.A. or B.S.
45 "I'll take that as ___"
46 Chess pieces that can jump over other pieces: abbr.

Down

1 Including everyone, in an old phrase
2 Weather phenomenon
3 Astronaut on Ohio's state quarter
4 Lasting forever
5 Musician on D.C.'s state quarter
6 Ending for farm
7 Explorers on Missouri's state quarter
8 Twist in a plot?
9 Sheets, pillowcases, etc.
23 Actress Farrow
24 "Little ol' me?"
26 "Agreed"
27 Capital of Spain
28 Jerry's ex, on "Seinfeld"
30 Close the deal
31 Mary-Kate and Ashley
33 Jamaican with dreadlocks, often

237

Across

1 Farmer's measurements
6 New Delhi's nation
11 Charlie or Martin of Hollywood
12 Words like "cat" and "catnip"
13 Kind of attraction a guidebook may warn you about
15 Spare ___
16 Word on bills
17 Female sheep
18 Highest heart or spade
19 Omelet ingredient
20 ___ Diego Chargers
21 Longings
23 Highfalutin'
25 Ms. Winfrey
27 Word before code or colony
29 "Uh-huh"
33 Battering ___
34 CD-___
36 To and ___
37 Eugene's st.
38 Kind of battery
39 In favor of
40 How the attraction in 13-across may be described
43 Pond growth
44 Kind of code
45 Necessities
46 Web locations

Down

1 On the wrong path
2 Decision
3 Sandwich in a deli
4 Ending for mountain or musket
5 Snippy, as a remark
6 Acura model
7 "You Are ___ Alone"
8 Intense pressure
9 You might say
10 Colorado resort
14 Rio de Janeiro's ___ Mountain
22 Father's boy
24 "Honor ___ father"
26 Street celebrations
27 Time out of prison
28 Come to the forefront
30 Get an A for ___
31 Stir up
32 Stallions
33 Martin's comedy partner
35 Superior ladies
41 Lass's friend
42 Me: Fr.

Across

1 Dickens hero
4 "For ___ a jolly ..."
7 "___ moment"
8 "The Three Faces of ___"
9 "You stink!"
12 European country whose capital is Tallinn
14 Brouhaha
15 "My Name Is ___"
16 King or queen, e.g.
17 Mr. Seinfeld
19 Blasé
20 1997 U.S. Open champ
21 Eng Bunker's twin
23 20-20, e.g.
24 Basketball's Jeremy ___
25 Victorian, for one
28 Car dealer's offering
30 End
31 Disgrace
33 Theater name
35 Thing
36 Army fatigues, for short
37 When it's broken, that's good
38 Source of sudden wealth
41 "Quiet down!" sounds
42 "Raiders of the Lost ___"
43 Long, long time
44 "Absolutely!"
45 ___ sauce

Down

1 Creepy author
2 ___ and outs
3 "Pink Panther" actor
4 Famous American orator
5 Not good
6 Caribbean, e.g.
9 British woman with a famous diary
10 Exude
11 Didn't have enough
13 Propel, in a way
16 Gabriel, for one
17 Boeing 747, e.g.
18 QB Manning
19 "Marry Poppins" kid
22 Not hers
26 "Flying Down to ___"
27 "The Simpsons" storekeeper
29 Shade tree
31 Doesn't guzzle
32 Provo's state
34 "___ Believer"
36 Apple center
38 The Chesapeake, e.g.
39 Animal house
40 "___ calls?"

Across

1 Zero

4 Dot-___ (internet company)

7 "___ a Man of Constant Sorrow"

10 An obnoxious person may have a large one

11 A, in Argentina

12 Real, cutesy-style

13 Place

14 Apiece

15 Hundredths of a dollar

16 Part of a magician's outfit, often

17 Peach center

18 Yes, in Quebec

19 Away from WSW

20 Ms. DiFranco

21 Coffee holder

22 More than battles

24 Non-digital clock

26 "That OK?"

28 African tribe that's also a dance

30 Goon

33 ___-Wan Kenobi

34 Kind of camera: abbr.

36 Monkey's uncle?

37 ___-A-Fella Records

38 "Beautiful job!"

39 School org.

40 S. ___ (st. whose capital is Pierre)

41 Not here

42 Golf course score

43 Before

44 Debtor's letters

45 ___ out a living

46 Banned pesticide

47 Come-___ (sales techniques)

48 Dad of Rod and Todd Flanders

Down

1 Male in a family tree

2 Green lizard

3 You might buy one, hoping to win a lot of money

4 Coffee serving, casually

5 What your odds of winning may be

6 Drink with an olive

7 But still, you never know...

8 Maestro Toscanini

9 Wondering

23 ___'wester (kind of storm)

25 Tiny crawler

27 Famous nuclear submarine named for a state

28 Phrased

29 "All ___!" (train conductor's shout)

31 Slow on the ___

32 Aimed (towards a certain audience)

35 Romulus's twin brother

240

Across

1 Scary snake
6 Final notice
10 Car dealer's offering
11 Taboos
13 Dessert named for a state
15 Sky sight
16 "First of all..."
17 Hard throw, in baseball
18 Came into contact with
19 Train stop: abbr.
20 Gasteyer formerly of "SNL"
21 Catch
23 Several czars
25 Colorado resort
27 Baffled
29 First-rate
33 Morning moisture
34 ___ Wednesday
36 Fond du ___, Wisc.
37 Gold, in Guatemala
38 Man's name made up of an alphabetical sequence
39 "Am ___ believe ...?"
40 TV show named for a state
43 Composed
44 Michigan city
45 "Jane ___"
46 Blind parts

Down

1 "Abbey Road" and "Revolver"
2 Make unable to hear
3 North ___ (Minot's state)
4 Language suffix
5 Second tries, casually
6 Away, in a way
7 ___ constrictor
8 From wing to wing
9 Arcade coins
12 Long story
14 Italian appetizers
22 Neon or argon
24 Little picnic pest
26 Shore
27 Put air into
28 Like some streets
30 Wilde or Newton-John
31 Inventor's claim
32 Moves along
33 Homer Simpson shouts
35 ___ and puffs
41 Balloon filler
42 "___ say!"

241

Across

1 Computer key
4 Latest craze
7 Former Bush aide Fleischer
8 Find work for
9 Baseball's Ripken
12 Tropical disease
14 Nutrition amt.
15 Woody Guthrie's kid
16 "But still..."
18 Eric Clapton classic
20 Small piece of land
21 And so forth
22 Foot problem
25 Hitchcock movie, or a woman's name
27 Salary scale
29 High shot in tennis
32 Plus
33 Presidential nickname
35 Is admitted
38 Expansive
39 Juan Peron's wife
40 Not likely to betray
42 Md. neighbor
43 Mauna ___, Hawaii
44 Spy novelist Deighton
45 The heavens
46 Some H.S. students

Down

1 Mexican food made of corn
2 Where Noah landed
3 Frequent host of the Oscars
4 Animal's hair
5 Largest of the continents
6 College head
9 What fortune tellers look into
10 "Rolling in the Deep" singer
11 Not now
13 Popular ISP
17 Part of CD
19 Palindromic band from Sweden
23 Permit
24 Word before tea or coffee
26 God of love
27 Looked for over the intercom
28 Rival of Tylenol
30 Clam's cousin
31 Marching band sticks
34 Charlottesville sch.
36 Societal troubles
37 Breakfast area
41 "Yippee!"

242

Across

1 Cry uncontrollably
4 Weasel's sound, in a song
7 Computerized task performer
10 In favor of
11 Day: Sp.
12 "___ you for real?"
13 Not-even-close shot in basketball
15 Cold War org.
16 "Cup or ___?" (ice cream parlor question)
17 Prepares ham or salmon
19 Inventory ___ Whitney
21 Grape's home
22 Barbie's buddy
23 Skills
26 Divided in half, as a TV show
28 Like some buildings or pipes
30 Not him
33 Got every question right on
34 Part of a play
36 Stirs to action
39 "No ifs, ands or ___!"
40 Physicians: abbr.
41 Time-tested
43 Mediterranean or Caribbean
44 Horse's food
45 Good first name for a cook
46 Have debts to pay
47 Bread used in a deli

Down

1 Actress Sissy of "Carrie"
2 Baltimore bird
3 Bruce Springsteen album of 1984
4 Hand-held device, for short
5 Sesame, coconut and peanut
6 ___ Sunday
7 Beatles song off "The White Album"
8 "Murder on the ___ Express"
9 Makes fun of
14 Arthur of "The Golden Girls"
18 Completed
20 Octagonal street sign
24 King Kong, e.g.
25 Young fellows
27 Large handfuls, as of cash
28 Cooking fats
29 Make a goal
31 Being
32 Save from injury
35 "60 Minutes" network
37 Reverberating sound
38 Cole ___ (picnic food)
42 Yes, to a sailor

243

Across

1 Football measurements
6 Incurred
11 Kindle buy
12 "La Bohème," e.g.
13 Philadelphia's state is named for him
15 "Cut it out!"
16 "Do the Right Thing" pizzeria owner
17 Dutch beer
22 Fight back against
25 "Another Green World" composer
26 Javelin, e.g.
27 Bring up the rear
29 Kipling's "Gunga ___"
30 Actress Plummer
31 It's hard to break
34 Solid ___ rock
35 Story
39 No liar
43 Bank
44 "Take your hands off me!"
45 Category
46 They croak

Down

1 Evergreens
2 Not much
3 Candy with caramel from Hershey's
4 Graceful ocean creature
5 Schuss, e.g.
6 From Italy's capital
7 Big name in computers
8 Born, in bios
9 Ashes holder
10 Give a bad review to
14 ___ were
18 "C'___ la vie!"
19 New Jersey's ___ University
20 Oklahoma city
21 "The Big Easy"
22 Change
23 Not good
24 E-mail, e.g.
27 "More than I needed to know," when texting
28 Scary snake
30 Blind as ___
32 Abominates
33 Contents of some urns
36 A chorus line
37 ___ Mason (financial services company)
38 "Aeneid" god
39 Special attention, for short
40 Bill of Rights subj.
41 Charlottesville sch.
42 Christmas character

244

Across

1 Bakery supply
6 "Planet of the ___"
10 Movie star
11 Apple leftover
12 Kind of bread
14 Alphabet trio
15 Borscht ingredients
16 Coaster
17 A, in Acapulco
20 Needing a key
23 It's over the eye
24 Contents of some urns
25 "Silly" birds
26 Not fast
27 Defeats
28 "___ bad!"
29 First aid ___
30 Fine dinnerware
32 A.T.M. need
35 Captain Ahab's quarry
37 Breed
38 Sit in on
39 Baby kangaroo
40 Affirmatives

Down

1 Show boredom
2 Bounce back, in a way
3 Above
4 Costa del ___
5 Multiplies by three
6 Hurt
7 Keats, for one
8 Crossword puzzle
 features, sometimes
9 Part of a tennis match
13 Garden intruder
16 Bias
18 Barely beat, with "out"
19 Has a mortgage
20 Bringing up the rear
21 Norway's capital
22 Train's sound
23 Harry Truman's wife
25 Escaped
27 Short ___ (Monopoly property)
29 Baby cat
31 Bring on
32 Stationer's stock
33 Tennis star Nastase
34 Brings home
35 NYT rival
36 Color

245

Across

1 Killer whale
5 Butcher shop tool
10 Chimney blackener
11 Hank who hit 755 home runs
12 Earring's place
13 Evaluate
14 Vegetable fried down South
15 "Be quiet!"
16 Quickly
18 Recedes, like the tide
22 Bakery-cafe chain
24 Sweater stuff from sheep
25 Ancient
26 To and ___
28 "Much ___ About Nothing"
29 Customer
31 President Jackson
33 Went on a boat or a plane
34 Not bad at all
35 Greek consonant
37 Is in possession of
40 Mike and Cicely
43 Get a terrible grade on
44 Home ___ (store chain)
45 Arm bone
46 Each of this puzzle's three long down answer's starts with one
47 Corrupt, as results of a test

Down

1 Capital of Norway
2 Second most-powerful chess piece
3 Like products with two different sponsors
4 "Relax, sergeant!"
5 Robe closer
6 Curved nut
7 "We ___ Family"
8 ___ Angeles Lakers
9 Navy rank: abbr.
13 Vegetable that comes in spears
17 Dog's bark, in the comics
19 Most expensive Monopoly property
20 Portend
21 Not fast
22 Do a bartender's job
23 Plus
27 Lennon's love
30 Captured back
32 Idiot
36 Chips before the poker hand
38 Late dinner hour
39 Cole ___
40 6-point plays, for short
41 Tokyo money
42 Place for a pedicure

246

Across

1 Rascal
6 Quarrels
11 Hot chocolate
12 Hosts at one's apartment
13 Send a warning to
14 Unexpected event
15 "The Andy Griffith Show" deputy
17 New Jersey basketball team
18 Train stations
22 Country neighboring Iraq
26 Kitchen appliances
27 Egypt's capital
28 Sage or oregano
29 Male or female
30 Employer
32 Large musical instrument
38 Mediterranean island nation
39 Stadium
40 Knight's protection
41 Dryer materials
42 Exact copy
43 Frighten, as a horse

Down

1 Wound covering
2 Coca-___
3 Computer brand
4 Time before noon, in poems
5 Inventors may be granted them
6 8-hour work period
7 Person who lives in France's capital
8 Since
9 "Name That ___"
10 Stratego piece
16 "Uh-huh"

18 Homer Simpson shout
19 Adam's madam
20 Apiece
21 How to get a machine to start working
23 Free (of)
24 "___ we alone?"
25 Oslo's country: abbr.
27 Cocoa Puffs and Shredded Wheat
29 Shaving cream type
31 Look unswervingly
32 Marx or Malone
33 Tickled doll
34 Coffeemaker's sound
35 Nevada city
36 "Do ___ others..."
37 Part of a Halloween costume
38 Apple computer

247

Across

1 Blueprint
4 Cow, maybe
7 Go downhill
10 Betraying your country
12 ATM need
13 New Hampshire neighbor
14 "That's ___ ..."
15 "What's gotten ___ you?"
16 "___ to Billie Joe"
17 Crush
20 "Fantastic" Roald Dahl character
22 Kind of pie
23 "Chicago" lyricist
24 Alabama neighbor
30 Nods, perhaps
31 ___ center
32 Rodeo sight
35 By oneself
37 Howard of "Happy Days"
38 Former home to the Hawks, with "the"
40 Publicity, slangily
41 Colorado neighbor
45 "Get it?"
46 Delivery shout
47 Be nosy
48 Not just "a"
49 "Delicious!"

Down

1 Channel with videos
2 "___ we having fun yet?"
3 Apiece
4 All together
5 Custom
6 Puts in a mausoleum
7 Parody
8 Buddy
9 One of the fingers
11 During
17 "Let me see..."
18 "Certainement!"
19 Country rtes.
21 Baseball card stat.
23 Ending for steward
25 Boar's mate
26 "Here's the answer!"
27 Ace
28 Ballpoint, e.g.
29 "Rocks"
32 Like good potato chips
33 No social animal
34 In tune
35 Win by ___
36 Peru's capital
39 Story
42 "Think" company
43 ___ de plume
44 High school class

248

Across

1 Bad part of town
5 Touched lightly with a cloth
11 "Que ____?" (greeting in Spanish)
12 Mistakes in a book
13 "The First Time ____ I Saw Your Face"
14 Biblical mountain
15 "North by Northwest" actor
17 Actress Tomlin
18 Pollution fighting govt. branch
21 New York's capital
24 Got bigger
25 Words like "crossword" and "puzzle"
26 Birds that fly in a V formation
27 Famous pirate Captain William ____
28 Beachfront properties, maybe
29 Additionally
30 Ice cream parlor item
31 "To Kill a Mockingbird" author
36 "Stop walking for a minute!"
38 Surrounding glow
39 Not on the porch or the lawn
40 Lion's home
41 Talk incessantly
42 Brings to court

Down

1 On ____ (without a contract)
2 Stuff that flows down from a volcano
3 Computer owner
4 Baltimore's state
5 Pay ____ (have to cough up a lot of money)
6 Wide selection
7 Word in many cereal named
8 Swapped
9 Greek letter
10 "Tru ____!"
16 Clear liquors
19 Mexico's currency
20 Blows away
21 Paul who sang "Put Your Head on My Shoulder"
22 Butcher's cut
23 Zen ____
24 What this puzzle's two long theme entries end with
26 Departed
28 Metal old pennies were made from
30 Inelegant
32 Working hard
33 Hawaiian party
34 One of the Great Lakes
35 Pair near the hair
36 Not a loss
37 Santa ____, California

249

Across

1 Baltic capital
5 No meat or cheese eater
10 Horace volume
11 ___ Lodge
12 Clever solution to a problem
14 In bed
15 Call, as a game
16 Key for some compositions: abbr.
20 Too uptight
23 Computer info
24 Order between "ready" and "fire"
25 Gossipy Smith
26 Attempt
28 Spray
31 18-wheeler
32 ___ green
33 Chinese restaurant offering
38 Just be joking
40 Circus employee
41 Annul
42 Bottomless pit
43 "___ of the D'Urbervilles"

Down

1 Column crossers
2 "American ___"
3 Richard of "Pretty Woman"
4 Question posers
5 Make sure
6 Coll. major
7 Overcharged
8 Cape ___, Mass.
9 Affirmative indication
13 "Planet of the ___"
17 African nation
18 Arguing
19 Utah basketball team
20 Hail Mary, e.g.
21 Baptism, for one
22 Mosque V.I.P.
27 Having two spouses at once
28 Britney of pop
29 Equal
30 Expired
34 Bakery selections
35 Air
36 Aims
37 Bothers
38 "Harper Valley ___"
39 Family dog, for short

250

Across

1 Respectful title for a woman
6 The Mamas & the ___
11 To the left or the right
12 Extremely
13 One cause of the American Revolution
15 Go down, like the sun
16 Caribbean liquors
17 Goodyear product
18 Your, in the Bible
21 Your region
23 Actor Thicke
25 Hockey setting
26 "Yes, my friend," to a Mexican
30 ___ talk (booster)
31 Jay of late-night talk
32 Gun sound, in comic strips
33 Mauna ___, Hawaii
36 Each of the three long across entries conceals a 5-letter one of these
40 Bizarre
41 Sample, as of food
42 Electrical threads
43 Someone ___ (not yours)

Down

1 Yoga equipment
2 Arthur of tennis
3 Health regimen
4 TV revenue sources
5 ___ system
6 Beat badly, as in a game
7 Swiss peaks
8 School org.
9 Semicircle
10 Stopped standing
14 Glow
17 Novelist Morrison

18 Threesome
19 Female chicken
20 Jabber
21 Light bulb's home
22 Jason's ship, in mythology
23 Scary snake
24 Falsehood
27 Friends
28 Medieval drink made from honey
29 Prisoner
32 Spreadable French cheese
33 Accompaniment to a hug
34 Ending for cigar
35 Yeses, at sea
36 Not many
37 Hawaiian necklace
38 Bobby of hockey
39 Silent ___ (nickname for President Coolidge)

251

Across

1 Gender abbr.
5 Pass on
10 Bounce back, in a way
11 Negra ___ (beer brand)
12 Small particle
13 Kind of band
14 In person
15 Big drinker
16 Dine at home
18 "___ a chance"
21 ___ lava
23 "Much ___ About Nothing"
24 "___ Blue?"
25 ___ roll
27 Crime family head
28 Barbie's beau
29 Introverts
31 Chang's Siamese twin
32 Bill of Microsoft
33 Air
35 Alone
38 When the clock strikes twelve
40 Popular herb
41 Snares
42 Knowing, as a secret
43 "___ Defeats Truman"
44 Halftime lead, e.g.

Down

1 Breakfast, lunch or dinner
2 Broadway opening
3 Kid's wintertime employment
4 Attack
5 Robert De Niro movie
6 Garden of ___
7 Kid's summertime employment
8 Pie ___ mode
9 "Silent Night" adjective
11 Kid's summertime employment
17 Golf peg
19 Aroma
20 2,000 pounds
21 Construct
22 Black cat, maybe
26 Caught
30 Mythical Scottish creature
32 Like caramel
34 Garden squirter
36 All excited
37 Characteristic carrier
38 "Go on ..."
39 "For shame!"

Across

1 Fathers
5 Holiest city, in Islam
10 Small intestine section
12 ___ movements (military maneuvers)
13 "I Love Lucy" actress
15 "Nice job!" reply
16 Zeus or Poseidon
17 The other way around
21 Chemical ending
22 "For shame!"
23 Bridal path
26 Cough up
30 New age chant
32 Singer Charles
33 Verbal election
36 Chemical ending
38 Coagulate
39 YouTube hits
44 Mosey
45 Expertise
46 Crows' homes
47 Rooney of "60 Minutes"

Down

1 Math operation: abbr.
2 "Aladdin" prince
3 Tools
4 Hotel offering
5 Cable channel
6 Victorian, for one
7 Kind of line
8 Chanel of fashion
9 Acted like
11 Sportscaster ___ Albert
14 Da's opposite
17 ___ Appia

18 ___ Amin
19 Fish eggs
20 Census datum
24 Bathroom, to Brits
25 Big record label
27 Red meat provides it
28 "Dig in!"
29 Soap ingredient
31 1205
33 Action words
34 "___ Coming" (1969 hit)
35 Clear liquor
36 "Terrible" czar
37 Kind of store
40 Cockpit abbr.
41 Guitar pioneer ___ Paul
42 Aged
43 Arch

253

Across

1 Egypt's capital city
6 African country whose capital is Accra
11 Wood used to smoke bacon
12 Word before space or limits
13 Some people put it in coffee
15 Compass dir.
16 ___ Alamos
17 Where injured baseball players are put: abbr.
18 Differently-___ (handicapped)
20 Flower that's also a woman's name
23 Blood problem
27 Very close, as two participants in a race
29 More sore
30 Conception
31 "___ I might..."
33 Taylor or Phair
36 Scottish form of the name John
37 Not morning: abbr.
40 Repeatedly
43 The wife on "The Brady Bunch"
44 Slowly disappear, as a coastline
45 Has the information
46 Get the feeling

Down

1 Lyricist Sammy
2 Actor Arkin
3 Not doing anything productive
4 B-ball official
5 Toothbrush brand
6 Gift from above
7 "What?"
8 Not much
9 Little ___ (Charles Dickens character)
10 Comic book dog barks
14 Longtime Astros pitcher
18 Pose a question
19 Patron saint of France
20 One ___ million
21 Word before center or room
22 "___ bin ein Berliner"
24 Club ___
25 It may be crushed or cubed
26 Police blotter letters
28 Overhead photos
32 South American mountain range
33 Key's target
34 Tennis great Lendl
35 Number before one
37 Stratford-upon-___ (Shakespeare's home)
38 U.S. government agents
39 Elm or oak
41 Line of seats
42 State north of Calif.

Across

1 Up to this point
6 "God ___ America"
11 Neighbor of Neptune
12 Arabian Peninsula nation
13 Sits around doing nothing
14 Italian island a style of pants are named for
15 Tex. city
16 Canyon or ranch ending
18 Waiter's money
19 Narcissist's problem
20 Actor Mineo
21 Talk nonstop
22 Football game "zebras"
24 Fall into line
26 Irritating kind of person
28 Followed closely
30 Zeus, Poseidon, etc.
33 Give weapons to
34 Home to a pig
36 Guys
37 Some college degs.
38 Creepy author of "The Pit and the Pendulum"
39 ___ cream sundae
40 Needing to shed a few pounds
42 On the ocean
44 Edmonton hockey player
45 Middle East big shot
46 Where valuables are kept
47 Irritable

Down

1 Tarantula or black widow
2 Later years
3 What the haughty politician was?
4 Consumed
5 Romantic flowers
6 How paints are sorted in a store
7 Stage actress Salonga
8 What he gave people to get elected?
9 ___ number (product identifier)
10 Short, as a response
17 Tried to reach quickly
23 Another word for the Sun
25 Actress Ryan of "Sleepless in Seattle"
27 Evening prayers
28 Subjects too sensitive to discuss
29 "Lawrence of ___"
31 Trickery
32 Underhanded
35 It makes bread rise
41 Get a look at
43 Word in many band names

255

Across

1 "See ya!"
4 Take a chair
7 Split ___ soup
10 Computerized task performer
11 Org. for Tiger Woods
12 ___ drop soup (Chinese menu item)
13 Musical instrument blown by a wacky bird?
16 Playful animal in the water
17 Eskimo's new home, if he moved to China?
23 Spaceman
24 Rose's danger
25 Tyrannosaurus ___ (big dinosaur)
26 "The Raven" author
27 Turning on a fixed point
30 Handed over, as money
32 Park that only houses Australian animals?
34 European river
35 What you can get on your arm to show your search engine loyalty?
41 Female sheep
42 Rowboat mover
43 Not just my or your
44 Gender
45 Sheet music markings
46 Oinking creature

Down

1 English channel?
2 Not me
3 And so on
4 Exactly correct
5 Patsy Cline's "___ Pieces"
6 "Here!"
7 Candy that has its own dispenser
8 It may get bruised or inflated
9 In the past
14 Basketball great ___ Bryant
15 Cry of frustration
17 Ehud of Israel
18 Billy Joel song "The Downeaster ___"
19 Add, when following a recipe
20 Jennifer of "Gigli"
21 University of Maine city
22 ___ a customer
28 Farmer's prefix
29 Obama cabinet member Ray
30 Submarine detectors
31 Robert Frost or Walt Whitman
33 Hayworth and Moreno
35 "What can I do for you?"
36 Amazement
37 Place a curse on
38 Toy that spins
39 Yes, in France
40 Assn.

Across

1 "Such a pity!"
5 Coffees that won't keep you up
11 Type of type
12 Not knowing right from wrong
13 Border
14 Between eighty and one hundred
15 Shed some tears
16 "___ be hilarious!"
17 Be defeated
19 Praising words
23 New York city
26 Suffix for student e-mail addresses
27 Bring together
28 Expert
30 Rd. crossings
31 Hurting on purpose
33 Foil-wrapped chocolate dessert
35 "___ have to do"
36 Henpeck
38 Pair on the body
41 Happen to
44 Hammer's target
45 Result of a punch
46 Model/TV host Banks
47 Bugs Bunny's favorite food
48 With great speed, in letters

Down

1 Some
2 Mother ___ (gold prospector's hope)
3 Aquarium swimmer
4 Disembark from, as a plane
5 Webster or Radcliffe
6 Give off
7 Purchased apartment
8 "We ___ the World"
9 Part of bacon
10 Sneaky
18 Vocalizes
20 Fish Tampa's baseball team were originally named for
21 Temptation location
22 "Song ___ Blue"
23 President before and after Clinton
24 "Do ___ others..."
25 Leave out
29 1996 Summer Olympics city
32 Tiny oinker
34 Radio station sign
37 In addition
39 Actress Sorvino
40 Hit with an open hand
41 London-based TV network
42 Time of history
43 Cat's coat

257

Across

1 Up to this point
6 Not higher
11 TV sitcom set at a diner in Arizona
12 "Someone Like You" singer
13 Parking penalties
14 Wood used to make chests
15 Actress ___ Marie Saint
16 General ___'s chicken
   (Chinese menu item)
18 Six-sider roller in Vegas
19 Wrath or envy
20 Rd. crossings
21 Once ___ lifetime opportunity
22 Folded Mexican food
24 Made up (for)
26 One sank the Titanic
28 "___ be the day!"
30 Pops a question
33 Actor Holbrook
34 ___ Lingus (Irish airline)
36 Spicy
37 Fall back
38 Not post-
39 Valuable mineral
40 King and Norman
42 Less
44 Photography technique
45 Clarifying phrase
46 Cigarette remnants
47 Goes left or right

Down

1 Least risky
2 Wilde or Newton-John
3 You can lose all your money in
  one, but you won't get wet

4 Part of a royal flush
5 Takes a breather
6 Izod ___ clothing
7 Praising poem
8 You can bring presents to one, but you won't get wet
9 "Seinfeld" lady
10 Look over again, as an article
17 Less likely to fall over
23 Tenth month: abbr.
25 "Are you a man ___ mouse?"
27 Goes by, as time
28 "___ & Louise"
29 ___ corpus
31 Language spoken in Seoul
32 Backs of boats
35 Deck out anew
41 Highway: abbr.
43 Bird whose meat is eaten by Australians

258

Across

1 Disallow to speak
4 "Casablanca" pianist
7 "___ y Plata" (Montana's motto)
8 Victorian, for one
9 Keep out
12 Calls the shots
14 Before
15 "What ___ now?"
16 Hebrew "peace"
18 Gamblers' mecca
20 18-wheeler
21 ___ Wednesday
22 Nova Scotia's capital
25 Poseidon's weapon
27 New employee
29 "Monty Python" airer
32 "Oh, very funny!"
33 Appropriate
35 "Aha!"
38 Dayton's state
39 Teacher's org.
40 Worst
42 Finale
43 Work unit
44 Born, in bios
45 Kind of shot
46 Tooth doc's degree

Down

1 Chocolate brand
2 Crops up
3 "Be my guest!"
4 "Hold on a ___!"
5 Song and dance, e.g.
6 Beat to a pulp
9 Miss the bus
10 Bouquet
11 Dance track, often
13 In-flight info, for short
17 A ___ apple
19 Climb
23 Gator or orange ending
24 Bottom of the barrel
26 Brawl
27 Biblical possessive
28 Actor Seth
30 Teased
31 Shuts the doors
34 Blouse, e.g.
36 Any thing
37 Drive-___
41 ___ roll

259

Across

1 Helps with a crime
6 Cherry alternative
11 Lake pillar
12 Acquiesce
13 Out on the links
15 On, as a lamp
16 Animal that oinks
17 Only three-letter element
18 Charlotte-to-Raleigh dir.
19 Aloof
20 Chemical suffix
21 Arizona tourist city
23 Computer brand
24 Baddies
26 Film crew member
29 Sloth or panda
33 Confederate soldier, for short
34 Fashionable boot
35 "Yo te ___"
36 Absorbed, as a cost
37 Rapa ___ (Easter Island)
38 Teacher's org.
39 Kuwait's body of water
42 Poet T.S. ___
43 Like "The X-Files"
44 Unfree worker
45 Animal in a roundup

Down

1 Compare ___ to oranges
2 Author's name
3 Flying high
4 Cracker Jack bonus
5 Criticizing unfairly
6 Like parachute pants
7 One of a dozen
8 Arousing
9 Singer Dion
10 Hugh of magazine fame
14 Central American nation
22 "Alley ___!"
23 "___ Lay Me Down" (1995 hit)
25 Motors
26 Fruit that may be sour
27 Say again, as a story
28 Spain and Portugal
30 Fertilizer
31 Audrey Tautou movie
32 Casual shoe
34 Bring together
40 Part of USSR
41 "___ lost!"

260

Across

1 Minor fights
6 Went back, like the tide
11 Video game company of the 1980s
12 Selection
13 It may be left in the pan after cooking breakfast
15 Waffle brand
16 Got older
17 Lobster-eaters wear one
19 RBI or ERA
21 God of love
23 Capital of the country that ends 13-across, if you say it out loud
27 Froot ___ (breakfast cereal)
29 News shows, newspapers, etc.
30 Capital of the country that begins 41-across
32 Luxurious fabric, as for bedsheets
33 Boxing location
35 Cost
36 River that flows through Hamburg
39 Surrealist painter Salvador ___
41 Modern breakfast food
45 Space man
46 Cheri formerly of "Saturday Night Live"
47 Andrew ___ Webber
48 Put back to zero

Down

1 Computer button
2 "Give ___ chance!"
3 Site where you can "like" posts
4 Toad's cousin
5 Belts out a tune
6 Organ of hearing
7 Takes in oxygen
8 Boast
9 Simplicity
10 Recolored
14 "I've ___ Feeling" (Beatles song)
17 Actor Lugosi
18 "The Man in the ___ Mask"
20 Bank amenity
22 You may give one to a trusted neighbor
24 Buildings
25 World's longest river
26 "For Pete's ___!"
28 ___ Lanka (Asian island nation)
31 Tennis star Roddick or actor Garcia
34 Zsa Zsa or Eva
36 And others: Lat.
37 Break in activity
38 Verve
40 In the wee hours
42 Finale
43 Mined matter
44 ___-picking (petty)

Across

1 Stew in your own anger
6 Prefix with scope or economics
11 Live show
12 Infamous energy company
13 Rome's nickname, with "The"
15 Listening organ
16 Show set in many cities
17 Highest amount possible, for short
18 "___ you hear me?"
19 Abbr. in some city names
20 Before, in poems
21 Pig's food
23 Informative pieces in the newspaper
25 Actress ___ Michelle Gellar
27 Gambler's spot
30 Work with acid
34 One day ___ time
35 FBI's sister organization
37 Gold: Sp.
38 Fisherman's pole
39 Bouncers ask for them
40 Sweet tuber
41 Hit duet sung by Diana Ross and Lionel Richie
44 Hair stylist's business
45 Picky ___ (person who's tough to shop for at the grocery store)
46 Took a nap
47 Pretty birds

Down

1 Schnauzer and weimaraner, for two
2 Like mall shops
3 Go too far with
4 "___ Town" (Thornton Wilder play)
5 Judi of movies
6 Singer Manchester or actress Gilbert
7 Company letters
8 Peninsula where an 1850s war was fought
9 Town club
10 Dark quartz varieties
14 Space rocks
22 Greek letter
24 Not he
26 Word before Greece or Rome
27 Rub gently
28 Not harmonic, like music
29 Cowboy's seat
31 Prius and Camry makers
32 Depraved
33 Baseball blasts
36 Fools
42 Chop (off)
43 Society's rules

262

Across

1 Rank above capt.
4 Where driver's licenses are handed out
7 Australian non-flyer
8 Its U stands for "under"
9 Small battery
12 Some poems
14 Letters on warships
15 One of Donald Duck's nephews
16 Dances like an Argentinian
18 Put into effect, as a law
20 Mom's sister, say
21 Man's name made from three consecutive letters of the alphabet
22 Accumulates
25 Trapeze flyer
27 Let go
29 Question
32 Arabian Peninsula nation
33 Yellow fruit
35 Casual eatery
38 See who can get there first
39 Animal with antlers
40 The U.S.
42 Caribbean or Caspian
43 "We'll have a ___ old time"
44 Actor Beatty
45 Before, in poetry
46 Hospital sections: abbr.

Down

1 Fits well together
2 Total
3 State capital that starts with a summer month
4 President between HST and JFK
5 No purebred
6 MasterCard rival
9 State capital that starts with a summer month
10 In unison
11 Helpers: abbr.
13 The Big Apple initials
17 Space shuttle letters
19 Actress Reid
23 Vaughn and Udall
24 Cain's brother
26 Penny
27 Nighttime garments
28 Actor Hirsch of "Into the Wild"
30 World Cup sport
31 Works on bread
34 Go astray
36 Great anger
37 Actor Sharif or Epps
41 One of two viewers

Across

1 Lightning ___
6 Worked with hay
11 1935 Triple Crown winner, or a city
12 Chip away at
13 Japanese noodle dish
14 Clay of "American Idol"
15 Cash cow
17 "Amazing!"
18 "Christ of St. John of the Cross" artist
21 All excited
26 Smart ___
28 Greta of film
29 Succeeded
31 A bunch
32 Come ___ end
34 Posh dinner carriers
40 Third month
41 Beatles song, e.g.
42 Catlike
43 Kind of concerto
44 Alternative to a convertible
45 Artist's stand

Down

1 Five-time Wimbledon champ
2 "Rubáiyát" poet
3 Dalai ___
4 NBC reality talent show
5 Electronics name
6 Great grip
7 Song for one
8 Norse god
9 Paradise
10 Animal house
16 Blouse, e.g.
18 Beaver's work
19 ___ mode
20 Was winning
22 State flower of Mississippi
23 Ace
24 Fall back
25 Affairs
27 Cook's tour stop
30 One of ten on the feet
33 Beyond's partner
34 Dressing ingredient
35 Bone-dry
36 1995 NCAA basketball champions
37 Bothers
38 Game piece
39 Close, as an envelope
40 More, in Madrid

264

Across

1 Small woods
6 Big sheet of paper
11 Zoo dart, for short
12 "Reversal of Fortune" star
13 Basketball coaching great
15 Bundle
16 Kid's cry
17 007, for one
20 "Check this out!"
22 Length x width, for a rectangle
24 Spain's continent
28 Phone book
30 Diver's sound
31 Connive
32 Ariz. neighbor
34 Armageddon
35 "I see!"
38 Utah city
40 Environmentalist's concern
45 Fixed a squeak
46 Early year
47 Nerves
48 Makes dull

Down

1 Bull's-eye: abbr.
2 Bauxite, e.g.
3 Crash site?
4 Become unhinged
5 Outfit
6 Excites
7 Sun, e.g.
8 Good soil
9 Ancient Andean
10 Dept. of Labor arm
14 Not here

17 "___ who?"
18 Get ready, for short
19 Cry
21 Mouth, in slang
23 1984 World Series MVP Trammell
25 Eye
26 Hacienda hand, maybe
27 Cornerstone: abbr.
29 Donny and Marie
33 Arc lamp gas
35 All excited
36 Opera song
37 Hot spot
39 Children's ___
41 Moray, e.g.
42 "Losing My Religion" rock group
43 Shoot the breeze
44 Football distances: abbr.

265

Across

1 Nebraska city
6 Froot ___ (breakfast cereal)
11 Party toy
12 Creepy
13 Food made from potatoes
15 Title for a knight
16 "The Cat in the ___"
17 After Sept.
18 Ending for descend
19 Plug-___ (computer patches)
20 Bruce of martial arts
21 Prepared a salad
23 Supreme
24 Writing assignment, often
26 Cole ___
29 Quiet down, as rumors or speculation
33 Beachgoer's acquisition
34 CD-___
35 India pale ___
36 Before Sept.
37 "Gross!" sounds
38 Dried river bed
39 Grocery store section where you'll find 13-across
42 Wild, as cats
43 Tiny hooting bird
44 Hits with the hand
45 Marshland growths

Down

1 Counteract
2 Miami Dolphins great Dan
3 Dodges
4 Darlin'
5 Bunker and Griffin
6 Some turns
7 "Love, Reign ___ Me" (Who song)
8 Maryland's state bird
9 Reese's ___
10 Group of six
14 Without question
22 Stitch up
23 Drive-___ (quick touring visits)
25 Tries to hit
26 Groups of personnel
27 Hardy's comedic partner
28 Kind of sweater
30 Time away from prison
31 Skipped over, as a sounds
32 Smallest amounts
34 Movie holders
40 Get with a laser gun
41 Need to pay

266

Across

1 "Chasing Pirates" singer Jones
6 Nation once called Persia
10 Speed skater ___ Anton Ohno
11 Hawaiian island
12 "The Color of Money" actor
14 Computer key
15 Get a hold of
16 Go downhill for fun
17 Patron saint of Norway
21 "Star Trek" character
25 ___ Dhabi
26 Holy ___ Empire
27 Jane and John
29 E-mail address ending
30 Moan and groan
32 Colleges award them: abbr.
34 Frigid
35 Get ready for a trip
37 In the manner of
40 "Immortal Beloved" actor
43 "Understood!"
44 Put up, like a building
45 Ladies
46 Male and female

Down

1 California valley noted for its wines
2 October birthstone
3 Crushing victory
4 Every last bit
5 Island off the coast of China
6 State associated with corn
7 Sylvester Stallone title character
8 Cry of discovery
9 Woman in a habit
13 Dickerson or Idle

16 Place to get a facial
18 Gentle animal
19 Cain slew him
20 Join together
21 Talking horse of TV
22 Took a trip on
23 Self-satisfied
24 Hand parts
28 Grant or Tan
31 Puerto ___
33 Wild shopping trip
36 Navy replies
37 MC rival, at the cash register
38 Queen Anne's ___ (flower)
39 Creatures in a colony
40 Soldiers, for short
41 ___ Wednesday
42 Rap's Dr. ___

267

Across

1 Songbirds
6 Data
11 "You can't fire me, ___!"
12 Author ___ Ingalls Wilder
13 Hilarious
14 "Wowzers!"
15 Professor's helpers: abbr.
16 Produce, as an egg
18 Super Bowl highlights?
19 Style for a stylist
22 Incite, as passion
24 Fraternal or identical sibling
28 Up, on a map
29 Vampire killer
30 Inflict upon
31 Prepared to eat a banana
32 Author of one of the Gospels
34 Sis's sib
37 Burro's relative
38 Kid's game
41 "Chill out!"
43 More than just mad
45 Confuse
46 :
47 Medicine amounts
48 Seaweed varieties

Down

1 Raise upward
2 Light blue shade
3 Become scarce in supply
4 One's relatives
5 Fashionable
6 Pink ___ (rock group)
7 "Ooh! ___!"
8 Havana's island
9 Walked (upon)
10 Simon ___ (another kids' game)
17 "___ you pulling my leg?"
20 Fords and Fiats
21 Fish-eating creature
22 "What else?"
23 Australian jumper, for short
25 Be proud of who you are
26 Pres. Eisenhower
27 Mr. Flanders
29 Feeling bad on a boat
31 Winston Churchill and Tony Blair, for two: abbr.
33 Money for the government
34 Actor Pitt
35 Try again on
36 Former GM make
39 Perched on
40 Military leaders: abbr.
42 The A of IPA
44 Eggs on a sushi menu

Across

1 100 centavos
5 Visit
11 "Terrible" czar
12 "Seinfeld" gal
13 ___ noir
14 Maybe later
15 The A of ABM
16 Simple shirt
17 Fashion magazine
19 Train stops: abbr.
23 Former U.S. president Zachary
25 Ball field covering
26 Death on the Nile cause, perhaps
27 Spaceship, maybe
29 Cloak-and-dagger org.
30 Ado
32 "Everything's fine"
34 Hawaii's ___ Coast
35 "My Name Is ___"
36 ___ Aviv
38 Brings home
41 Ancient
44 Not much
45 Examine closely
46 Strengthen, with "up"
47 Move unsteadily
48 Final, e.g.

Down

1 12-point type
2 Author ___ S. Connell
3 Kind of attacher
4 "Mourning Becomes Electra" playwright
5 Baseball player way behind the pitcher
6 Soothing herb
7 Most recent
8 Author ___ Yutang
9 "Walking on Thin Ice" singer Yoko
10 "What's ___?"
18 "Skip to My ___"
20 Fisherman's container
21 Opera song
22 Fix, like a cat
23 Charge
24 About
28 Grandma, to Germans
31 Turn in, as an accomplice
33 Highly decorative
37 Other
39 Louise of "Gilligan's Island"
40 Flower part
41 Appropriate
42 "Fancy that!"
43 Prior to

269

Across

1 In a happy way
6 ___ in the pan (one-hit wonder)
11 Sailing the waves
12 Flood blocker
13 Marsha Mason title role of 1977, with "The"
15 Economist's stat
16 Exchange punches in the ring
17 Be sick
18 Mr. DiCaprio
19 "What ___ doing?"
20 "The ___ of Pooh"
21 Whirlpool
23 Prepares to pray
25 Friend, to Francisco
27 Refuse to speak
30 Takes a chair
34 Gun (the motor)
35 Health resort
37 Officer
38 Put away
39 Ancient Egypt's King ___
40 Female flock member
41 Lynda Carter's most famous role
44 Powerful gun
45 Oscar or Emmy
46 Gets madder and madder
47 Tears apart

Down

1 Group of geese
2 Made up (for)
3 Kind of crustacean
4 Was headed for victory
5 "___-Dabba-Doo!"
6 Showing off one's muscles
7 Section, as of a race
8 Fly
9 Word before number or killer
10 Standard greetings
14 Jewish holiday
22 It's like a sweet potato
24 Goddess of the dawn
26 Puts together, as an army
27 Moves on all fours
28 Release
29 Retaliate for
31 "The ___ Cometh" (Eugene O'Neill play)
32 In the direction of
33 Throws around, as money
36 Fighting
42 Meadow drops
43 Be indebted to

270

Across

1 "Great" dog
5 Girl in Wonderland
10 Ready for customers
11 Taboo acts
12 Tricky Trojan War offerings
14 "The ___ Squad"
15 In addition
16 Whoever
18 "The Amazing ___"
22 Puts to work
24 Wish you could take it back
25 The Taj Mahal's country
28 Monopoly purchase
30 24 hours
31 Loretta of "M*A*S*H"
33 Had debts
35 Moose's horn
39 Farm measurement
41 Exist
42 You can see them all over Europe
45 Came up, as a subject
46 In a ___ (irritated)
47 ___ down (muted)
48 Gets a look at

Down

1 Standard theory
2 It may say "Kiss the chef"
3 Impoverished
4 Away from WSW
5 Director of "Crouching Tiger, Hidden Dragon"
6 Superman's love ___ Lane
7 "You're ___ a surprise!"
8 Army bed
9 Feminine ending
13 Topeka's state
17 Yes, to a Frenchman
19 School class
20 Pool stick
21 Long fish
23 Black eye
25 Wedding phrase
26 "I don't think so"
27 Make hair a different color
29 Baseball great Mel
32 Gave a heads-up to
34 Matt of "The Bourne Identity"
36 Last name that sounds like a street
37 Kovacs or Els
38 Takes a breather
40 Just in ___
42 Year of the ___ (1972 or 1984, on the Chinese calendar)
43 Gold: Sp.
44 Letters on aircraft carriers

Across

1 "Green ___"
6 Arm of the sea
11 Get red in the face from embarrassment
12 She was turned to stone, in a Greek myth
13 Largest newspaper in Massachusetts
15 Baseball great Mel
16 Not 'neath
17 Relatives
18 Most common word in English
19 Airline until 2011
20 Connections
21 Williams and Knight
23 Ungenerous with money
25 Implored
27 Someone who drinks slowly
30 Phoenix basketball team
34 Self-worth
35 Lawn clump
37 Edge
38 Greek letters
39 Calendar abbr.
40 Singer DiFranco
41 Newspaper Clark Kent and Lois Lane work at
44 Up to the time that
45 Petty
46 Glue alternative
47 Sticks around

Down

1 Costello's comedy partner
2 Give shirts and pants to
3 Like a rake left out in the rain
4 More than -er
5 "Darn it!"
6 Unthankful person
7 Zero, in soccer scores
8 Peer through, as a window
9 Going back, like the tide
10 Itty-bitty
14 Internet feed
22 Eat well
24 Drivers licenses, passports, etc.
26 Give a makeover
27 Do a parody of
28 Lizard some keep as a pet
29 Assumes for the sake of argument
31 One of the Muses
32 What the number XC is in Roman numerals
33 Strikes down, in the Bible
36 Back muscles
42 Ignited
43 Museum stuff

Across

1 Address, as a person
6 Nation with pyramids
11 Hello, in Hawaii
12 Not poetry
13 Newsman Matt
14 Reason
15 Michelin product
16 Former Virginia governor Chuck
17 Shore bird
19 Societal rule
22 Not spontaneous
24 Prefix meaning "green"
25 Big roll, as of cash
26 "Survivor" network
28 "Never heard of him"
29 Leg's neighbor
30 Sat ominously on the horizon
32 Give money to
33 Hilarious
34 Facial feature of Madonna
36 Give off
39 Capital of 6-across
41 Friend
42 "___ of God"
43 How lemonade tastes
44 Extinct birds
45 Griffith and Williams

Down

1 Pepper's partner
2 Jai ___ (ball game)
3 "That's just what I was thinking!"
4 It may have come first
5 Paddle's cousin
6 Orlando's ___ Center
7 Snatch
8 "That was incredible!"
9 Letter afterthoughts
10 Kickoff tool, in football
16 Another term for "purple" -- and two colors that sound like they appear in the long down entries
18 ___ room (fun place in the house)
20 Hurt sorely
21 Teak or cherry
22 Trade
23 Plantation in "Gone With the Wind"
27 Male kid
31 "___, one vote" (old saying about election rights)
33 Dental ___
35 Black-and-white cookie
37 Rock's ___ Pop
38 Presents for kids, often
39 Misbehaving type
40 In the past
41 One ___ time

Across

1 Fitting
4 Vehicle with a meter
7 "___ favor"
8 In the manner of
9 Fuel for a Ford Fairlane
12 So all can see
14 Devoured
15 Numbered groups
16 Wild binge
18 Reverberating sound
19 Website for bidding
20 Prepared
21 School project creation
24 Not wall-to-wall carpeting
26 Jack of fitness
28 Watch closely
31 Strong trees
32 Big theater
33 Journeys
35 Walk loudly
36 Huge amount
37 Chow down on
39 Director Lee
40 "Much ___ About Nothing"
41 ___ Aviv (city in Israel)
42 Kitten's sound
43 "48 ___" (Eddie Murphy movie)

Down

1 Red fruits
2 Cops
3 Disparaging your opponent during a sporting event
4 Food containers
5 Every last bit
6 Chesapeake and Charleston
9 Person who curses a lot
10 Mr. T's group of the 1980s
11 "Later!"
13 O.J. Simpson trial judge
17 Country in the Andes Mountains
21 Room of the house
22 James Bond creator ___ Fleming
23 Miner's stuff
25 Voice feature
26 "Whole ___ Shakin' Goin' On"
27 Burr or Neville
29 Talk nonstop
30 Kicks out
32 "___ My Party"
34 Con job
35 Winter whiteness
38 "___ to Billie Joe"

Across

1 Computer programs, for short
5 Girl's name that can also take an H
10 Actor's goal
11 "Tomorrow" musical
12 Where inmates exercise
14 Memorial designer Maya
15 "Now!"
16 Break
18 Active
22 Noblemen
24 Wish you hadn't
25 Clean
27 People of Mecca
29 Author Umberto
30 Aden's land
32 Animal shelters
34 Cut a little while shaving
37 Utah ski resort
39 ___-mo
40 It's read for a bill
43 "Home ___"
44 Eat like a bird
45 Dentist's direction
46 Affectedly creative

Down

1 Big name in computers
2 Romeo's rival
3 Ivy League school
4 John, Paul and George: abbr.
5 Fireplace area
6 Irish singer
7 No-see-ums
8 Balloon filler
9 Actor Beatty
13 Fish hawk
17 "I see!"
19 Joking type
20 Massage
21 "Absolutely!"
23 Seuss declaration
25 Fourposter, e.g.
26 Trick taker, often
28 ___ center
31 Access
33 Crushed, perhaps
35 Bumper sticker word
36 Nerdy
38 Contact, e.g.
40 "This means ___!"
41 "Aladdin" prince
42 Antipollution org.

275

Across

1 Scary beasts created by J.R.R. Tolkien
5 Threw
11 Painful affliction
12 Seem
13 Red gemstone
14 ___ mix (sleet, snow and rain)
15 List-ending abbr.
16 High card
17 Strauss of jeans
19 Not tons
23 TV show named with initials
25 Assistance
27 Wedding day phrase
28 Massage
29 "The Way," in Eastern philosophy
30 Aniston, to friends
31 Go wrong
32 Eddie Murphy's old TV show, briefly
33 Sign, as a contract
34 Judge
36 Farmer's tool
38 Flightless bird of Australia
40 Taverns
43 Big bird of prey
46 Sitting on
47 Syrup once used in cases of poisoning
48 Arizona city
49 Inhalation
50 God of war

Down

1 Shrek is one
2 Easy victory
3 Alcoholic drink named for an island
4 Work on someone's hair
5 Kids' drink named for an island
6 Of Biblical proportions
7 Sleeping concern
8 Doggie doc
9 You listen with it
10 Arid
18 Brewery containers
20 Posh beverage brand named for an island
21 Garden of ___
22 Policy ___ (D.C. expert)
23 Street ___ (rep)
24 "Absolutely!"
26 Barbie or Ken
35 Holiest city, to Muslims
37 Bush successor
39 Castle's protection
41 Valentine's Day flower
42 Places for massages
43 Little lie
44 Fourth mo.
45 Director Ang

276

Across

1 Secret meeting
6 Noisy clock feature
11 Steam room
12 Latest craze
13 Schindler of "Schindler's List"
14 Defeat
15 Approved
17 "Penny ___" (Beatles song)
19 Toes the line
22 Food that comes in a carton of 12
23 Activity for black belts
25 Miracle ___
26 "Help!"
27 He's a doll
28 Italian frozen treat
30 In the same place: Lat.
31 Buzz Aldrin's real first name
32 Rifles and pistols
33 Name, as to a position
35 Ocean killer
38 Part of TNT
41 Accord and Civic maker
42 It may be ordered rare or medium rare
43 It makes bread rise
44 Presidential periods

Down

1 General on a Chinese menu
2 Dormitory overseers: abbr.
3 Variety of potato
4 Slithering creatures
5 Actress Reid
6 One-celled organisms
7 Estee of perfume
8 Small crawler
9 Free (of)
10 Chinese dictator
16 John Lennon's love
17 ___ Mason (financial company)
18 See it the same way
20 Spread found in Asia
21 Big beer mug
24 Finales
26 Be unskilled in, slangily
29 Academy ___ (Oscars)
30 Set on fire
34 Part of MIT
35 Hardly outgoing
36 Farming tool
37 Santa ___ Winds
39 Animal of the constellation Aries
40 Gives approval to

277

Across

1 Alternative to glue
6 Not south
11 Book of maps
12 Informed
13 Rugged individuals
15 Last part
16 Make a blunder
17 "20/20" network
18 Section, as of a race
19 Self-importance
20 ___-wee baseball
21 "Hold on ___!"
23 Kindle buy
25 Golfer Palmer
27 Henry ___ Lodge
29 Massages
33 Enjoyed the couch
34 "___ the season to be jolly"
36 Tic-___-toe
37 Decide
38 Colony crawler
39 Mined minerals
40 Writing instrument that needs to be dipped in ink
43 Musical with the song "Tomorrow"
44 Ruckus
45 Movie holders
46 Irritating little bugs

Down

1 Hit ballad by Toto
2 Makes up (for)
3 Gunk
4 Light brown
5 Lauder of cosmetics
6 Kenya's capital
7 Have
8 New Jersey city or college
9 Alex of "Jeopardy!"
10 From now onward
14 Country whose capital is Buenos Aires
22 Taxi
24 Above, in poetry
26 Turns on an axis
27 Noted gangster Al
28 Coordinate
30 Perfect world
31 Least covered
32 Movie parts
33 Up to this point
35 Bee's "bite"
41 Zero
42 ___-smoking (restaurant section)

Across

1 Not working today
4 Ad ____ (improvise)
7 Part of WWW
10 Belonging to both of us
11 Guacamole is made from it
13 Coin you can save if you find a bargain
15 Hard rain
16 No longer living
17 Roman with a salad named for him
20 Naughty Ms. West
22 Major record label
26 Coin something might not be worth
29 Made a shrill cry
30 Passports and such
31 Fashioned
34 Word after coffee or pound
37 Negated the effects of
40 Coin you won't see from a defiant creditor
43 Hit on the radio
44 Playful bite from a pup
45 Picnic pest
46 Chemistry suffix
47 Economist's stat

Down

1 "Uh-oh!"
2 Fold up, as a flag
3 Card game on the computer
4 Coffee drink that simply means "milk" in Italian
5 Wall-climbing plant
6 Jazz offshoot
7 Fall back
8 Poet ____ St. Vincent Millay
9 Woody's last name, on "Cheers"
12 ____ the Entertainer
14 Lipton drink
18 Like beaches
19 Mr. Onassis
20 Fifth month
21 Mimic
23 Result of hitting the brakes too hard
24 Rock star Nugent
25 Pacino and Gore
27 Shocking wins
28 Came into contact with
32 Dive (for)
33 Last part
34 Club in a Barry Manilow hit
35 Unsigned, as a poem
36 Held on to
38 Volunteer's phrase
39 "Pirates of the Caribbean" star
41 Tool for a farmer
42 Place to stay for the night

279

Across

1 Sections
6 Four on a car
11 Prepare for the arrival of
12 "___ we all?"
13 Official name for a nose job
15 Joke around
16 Buddy
17 Not before
18 Brewski
19 Place for a pig
20 Prior to
21 Medieval worker
23 ___ Island
25 The five main vowels
27 Achiever's attitude
29 Baseball field covering
33 Professor's degree
34 "___ now or never!"
36 Actor Kilmer
37 ___ Paulo
38 ___ for tat
39 Actress Gardner
40 ___ Oath (what a doctor takes)
43 Tycoon who died on the Titanic
44 Silly
45 Bridge positions
46 Cuts the peel off

Down

1 Raincoats
2 Some time
3 "Lara Croft: Tomb ___"
4 Element in a "Wizard of Oz" character's name
5 Cuts it out
6 Fox hunt cry
7 Nest egg money
8 Took a load off
9 Total
10 Fashion
14 Likely to salute the flag
22 Supporter
24 Away from home
26 Magazine staff members
27 ___ longue
28 Takes as one's own child
30 James Cameron movie of 2009
31 Gully
32 Locations
33 "Horse hockey!"
35 Las Vegas area, with "The"
41 Flower's home
42 Comedic actress Gasteyer

280

Across

1 Heirloom location
6 "Beat it!"
11 Chow line?
12 "And I ___"
13 13 or 29, e.g.
15 Babysitter's handful
16 Caribbean, e.g.
17 Grocery store container
18 Born
19 Toni Morrison's "___ Baby"
20 Ending for Japan or Siam
21 Cut, maybe
23 Brought up
25 Language spoken in Great Britain
27 Flower lover's field
30 Dangerous biters
34 Compass dir.
35 Bar bill
37 Congratulations, of a sort
38 Addis Ababa's land: abbr.
39 "___ say!"
40 Gold: Sp.
41 Alpha, in the Greek alphabet
44 Inbox contents
45 Not a soul
46 Crowded
47 Auto damages

Down

1 Of Switzerland, perhaps
2 Called
3 Taiwan's capital
4 Ending for real or classical
5 Treasury
6 Chessboard places
7 With: Lat.
8 Thief
9 "Relax, and that's an order!"
10 Joined
14 Almost everything
22 Former airline
24 "Bingo!"
26 Authorize
27 Bellyached
28 In installments
29 Iran's capital
31 Perfect
32 Bring up
33 Mall places
36 Mixture
42 Bro's sib
43 "For shame!"

Across

1 "And that's a ___!"
5 First part of a song
10 Color that means "water" in Latin
11 Zsa Zsa or Eva
12 It removed paint
14 One way into a house
15 Title for a knight
16 Idiot
20 Showed respect to a superior officer
24 ___ double take
25 "In a perfect world..."
26 Some golf clubs
28 Coolest temperature of the day
29 Break into two paths
31 Soapmaker's materials
33 "Give ___ break!"
34 Workplace divisions
39 Full of twists and turns
41 "Sweet Love" singer Baker
42 Leave out
43 Office ___ (store chain)
44 Some checkers pieces

Down

1 "Blueberry Hill" singer ___ Domino
2 Here: Sp.
3 Cheese item
4 Stabilizes, as a splint
5 Pretend to be nonexistent
6 Cold War side: abbr.
7 Classic Ford
8 "A Beautiful Mind" director ___ Howard
9 Portland's state: abbr.
13 Worked on, as a newspaper article
17 Stench
18 Simple video game
19 Simplicity
20 Window ___
21 Hello, to sailors
22 Rob of "Wayne's World"
23 Enter quickly, as the pool
27 Nuclear structure
30 Exhausted person's utterance
32 Paper money
35 "It's ___ you" ("Not my decision")
36 Green fruit
37 Oklahoma city
38 Tennis match parts
39 Pathetic
40 Direction away from WSW

Across

1 Big name in computers
6 Caught some Z's
11 Seuss character
12 Eiffel ___
13 One of the deadly sins
14 Each
15 "Hold on a ___!"
16 Pink, as a steak
18 Pop great ___ John
20 Vietnamese soup
23 Delicate
25 Lisa of "Friends"
27 Mature person
29 Acadia National Park locale
30 Electorate
32 The Untouchables, e.g.
33 Donkey's cousin
34 Pond buildup
36 "Hey!"
37 Pool stick
40 "___ disturb"
43 Pitcher's place
45 "Remember the ___!"
46 Certain print
47 Block
48 Firestarter's crime

Down

1 "The Sound of Music" backdrop
2 Small hole
3 Store reductions
4 Boy
5 Apply, as pressure
6 Chest protector
7 Zero, on the tennis court
8 Female sheep
9 Each
10 "Don't give up!"

17 "All systems go"
19 Singer Lovett
20 Butcher's best
21 Better
22 "A Prayer for ___ Meany"
23 ___ lamp
24 Bothers
26 Computer info
28 Turncoat
31 Arch
35 Beta follower
36 "Where the heart is"
38 "Do ___ others as..."
39 Paradise
40 "Dear old" guy
41 "Bravo!"
42 ___ King Cole
44 Rowboat mover

283

Across

1 Sports venue
6 The five of hearts and the six of spades, e.g.
11 Printer stuff
12 Sydney ___ House
13 TV show set in Massachusetts
15 Big flightless bird
16 E-mail address ending for a general
17 Letters before a crook's name
18 Title of respect
19 Great serve, in tennis
20 Was winning
21 Golf pegs
23 Way out
25 Woods of golf
27 Campfire brand
30 Wound reminder
34 2,000 pounds
35 Show no respect for
37 Kind of poem
38 Select
39 Newspapers have to buy it
40 Not working any more: abbr.
41 TV show set in Illinois
44 The K in DKNY
45 Uncles' mates
46 Part of a process
47 Not most

Down

1 Most optimistically
2 Person you share an apartment with, casually
3 Make 100% positive
4 Equipment for soccer or badminton
5 Scent
6 University
7 Baboon's cousin
8 Mesmerize, as with great stories
9 Pastry brand
10 Healthy lunches
14 "Well done!"
22 Narrow waterway: abbr.
24 Shore Line and B&O, in Monopoly
26 Native Americans
27 Shares in the company
28 Tuxedo wearer's headwear
29 Whole
31 Mexican brand of beer
32 Experts
33 Second try at the exam
36 Danish toast
42 Hat
43 Color

284

Across

1 Roger who hit 61 home runs in 1961
6 Garment in Ancient Rome
10 Layer for environmentalists
11 Throws, as a pitch
13 Back up one's words with action
15 Not feeling well
16 Drink that may be white or black
17 Boston cream or lemon meringue
18 Prefix with liberal or conservative
19 Horse morsel
20 Church seat
21 Crew
23 Certainly doesn't look forward to
25 Game show host, e.g.
27 Arm art, maybe
30 Ear area
34 Sch. founded by Thomas Jefferson
35 Part of the face
37 Smoked salmon
38 Tell a lie
39 Cold cubes
40 One of the Seven Dwarfs
41 Be unbeatable
44 ___ pad (kind of tablet)
45 Head of cattle, to a rancher
46 "When Irish ___ Are Smiling"
47 Quickness

Down

1 Doing the lawn
2 Popular shrub
3 Deodorant type
4 Fluid for a 27-across
5 ___ music (write a score for)
6 Shakespearean building
7 Not at home
8 Italian liqueur
9 Fighting alongside one another
12 Makes inaccurate, as survey results
14 Decision maker for a sports team
22 Come into possession of
24 Slick fish
26 Drinks made with rum and mint
27 Boston-area college
28 Take to the skies
29 It indents your text
31 Later years
32 He takes bets
33 Go over
36 Gardener's irritations
42 Compass dir.
43 Police officer

285

Across

1 Toy with a string
5 Talked and talked and talked
11 Sailor's hello
12 Too
13 18-wheelers
14 "Mapped" human structure
15 "I dare you!"
16 Drink dispenser
17 Grizzly or Kodiak
19 Peeping pair
23 Year of ___ (1996 or 2008, to the Chinese)
25 Bird that's a symbol of peace
26 Not him
27 Owner of the Kwik-E-Mart
29 Understand
30 Pair in a rowboat
32 Indians and Japanese, e.g.
34 Great Salt Lake's state
35 Weekend warrior's org.
36 TV title alien
38 Plus
41 Earhart or Bedelia
44 Put (down), as kitchen tiles
45 First notes of the scale
46 Small speck of land
47 County of England
48 Poses a question

Down

1 Three feet
2 Cincinnati's state
3 Baseball catcher known for his contradictory witticisms
4 Clams' cousin
5 Dessert made with fruit
6 State before the court
7 Was the author of
8 Paid athlete
9 "A Nightmare on ___ Street"
10 Hair coloring
18 Little battery size
20 Where you might do the Warrior Position or Child's Pose
21 Like the numbers 2 and 22 and 222
22 Becomes hard, as concrete
23 Holier-than-___
24 Not cold
28 Gp. known for its entertainment tours
31 Some stones
33 Roma's country
37 Citrus fruit
39 Smooth fabric
40 Some Keats poems
41 Toss into the bargain
42 Cow's sound
43 Misstep

Across

1 Ending for Kafka or Beatles
6 Chef's hat
11 Single-family dwelling
12 Explode, like a volcano
13 Salesman's pitch
14 Chimney darkeners
15 Tomb
17 Kite or yo-yo
18 Big boats
20 Sicilian
22 Game played with pegs
23 Hit, as one's toe
26 Honda name
28 Casino name
29 Buzzing home
31 Ending for Japan or Sudan
32 Song for one
33 Eliminated from the tournament by the officials, for short
34 Its first letter stands for "early"
36 Louisiana wetlands
38 Company with a lizard as its mascot
40 Keep away from
43 Scent
44 Evoking nostalgia
45 "Eternal Sunshine of the Spotless Mind" actress Kirsten
46 Night vision?

Down

1 Hesitant syllables
2 Soak (up)
3 Reporter's
4 Computer owners
5 Slippery
6 Cylinder in a lab
7 ___ y plata (Montana's state motto, meaning "gold and silver")
8 Memorable line
9 Planning
10 Online store for handicrafts
16 Cat of the house
18 Captain ___ ("Moby Dick" character)
19 Shrimp fried ___
21 Miami Heat, Oklahoma City Thunder, etc.
23 Regatta entrant
24 "What ___ is new?"
25 Made a new color
27 Greek letter
30 Radio org.
33 Delaware's capital
34 "My word!"
35 South American nation
37 Place to play
39 They're shorter than inches: abbr.
41 Money for the golden years: abbr.
42 Actor DeLuise

Across

1 Ripken at shortstop...
4 ...and a piece of equipment for him
7 Folk-rocker DiFranco
8 Inventor Whitney
9 Tiny bit
12 Nerdy type
14 "Curb Your Enthusiasm" channel
15 Section of London or New York
16 Shiny disc on a dress
18 Change
20 Delete
21 Took off
22 Longtime employee, say
25 Person who doesn't even say "thank you"
27 Patronizes, as a restaurant
29 Baseball stat
32 Rim
33 Some noblemen
35 Heart rate-increasing exercise
38 "Black diamonds"
39 Gold, in Guatemala
40 Indulge (in)
42 Kind of wine
43 "Now I get it!"
44 ___ Moines, Iowa
45 Do voice-over work

Down

1 Julius or Augustus
2 Portuguese-speaking African country
3 Item on the roof of a house or building
4 Spelling competition
5 "Such a shame!"
6 Low, high or ebb
9 1975 Bruce Springsteen song
10 Tolerate
11 Giver of money
13 Long-handled tool
17 Throw in the towel
19 Fixes, as an election
23 Gun rights org.
24 Make happy
26 Require
27 Curtains, pictures, etc.
28 "___ you!" (challenging words)
30 Robert of "Baretta"
31 The British ___ (Great Britain, Ireland, etc.)
34 Take to the stage
36 Walkman's successor
37 Honolulu's island
41 Steal from

Across

1 Puckish person
4 Mindreader's claim
7 Difficult decision
9 Horse height measurements: abbr.
12 Language spoken in Siena
13 Gold: Sp.
14 Shout
15 Conductor Stravinsky
16 Rock band named for an electrical term
18 Class for mothers-to-be
20 Singing pair
21 Utensil for cereal
22 Rep. rival
23 Inmate
24 Secret agent
27 Madder than mad
29 Tool to get rid of weeds
30 Country with a famous canal
32 Coming up
33 Tool to get wrinkles out of clothes
34 Norse god with lightning bolts
36 Golfing great ___ Trevino
37 Evict unceremoniously
40 ___ Vegas, Nevada
41 Take over from, as shift duties
42 Ending for social or capital
43 John Coltrane instrument

Down

1 ___ Amin, dictator played
   by Forrest Whitaker
2 Harvard rival
3 Enjoy a game of Mexican Train, e.g.
4 Olympic runner Zatopek
5 Hardly a big deal
6 Give a bad review to
8 Part of GE
9 Sitcom set in a WWII prison camp
10 TV physician
11 Aching
15 "That's what I think," when texting
16 Toss in
17 Pool stick
19 Top of the heap
21 Get-rich-quick scheme
25 Word after chicken or small
26 Up to now
28 Skedaddled
30 Tablet
31 Section
32 Phrase of denial
35 Late rock star Levon ___
37 Man's nickname
38 Charlottesville sch.
39 ___-Mex cuisine

Across

1 Personal ad abbr.

4 Fall back

7 "___ the fields we go"

8 Sandra of "Gidget"

9 Miami's st.

12 Gives a creepy look to

14 Howard or Paul

15 Cabinet dept.

16 Ability

18 Center

20 "Othello" role

21 "The Matrix" hero

22 Person from Anchorage or Juneau

25 Stepped to the side

27 Out of line

29 Alpine sight

32 Hop, skip or jump

33 Dreary sound

35 Fly a plane

38 Cabal

39 "Do the Right Thing" director

40 South American nation

42 12th graders: abbr.

43 Checkup sounds

44 "___ we having fun yet?"

45 Hawaii's Mauna ___

46 "Are we there ___?"

Down

1 Serious

2 Hot dog

3 Briefly renamed food of the 2000s

4 Masthead contents, briefly

5 Doozy

6 ___ carotene

9 2003 Lindsay Lohan movie

10 Vowel sound in "Bates"

11 Susan of "Goldengirl"

13 Four Monopoly squares: abbr.

17 Mona ___

19 "Behold!"

23 "___ Miserables"

24 Blown away

26 "Chiquitita" quartet

27 Tracks

28 Flu symptom

30 Slight, in a way

31 Wish undone

34 Bank offering, for short

36 Blue hue

37 Bounce back, in a way

41 South of Canada

290

Across

1 Graceful birds
6 Try to achieve, as a goal
11 Put on the corkboard
12 By oneself
13 Cream of the crop
14 Playoff spot
15 Shady tree
16 Low point
18 Even score
19 Cold War org.
20 Soft N' ___ (deodorant brand)
21 Actress Thurman
22 Grasped
24 Trapped, like a butterfly
26 German city, or a perfume
28 Airport area
30 Get-rich-quick idea
33 Time of history
34 Half a dance
36 Ending for pay or Cray
37 Semicircle
38 "___ the ramparts..."
39 Time-tested
40 ___ Peak, Colorado
42 Posed a question
44 Out in the open
45 Light brown shade
46 ___ Haute, Indiana
47 Grab the wheel

Down

1 Politician's talking
2 Country great Nelson
3 Lion or elephant a kid can eat
4 Cashew or almond
5 Go too fast
6 Just shooting the breeze
7 "Bravo!"
8 Chinese restaurant finale
9 Not late
10 Put in the microwave
17 Fancy bread
23 Actor DeLuise
25 Part of Q & A
27 Izod ___ (clothing brand)
28 Chai server
29 Get there
31 Make accusatory statements
32 More irate
35 People of Mecca
41 Make a mistake
43 Prepared

Across

1 Sold aggressively
7 Blockhead
11 Terry McMillan's "Waiting to ___"
12 Helper
13 Land, as a fish
14 Enlist in
15 After expenses
16 Bright
17 Software program, briefly
19 "Baseball Tonight" channel
21 ___ tai
22 Ignore
26 Grade A food
27 See 3-down
28 Court
29 Lipton rival
31 Aggravate
32 Swearing-in words
34 Born, in society pages
35 "Darn!"
38 "I ___ you one"
40 Toot the horn
41 Curb
44 "What've you been ___?"
45 Helen of "The Miracle Worker"
46 Advertising sign
47 Refer

Down

1 "___ Town Too"
2 Can
3 Never, with 27-across
4 Bucks
5 A-list
6 Animal house
7 Some Louisianans
8 Animal with a mane
9 Norse god
10 Contradict
16 Fix, in a way
17 "Absolutely!"
18 Beep
20 Comics sound
23 Scary strain
24 Yawn inducer
25 Bind
27 Accomplishment
30 Assumed
33 Monopoly purchase
35 Avoid
36 Pray
37 "I'm ___ you!"
39 Has the intention of
41 Calypso offshoot
42 Was winning
43 Prior to

Across

1 "Friends" guy
5 Light lunch
10 Similar
12 Copy exactly
13 Dallas trio who sang "Wide Open Spaces"
15 "___ heard!"
16 British bathroom
17 Mountain like the Matterhorn
18 Title for a knight
19 Bald Brynner
20 "Titanic" name
21 Door lock part
23 Hardest to find
25 Opening part, as of a song
27 Beamed
30 Second Greek letter
34 DDE beat him twice
35 "___ the Dog"
37 "Platoon" setting, for short
38 AARP members
39 Train stop: abbr.
40 "I ___ Rock"
41 Neil Young hit of 1973
44 "Old MacDonald" refrain
45 Triangular road sign
46 Carpenter's piece
47 "Not guilty" or "guilty"

Down

1 Root vegetable
2 Singer ___ Newton-John
3 Philadelphia's basketball team, for short
4 Compete in the Winter Olympics, maybe
5 Wise student
6 Boxing champ
7 Setting
8 Foot joints that may get sprained
9 Dictator
11 Slick, like some fish
14 When to appear before the judge
22 Code at an ATM
24 Steal
26 It may have just premiered on TV
27 Talks back to
28 Above and beyond the call of duty
29 Promoter, as of bonds
31 Tooth covering
32 Mexican food that comes wrapped in a corn husk
33 Woman's name that means "she must be loved"
36 Actor Sinise or Oldman
42 Even score
43 Small sip, as of liquor

293

Across

1 Informal greeting
6 Dillon or Damon
10 "La Bohème," e.g.
11 Theater worker
13 Not our
14 Motif
15 Passbook abbr.
16 Draft org.?
18 Bean counter, for short
19 "Aladdin" character
20 "My boy"
21 CD-___
22 Very small
24 Lawyer: abbr.
26 Excited
28 Nothing-but-net sound
31 Half a fortnight
33 "Green Gables" girl
34 ___ tai
36 Breed of dog, for short
38 Come together
39 "Is that ___?"
40 Affirmative vote
41 Beauty
42 Watch brand
44 Astound
46 Not these
47 Cleanser brand
48 Amazes
49 Obeys

Down

1 Saturday night event
2 Shakespearean woman
3 Beautiful tree
4 Soft & ___ deodorant
5 Tall tales
6 Space creatures, maybe
7 ___ Wednesday
8 1993 film with Stephen Rea
9 Beat
12 Paper amount
17 ___ constrictor
23 "___-Haw!"
25 Airline until 2001
27 Takes it easy
29 Needed a tissue
30 Soldiers' head coverings
32 Mary ___ cosmetics
34 Store
35 Hawaiian hello
37 Sandy place
43 Ending for Sudan or Taiwan
45 "The Simpsons" bartender

294

Across

1 Infield coverings, when it rains
6 Chairs
11 Came up in conversation
12 Mass ___
13 Tom Cruise's wife
15 Time of history
16 Selling quickly
17 They often include a photo
18 Plague-carrying animal
19 Before
20 Bread for a reuben
21 Heads of cattle
23 Requirement
24 Chompers
26 ___ legs (cat's pair)
29 Infrequent
33 Meat eaten by Aussies
34 That lady
35 Stock abbr.
36 Tire or record abbr.
37 2,000 lb.
38 Resort type
39 2012 Masters winner
42 Lost badly, in slang
43 "Silly" birds
44 It goes around a skyscraper
45 Finished

Down

1 People who accept an offer
2 Biblical peak
3 Turn
4 Greek consonant
5 "Now you listen to me!"
6 Struck
7 Fish found in sushi restaurants
8 Wish to emulate
9 Color a hippie's shirt
10 Talked back to
14 Where riders show off mares
22 Airport abbr.
23 Washington Capitals, New York Islanders, etc.
25 ___ Mutant Ninja Turtles
26 Like some teas or remedies
27 Read into, as motives
28 Made unable to feel
30 Showed no respect for
31 Go against
32 Whined
34 Kansas or Missouri
40 Enormous
41 Age for a fifth-grader, maybe

295

Across

1 Big, fancy boat
6 Enjoys the sunshine
11 Old anesthetic
12 Musical about a redheaded orphan
13 "Basic Instinct" actress
15 May honoree
16 Sadness
17 Gives approval to
18 Roadie's equipment
19 Finish
20 Flower container
21 Chocolate company
23 "And time goes ___ slowly" (Righteous Brothers lyric)
24 In unison
26 Famous cookie maker
29 Native American symbols
33 Sought office
34 Dr.'s degree
35 Polka ___
36 TV show interruptions
37 Rock band ___ Speedwagon
38 Great anger
39 Woman who lives in the town of Bedrock
42 State famous for its potatoes
43 Worked with hay
44 Apple ___ (kitchen tool)
45 Threes, in a deck of cards

Down

1 Toady
2 Not out of the house
3 Tournament victors
4 "I Saw ___ Standing There"
5 Mason's tools
6 "___ on a true story"
7 Little crawler
8 "Peanuts" beagle
9 Copy store
10 Takes care of
14 The one and only
22 Prof. helpers
23 Make it interesting
25 "Absolutely!"
26 Language from which we get the words "admiral" and "magazine"
27 Eked out a living
28 GPS in a car
30 Good for consumption
31 ___ Safer (journalist who co-founded "60 Minutes")
32 Noble horses
34 Comic legend Richard
40 Definite article word
41 Saloon

298

Across

1 Common shout when you're on TV for just a few seconds

6 ___ California (Mexican peninsula)

10 Brockovich and Moran

11 Big test

12 Job application attachment

14 Say it didn't happen

15 Involuntary movements

17 Video recorder, for short

19 Berlin's country: abbr.

20 Palindromic movie house with a roaring lion as its logo

23 Animal that starts with a double letter

25 Big shopping trip

27 Hollywood superagent Michael

28 Acted out with no words

29 ___ Peninsula (part of Egypt)

30 Occupied

31 Compass dir.

32 Palindromic religious woman

34 Baltic or Aegean

35 Put up a struggle

37 It ends with a punch line

40 Take to the skies

43 Hot and dry

44 Went astray

45 Joins in holy matrimony

46 Helen who sang "I Am Woman"

Down

1 Not his

2 Extreme anger

3 Woman in an annual beauty pageant

4 "Movin' ___" ("The Jeffersons" theme song)

5 Publication started by Gloria Steinem

6 Where people snooze

7 Weapon in "The Shining"

8 "The Brady Bunch" girl

9 Singer Grant or novelist Tan

13 Suffix for Japan or Taiwan

16 1942 Best Picture winner

17 In the vicinity

18 One of the Chipmunks

20 "Mean" guy in a Beatles title

21 Silly birds

22 Jason's wife, in mythology

24 1959 hit for The Kingston Trio

26 One of ten for a bowler

33 Between Can. and Mex.

35 1981 Warren Beatty movie about communism

36 Be the father of

37 Face part

38 Portland's state: abbr.

39 Joke around

41 CNN founder Turner

42 ___'s ice cream

299

Across

1 Support, as a candidate
5 Agreements
10 Powerful anesthetic
12 Patriot ___ Allen
13 Scene of battle, or basketball
14 Replay camera
15 Get ___ of (eliminate)
16 Annoy
18 Mercury or Saturn
19 "Dear old" guy
20 Hawaiian necklace
21 "Beautiful job!"
22 Cole ___
24 Unavailable for review, as documents
26 "Killing Me Softly with His Song" singer Flack
28 Green Bay football player
30 On
33 ___ Wednesday
34 Big rd.
36 Laundry detergent brand
37 Find work for
38 100 yrs.
39 El ___ (1961 Charlton Heston role)
40 "Hasta ___" ("see you later")
42 Different
44 Firing offense?
45 Piggies
46 Flowers of the future
47 Decides

Down

1 Chin covers
2 Of a part of the heart
3 Yellow dairy product
4 Barbie's doll friend
5 More irritating
6 Georgia's capital: abbr.
7 Piece in a cookie
8 "Hot" mexican food
9 Slept loudly
11 Train travel
17 Book, as a table in a restaurant
23 Pan used in Chinese cooking
25 One day ___ time
27 Towers with warning lights
28 Comic Poundstone and singer Abdul
29 Promise
31 The ___ (eastern Asia)
32 San Diego baseball team
35 "The Dukes of Hazzard" deputy
41 Mercury or Saturn
43 Pair

300

Across

1 Talk about

8 ___ Aviv (city in Israel)

11 Toronto's province

12 Pie ___ mode

13 Dish with parmesan cheese and croutons

15 Prepares to pray

16 Nevada senator Harry

17 Skinny fish

18 Tube-shaped pasta

19 Alcoholic's affliction, for short

20 Computer accessory

22 Finnish steam room

23 Handsome

26 ___ Perignon champagne

29 Amusing water creature

30 He lost to Bush in 2000

31 Geek

32 Beautiful ladies

34 Sandwich bread choices

36 Never-proven mental ability

37 Place for F-16 fighter jets

38 "What can I do for you?"

39 Color that's also a Stephen King movie

Down

1 Decreased for a penalty, as pay

2 Caught, like fish

3 Strengthens (oneself), as for a shock

4 Situations

5 Risk territory named for a Eurasian mountain range

6 Respectable gentlemen

7 "Mayday!"

8 Natural skill

9 "Seinfeld" woman

10 Way up a wall

14 Scene of conflict

18 ___-pong

20 Sock grouping

21 Point, in baseball

22 Gets rid of, like extra pounds

23 Kind of animal Eddie Murphy voices in "Shrek"

24 In a relaxed state

25 Pieces of bacon

26 Rival of Hertz and Enterprise

27 "You won't like the alternative"

28 ___ up (botched the job)

30 Boston newspaper

32 Verve

33 Goes wrong

35 Lobe's home

301

Across

1 Bakery buys
6 Baseball or blue jeans features
11 Phantom's place, in a musical title
12 Expect eagerly
13 Kind of tooth
14 "Around the World in 80 Days" author
15 Ernie who's won the U.S. Open twice
16 Santa ___, Calif.
18 "First of all..."
19 Part of IPA
20 Take all of, as the covers
21 Zero, in soccer scores
22 Plays (around with)
24 Past, present and future
26 Hands over
28 Lacking much money
30 Word in Oscar categories
33 Longoria of "Desperate Housewives"
34 On the ___ (running from the police)
36 Fib
37 Basketball hoop
38 B-F links
39 He lost to 35-down at Gettysburg
40 "___ Mia!"
42 Best guests
44 Didn't visit a restaurant
45 "Inferno" author
46 Geeky types
47 Mystery writing award

Down

1 Attack
2 Moon-landing name
3 He played Dr. Frasier Crane
4 Time of history
5 Palin from Alaska
6 Brutes
7 She may have a little lamb
8 He produced "Fantasy Island" and "Beverly Hills 90210"
9 Mickey Mouse's mate
10 Reinforces (oneself), as for a shock
17 Tablet
23 Punk figure Vicious
25 Dull pencil point
27 Mr. Spock on "Star Trek," and others
28 Mr. Melville
29 Take to the skies
31 Nap in the afternoon
32 Harris ___ grocery stores
35 He beat 39-across at Gettysburg
41 Prefix with night or week
43 Young fella

302

Across

1 Marginally acceptable
8 Neighbor of Florida
9 Societal rule
12 Tourist
13 Boxing hero
14 Frigid cubes
15 Spring or autumn
17 Geeky types
20 Part of a movie or play
21 Barcelona's country
23 Street ___ (reputation)
24 Revolted
26 Go round and round
28 ___ the opinion (thought)
30 Beer amounts
32 Will names
34 Enter again, as data
36 Prefix with classical
37 Perfect serve
38 Reagan adviser Lee ___
41 "So's ___ old man!"
42 Circus acrobat's swing
43 Men of Mexico

Down

1 "You ___ a good time?"
2 "___ Restaurant" (Arlo Guthrie song)
3 It produces documents
4 Intelligence agcy.
5 Flying mammal
6 Famous ___ cookies
7 Has the nerve
9 Toy cats love to play with
10 Solo
11 ___ and dined
16 Point the finger at
18 Lovely and delicate
19 Palindromic girl
22 ___ Jersey Devils (hockey team)
25 Casual turndown
26 Mist
27 Rook or bishop, in chess
29 Stop in your tracks
31 Little arguments
33 Canker ___
35 To be: Fr.
39 Not healthy-looking
40 Part of military addresses

303

Across

1 Mexican warrior
6 Printing fluids
10 More than hate
12 Nosh
13 Involve
14 From the top
15 "What did I tell you?"
16 Spooky sounds
18 ___ Mirage, California
21 At a discount
23 Maple syrup stuff
26 Loud chewing sound
27 Company that's also a fruit
29 Chicago clock setting: abbr.
30 Surprise for students
32 Best-ever result
33 Do some arithmetic
36 Take down the aisle
39 Desktop image
40 Blood carrier
43 Pair on a mountain
44 Rookie, in computer-speak
45 Jekyll's counterpart
46 Where people "go" at night

Down

1 Beers
2 "The Twilight ___"
3 French fry alternative
4 Greek letter after zeta
5 Greek letter after phi
6 State bordering Montana
7 El ___ (weather phenomenon)
8 Leg joint
9 Uses a needle and thread
11 Put into political power
17 Inexpensive and low-quality
19 Biceps' place
20 Took a snooze
21 300, in Ancient Rome
22 Hesitant syllables
23 In his day, the shortest player ever in the NBA (5' 7")
24 Cosell interviewed him many times
25 Candy with its own dispensers
28 O-S links
31 Indian or Pacific
32 "Lather, ___, repeat"
33 Plate
34 Gross, to a kid
35 Word stamped on a bad check
37 Buffalo's lake
38 Like some blonde hair
41 No longer working: abbr.
42 Couple

304

Across

1 Fall behind
4 Animal in the family
7 Bobby of hockey
8 "This feels good!"
9 Kia or Miata
12 Head honcho
13 You, for one
15 "OK, I give up!"
17 Uncooked meal
18 Takes the wheel
20 At that point
21 Cheer
22 Ms. Morrison
23 Cloak wearer, perhaps
25 One of 435 in DC
27 Took off
28 "Silence!"
30 Kim's Hollywood ex
32 Utah ski resort
33 Bone ____
36 Decreases
38 ____ ghost (hallucinates)
39 Attendance
41 Father
42 Mimic
43 ____ Lanka (country near India)
44 Mike and ____ candies
45 "Lost" network
46 Little bit

Down

1 Point
2 "____ we all?"
3 Business with carts
4 With 26-down, question they
  may ask you at a 3-down

5 Piece of corn
6 "____ is the last straw!"
9 Another question you may be asked at 3-down...
  which boils down to the same question as 4-down
10 Wise goddess
11 Get under control
14 No purebred
16 Melissa ____, who cursed at the Oscars
19 Power for trains
23 Drink brand named for a mountain
24 Palindromic exercise
26 See 4-down
29 Goldie of "Cactus Flower"
31 Before
34 Japanese city
35 Went into the water
37 Sammy who hit 66 home runs in 1998
40 City, in slang

Across

1 Paid athletes
5 Confession phrase
11 The moon, in poetry
12 Secondhand transaction
13 "Family Ties" role
15 Perfect score, often
16 Blue jeans hole
17 Actress Gardner of "Mogambo"
18 Make a 14-down
20 Affable Mr. Affleck
21 Hi-Q pieces
23 Quite drunk
24 Varieties
27 Helps in a criminal act
29 Santa ___ Winds (California weather phenomenon)
30 "Slaves of New York" author Janowitz
32 Fond du ___, Wisconsin
33 Revved up, as a motorcycle
37 Wonderment
38 Before, to bards
39 Valuable mineral deposit
40 Actor who played 13-across
43 Texas hold 'em pronouncement
44 Madam
45 Starts a tennis point
46 Small bills

Down

1 Greek philosopher who wrote "The Republic"
2 12-inch stick
3 Standing upright
4 John Coltrane's musical instrument
5 Irritating
6 Adele's "Rolling in the ___"
7 "There ___ way out"
8 OK to see romantically
9 "That was excellent!"
10 Lease signers
14 Catholic cleric
19 Fitting
22 Clemens or L. Jackson
24 Italian sausages
25 Where a bird may perch
26 Palindromic vehicle
28 Total embargo
31 Sees it the same way
34 ___ of (disliking)
35 Eat away
36 ___ Midnight Runners ("Come on, Eileen" band)
38 Facility
41 AIDS cause
42 She used to go out with 20-across

Across

1 Power

7 Ruin

10 Popeye the Sailor has a tattoo of one

11 ___ and aft

12 Mother ___ (noted humanitarian)

13 Onassis and Emanuel

14 Tennis star Tommy

15 Leave the union

17 Web connecting businesses, for short

18 Sailing the waves

19 Prophet

20 Chaperone

21 Your planet

23 Prophet

26 Work units

30 Prejudiced person

31 Fix, as a medical condition

32 Extreme fear

34 Half-hitch or granny

35 Not new, like a car

36 Didn't dine at home

38 Palindromic candy company

39 Read through casually

40 Finale

41 Person who judges food

Down

1 Singer Johnny

2 Nervous feeling

3 Minor tiff

4 1950s-70s label known for blues, jazz and rock

5 ___ Angeles Lakers

6 Historical times

7 To a greater degree

8 More dry and hot

9 Find a new chair for

11 They spot false claims

16 "___ of Eden"

20 Previously

22 Choir voice

23 More than 90 degrees, as an angle

24 Candy company

25 "Amen!"

27 Leave in a hurry

28 Complain

29 Irish ___ (big dog)

33 At full attention

37 Chai or chamomile

307

Across

1 "Wheel of Fortune" host
6 Revels (in), as the sunshine
11 180-degree reversal
12 FBI worker
13 Golfer Palmer, to pals
14 Spirit in a bottle
15 Oakland football team member
17 Latvia's capital
18 Environmentalist's prefix
19 Caspian or Baltic
21 Unit of resistance
22 Zilch
24 Gives a warning to
26 Saying "Oh, that's just great!" when something bad happens, e.g.
28 Revenue minus expenses
30 Dad
33 You lose it when you stand up
34 Home for peas
36 Actress Farrow or soccer star Hamm
37 Farmland measurement
39 Send back
41 "___ We Dance?"
43 Hip and cool
44 Org. for smarties
45 Go in
46 "Take ___ off!" ("Relax!")
47 Chills out

Down

1 Ray of PBS's "NewsHour"
2 Disappear without ___
3 TV mobster role played by Dominic Chianese
4 Like much of Arizona
5 Leg benders
6 Grocery store container
7 Ending for teen or new
8 Forgetful times
9 Chess piece that leaps over other pieces
10 Prepares vegetables, in a way
16 Nuclear plant building
20 Pie ___ mode
23 Clumsy fool
25 Clairvoyant's ability
27 Tear
28 Blood component
29 "Friends" role
31 White ___ fence
32 Mythological half-men, half-goats
35 Put off until later
38 Actress Lanchester of "Mary Poppins"
40 When summer starts
42 Young guy

308

Across

1 ___ pole (Native American icon)
6 Tries for a field goal
11 Humorous ending meaning "big amount of"
12 "I'm on ___" ("Saturday Night Live" song)
13 Offer a counterargument
14 Prefix with surgery or transmitter
15 "The Sopranos" role, or part of RSVP
16 Give it a whirl
18 Company boss
19 "___ to a Nightingale"
20 Weeding tool
21 Like cool cats, in '60s-speak
22 Completely clueless
24 Cash dispensers
25 "What does it cost?"
27 X-ray ___ (novelty eyeglasses)
29 Decided
31 Hawaiian necklace made of flowers
32 Painter's deg.
33 Danger in Iraq, for short (hidden in PIEDMONT)
35 Tax-collecting org.
36 Towards the back, on a ship
37 ___ Lanka (country off the coast of India)
38 Songs and such
40 Amber source
42 Charging too much interest
43 Give off, as confidence
44 Sneaks a look
45 Olympic swords

Down

1 Trunk of the body
2 Tater tots brand
3 Put a decision off for a while
4 Meat source in Australia
5 One of the four Gospels
6 Rapper ___ West
7 "May ___ excused?"
8 Frame a decision in a certain way
9 ___ Abdul-Jabbar (basketball legend)
10 Bends down
17 Wander away
23 Chicago White ___
24 Pretend
26 Trapped, like kitty
27 Get thinner
28 Read through casually
30 Make fun of
32 Famous New York City department store
34 Eats out at a restaurant
39 Aggravate
41 Previous work: abbr.

309

Across

1 Opposite of "lower"
6 First Greek letter
11 Bartiromo or Sharapova
12 ___ bear (Arctic animal)
13 Garden store purchase
14 Dish
15 Pretty sneaky
16 Come from behind to win
18 Naples' nation
20 Holiday ___ Express (hotel chain)
23 Garments worn in ancient Rome
25 Leg bender
26 Geometry calculation
27 World-weary sounds
28 He doesn't speak at work
29 Preacher's perch in church
30 Airport guess: abbr.
31 The Lone Ranger's kemo sabe
32 "That's not going to happen!"
34 Paul and John: abbr.
37 Play the role of
39 Topic under discussion
41 Cool-headedness
42 Steam bath
43 Unexpected victory
44 Glue name

Down

1 Baseball game workers, for short
2 ___ Mall (cigarette brand)
3 Grasshopper lookalike
4 A, in Germany
5 The daily grind
6 Try to get the job
7 Sit (around)
8 Pretending to be dead
9 Wintertime wear
10 Exist
17 Roker and Pacino
19 Scrabble piece
21 Soda brand
22 House for a hawk
23 Not wild
24 Inch, foot or pound
25 Scottish "pants"
27 Daybreak
29 "The Raven" poet
31 Flatscreen, for example
33 Loosen, as restrictions
35 Song
36 Cook quickly
37 "The Simpsons" character
38 Policeman
40 Actor Mineo

310

Across

1 Vehicle that may have a bell on it
5 Country with a canal
11 "American ___" (singing show)
12 Slanted kind of type
13 Jump
14 Cash register button
15 Nickname for Los Angeles
17 Drunk ___ skunk
18 Zoo enclosures
22 Arm joint
24 The same
25 Father's Day gift, often
26 "This ___ joke, right?"
27 Former Russian leaders
30 Extend your subscription
32 Women-only part of a house, in the Ottoman Empire
33 Chopper's tool
34 End of a book
38 Japanese automaker
41 Mineral used in jewelry
42 French woman's name
43 Go to the bottom of the sea
44 Most rational
45 They can be poached or fried

Down

1 Gates of Microsoft
2 Conception
3 Australian animal that's really a marsupial
4 Texas city
5 ___ colada (drink)
6 Right away
7 NYSE rival
8 Pie ___ mode
9 A thousand thou
10 High card in the deck
16 "___ & Order"
19 Popular pet that's really a rodent
20 Loosen (up)
21 Cole ___ (side at a barbecue)
22 ___ A Sketch (red toy)
23 Ms. Minnelli
28 Tell, as a story
29 Stings a little bit
30 Mouse's cousin
31 Sensationalist news article
35 Beef fat used in cooking
36 Armed group
37 Fraternal organization
38 Part of iOS
39 Charlottesville sch.
40 Surgeon Carson or singer Folds

311

Across

1 One of the Seven Dwarfs
4 Letter between phi and psi
7 Shaving cream container
10 Mr. Nahasapeemapetilon
11 Word before center or room
12 Tribe for which Salt Lake City's state is named
13 Title for a knight
14 Bangs may cover it
16 Sage and parsley
18 Is overly critical
19 Up to this point
20 Brilliant boxer
21 Simple watercraft
23 Say "not guilty," for example
26 "___ tell you what..."
27 Hereditary material
28 Location
31 ___-yard line (center of a football field)
33 Actor Kilmer
34 Historical period, or a detergent brand
35 Higher than
37 Gun, as a motor
40 Without end
42 Undivided
43 Prior to
44 New Year's ___
45 Move the boat along
46 Take down the aisle
47 ___ King Cole

Down

1 Small amount, as of salt
2 Mayberry kid
3 Like some rice or ramen noodles
4 Reaches a high point
5 "Listen up!"
6 One covers Antarctica
7 Played the yes-man
8 Perched upon
9 The latest buzz
15 Golf or tennis item
17 Put money on it
21 Hole in a hipster's jeans
22 Every bit
24 Crawling critter
25 One-seventh of a week
29 Home to a bear, perhaps
30 "Ocean's ___"
31 Furry creature
32 Extreme anger
35 Not that many
36 Dull person
38 One, to Juan
39 Seat in church
41 ___ Marie Saint

Across

1 Sparta's ancient rival city
7 Not much
11 Hush-hush org.
12 Saturday night meeting
13 Gets, as revenge
14 Heavy metal
15 Palindromic kid
16 Second U.S. president
17 Hound's hand
19 1970s song with its own dance
21 H, in 1-across
22 Search and ___ mission
26 11th of 12: abbr.
27 Unsettled questions
28 Shocked sounds
29 Revealing bathing suit brand
31 Bathroom, in Bristol
32 Deli counter shout
34 UPS competitor
35 Japanese dressed in black
38 Manuscript count: abbr.
40 John Glenn's state
41 Steinway instruments
44 Theater award
45 Gas number
46 Resorts
47 Vegetable stand item

Down

1 Chowed down on
2 Note-ending abbr.
3 When air conditioners hum
4 ___ Domani (wine brand)
5 ___-gritty
6 Airline to Stockholm
7 Shoe brand
8 Actress Reid
9 Piece of platinum
10 Thieves' places
16 Deck foursome
17 Bic items
18 Perched on
20 "Fantastic" Roald Dahl character
23 When fireplaces crackle
24 "This isn't gonna be good..."
25 Class for foreigners, for short
27 Concept
30 Has fun with
33 More than once
35 Haves and have-___
36 Breakfast-all-day chain
37 One of Columbus's ships
39 Facts and figures
41 Palindromic music genre
42 Palindromic musician
43 But: Lat.

313

Across

1 Judge's field
4 Excellent athlete
11 Notable time period
12 Not quantity
13 Member of a Missouri baseball team, for short
15 "___ the night before Christmas..."
16 "Gosh!"
17 Sit around
19 Unhappy fan
21 Female sheep
22 Drench
24 Monarch in a nursery rhyme
29 They may clash
30 Zero, on the soccer pitch
31 Nagasaki's nation
34 Soup ___ ("Seinfeld" villain)
35 He beat Frazier in the "Thrilla in Manila"
36 Woody's last name, on "Cheers"
38 Up to me
43 Serious
44 Brazilian city
45 Groups of six
46 Slippery as an ___

Down

1 "___ Miserables"
2 Painter's field
3 Danced a certain dance
4 Blue shade that means "water" in Latin
5 San ___ Obispo, Calif.
6 "Leaving ___ Vegas"
7 Western metropolis, for short
8 Saint for whom Chile's capital is named (hidden in INERTIA GOING)
9 "___ Grows in Brooklyn"
10 Truck company, or actress Winona
14 Be in arrears
17 Zodiac sign
18 Tool for cutting holes in leather
19 Paper or plastic items
20 Great Plains metropolis, for short
22 It may say "stop" or "yield"
23 Yoko who sang "Every Man Has a Woman Who Loves Him"
25 Mauna ___, Hawaii
26 Having been challenged
27 Taylor or Phair
28 Inventor Whitney
31 "Me and Bobby McGee" singer Joplin
32 By oneself
33 Brad and William
34 Northern metropolis, for short
36 Word on a hitchhiker's sign
37 Valuable deposits
39 To this point
40 "First of all..."
41 Falsehood
42 "That's hilarious," online

314

Across

1 Gets an eyeful of
5 Attend
11 Alan of "M*A*S*H"
12 Birthplace
13 Bar on "Three's Company"
15 What the Titanic struck
16 Followers of a Chinese philosophy
21 Rains hard
25 Still sleeping
26 Car
27 Wax and ___
28 Biblical poem
30 Exploded in anger
31 Marathoner, wrestler or golfer
33 "___ of Sunnybrook Farm"
38 1986 Robert Redford/
   Daryl Hannah movie
42 Bluegrass singer Krauss
43 Pig's sound
44 Tourist attractions
45 Drunkards

Down

1 Women's garment in India
2 Part of GE
3 Rim
4 Former Swedish automaker
5 Snake with a hood
6 State whose capital is Salem
7 Farrow of "Alice"
8 ___ McMuffin
9 ___ the cows come home
10 Number after zero
14 "___ try this again..."
17 State south of Minnesota
18 Without a date
19 Song
20 Went too fast
21 Daddy
22 Kick out
23 Six-sided state
24 Toss of the dice
29 Red wine
30 Country singer McEntire
32 Former little kids
34 Driving forces
35 Advertising award named for one of the Muses
36 Word on a penny
37 Makes inquiries
38 ___ Vegas
39 Manning or Whitney
40 Job for a musician
41 End of a cigarette

315

Across

1 Karate studio
5 Get away
11 John, to Russians
12 ___ and groaned
13 Showed up
14 Wedding places
15 Voter's event
17 Take to the seas
18 Slightly open, like a door
22 Buffalo ___ (NHL team)
24 Rate of speed
25 "Now I understand!"
26 Greek letter
27 Lake's little cousin
29 Supported financially
32 Jekyll's counterpart
33 ___ League (Mideast group)
34 Phrase asked repeatedly in "Marathon Man"
38 Like some dresses
41 Take a left or a right
42 Stick (to)
43 Lou or Robert
44 Covered in trees
45 Valuable minerals

Down

1 They're rolled in Yahtzee
2 Shape of the president's office
3 Fictional government agent called "007"
4 Small, like a garage
5 Inbox contents
6 Alone
7 Quick snooze
8 Santa ___, Calif.
9 According to
10 Bradley and McMahon
16 Even score
19 Fictional government agent on "24"
20 Pain
21 Senator Harry or actor Tim
22 Year between freshman and junior, for short
23 Hello, to sailors
28 Heated up, like a frozen windshield
29 Prepared a fishing line
30 Museum stuff
31 Longtime Cuban dictator
35 Positive
36 At no cost
37 Finishes
38 "___ & Order"
39 Prefix with meter
40 Which person?

Across

1 The Crimson Tide
5 "Close but no ___"
10 Possessing a pulse
12 More than just love
13 Went quickly
14 Kitchen, parlor and study
15 -like
16 Stomach six-pack
18 Cube used in Yahtzee
19 Hawaiian stringed instrument, for short
20 Woman's name that sounds like a month
21 Currency in Kyoto
22 African nation that sounds like a woman's name
24 News
26 Drink in Dixie
28 In possession of
30 Unpleasant task
33 Fix, like an election's results
34 Rubber ducky's home
36 Close amigo
37 African animal
38 Choice in a bakery or a bar
39 "___ & Order: SVU"
40 "Au revoir!"
42 Chippewa or Cherokee
44 Art class drawings, sometimes
45 18-wheelers
46 Fashionable wheat
47 Lovers' quarrel

Down

1 Element drunk before an x-ray
2 Largest state in area
3 Restaurant diner's book (from France)
4 Big rd.
5 Kid carrier
6 Words to the bride
7 Famous airship
8 Nations' defenders
9 Hold against
11 Cheese from the Netherlands
17 Mr. Clean or Jesse Ventura
23 Here, to Henri
25 Kennedy or Turner
27 Give for safekeeping
28 The heart, the kidneys, etc.
29 Finish
31 "Lawrence of ___"
32 Famous advice from Horace Greeley
35 Vegas amounts
41 Fish that's a last name backwards
43 Thing: Lat.

317

Across

1 Cow comment
4 Outlaw
7 Cremains holder
8 Tabloid headline word
9 Sets in the living room...
12 ...and ratings used for it
14 Tiny
15 Dubuque's state
16 Finally got a victory
18 Applauds
20 Cute creature in "Return of the Jedi"
21 Funny thing to shout when passing bales of dried straw in a field
22 Yoga retreat sites
25 Appear before the court
27 Makes a mistake
29 Masseur's employer
32 Shoe string
33 The devil
35 Broken, as promises
38 Caffeine or cocaine
39 Novelist Rita ___ Brown
40 Actor Kurt
42 Cherry's center
43 Prez on a penny
44 Christmas ___
45 So far
46 Opposite of 'taint

Down

1 Bavaria's biggest city
2 Baltimore ___ (Maryland's state bird)
3 It's not for a round trip
4 City transportation
5 Several
6 Forbidden act
9 Give-and-take situation, in metaphor
10 Snake's poison
11 Looks for
13 Once around the track
17 Soft ball
19 Talk back to
23 Good name for a cook
24 Pair that may sway
26 Sword in the Olympics
27 Batter's low period
28 Porch named for a Hawaiian island
30 Pope from 1963-78
31 Geometric calculations
34 TV show stoppers
36 "Let us ___"
37 London's subway, with "The"
41 Prepared

318

Across

1 Buddies
5 Holler, or a hilarious person
11 Passing notice
12 Illinois city politicians want to "play in"
13 Arizona city
14 Stomach troubles
15 Captain Kirk's show
17 Spelling competition
18 White of "The Golden Girls"
22 Humble home
24 Mall tenant
25 It spins in the summer
26 Little bit (as of brandy)
27 Bail out, like a pilot might
30 "Later, Luis!"
32 ___ Works (Monopoly utility)
33 Chocolate ___ (popular dog)
34 Smith, Jones or Chang
38 Mouth moistener
41 Found a place for
42 "___ Restaurant"
43 Alternative to Google
44 Olympics prizes
45 "What ___ can I say?"

Down

1 Fuzzy little dogs, for short
2 Help with a heist
3 1980s actress whose name almost reverses to 19-down
4 Didn't avert one's gaze
5 Push (on)
6 Tabloid folk
7 Ship to outer space
8 Before
9 It goes in your lungs
10 More, in Managua
16 Casual shirt
19 1980s singer whose name almost reverses to 3-down
20 Threesome
21 Casual agreements
22 Not that many
23 ___ California (peninsula of Mexico)
28 Old Toyota
29 Go abroad, say
30 Computer key
31 River through Vienna and Budapest
35 Talk back to
36 Department store section
37 Small advantage
38 American "Uncle"
39 Kind of beer
40 Container's top

319

Across

1 Scientist's workplace, or a kind of dog
4 Financial newspaper, for short
7 Leno or Mohr
10 Hockey surface
11 Shopkeeper on "The Simpsons"
12 "___ of these days..."
13 "Now I understand!"
14 Apartment building residents
16 Movie critic
18 Make a mistake
19 Risque, as humor
23 Hot stuff?
25 Outback and Impreza automaker
26 Do some arithmetic
27 Part of many disguises
28 Piece of timber
29 Cuddly animals from Australia
31 Dog food brand
32 ___ Fudd (Bugs Bunny's hunter)
33 Poehler of "Parks and Recreation"
34 Strange folks
38 Mesabi Range minerals
41 Intention
42 Recycling ___
43 Lard or butter
44 Letters between L and P
45 Cow's word
46 Military bases: abbr.
47 Ask for alms

Down

1 "That isn't true and you know it!"
2 Dull pain
3 River-blocking structure
4 ___ Works (Monopoly property)
5 Gush (forth)
6 Southern flyer
7 Stewart of "The Daily Show"
8 Little crawler
9 "What is it?"
15 Man of Mecca
17 Anger
20 "I Know This Much Is True" novelist
21 Bit of rain
22 1980s car named for its country of origin
23 Phony
24 "American ___"
25 Bro's sib
27 Keep at bay
30 Kings of ___
31 "I ___ Man of Constant Sorrow"
33 Helps in crime
35 "Shoot!"
36 Actor's words
37 Pollution problem
38 Computer company
39 Brazilian city
40 Yoko of "Dear Yoko"

320

Across

1 Quick punch
4 J. Edgar Hoover once ran it
7 Halloween flyer
10 Big boxer
11 ___ room (place to play)
12 "That's gross!"
13 She did the album "Double Fantasy" with John Lennon
15 ___ Luthor (Superman's rival)
16 Prepare vegetables, maybe
17 Zero, to soccer fans
19 Record store section
21 ___ Virginia
24 Org. that includes the Cleveland Cavaliers and the Chicago Bulls
27 Woman's name that anagrams to "habitat"
29 Fajitas vegetable
31 Needed a kleenex
32 See 49-across
33 Biblical prophet
34 Stuff to change your hair color
36 "Aren't you ___ one who always said..."
38 Mexican restaurant freebie
42 Enjoy a winter resort
44 "It's a bet!"
46 Female chicken
47 Quarterback Manning
48 Down in the dumps
49 With 32-across, Christmas drink
50 Group of related items
51 Cloud's home

Down

1 Toronto Blue ___
2 Plenty
3 Two-wheeler
4 Entirely
5 "Argo" director Affleck
6 Image on your computer's desktop
7 Church publication
8 Era
9 Abbr. at the end of a note
14 Paddle's cousin
18 Victor's shout
20 Touched, like a dog or cat might
22 "Get away, fly!"
23 Drink for astronauts
24 Investor's letters
25 Mercedes-___
26 Warning
28 Surfer's clothing
30 Jacob's wife
35 Body part that produces wax
37 Peeping pair
39 Minus
40 Douse with water
41 "The ___ Griffith Show"
42 That lady
43 Beer container at a party
45 "Bravo!"

Solutions

1

```
P R O S A I C   S S T
A E R A T O R   T E E
D O W N T O E A R T H
D I E T S     A B A T E
E L L E     E T O I L E
D S L   A V I A T E
      A N E N T
    S P R A N G   D A G
M O R E L S     D E D E
U N I T Y     R E P O T
S N O O Z E A L A R M
T E R   E R I T R E A
S T Y   R E L A T E D
```

2

```
S T A K E S     B O S
T E R R E T   S I P E
E N C I N A   E D I T
N U T S   R E S E A T
C R I S     S A R T O
H E C K   R A M S E S
    R E E S E
A S S I S T   S A M S
S T I N T   T I O N
S A R G E S   R E D O
E D E L   P E E L E R
T I N E   A D E L L E
S A S   R E T O S S
```

3

```
A R B O R   C R E S C
L E R O I   C O X A E
A T O N E   L O T T E
B O K   L O A   R A L
A R E   S E M   A N O
M T N S   O P T O
A S H E N   S O R E S
    E W E S   M D S E
A S A   V I N   I T E
S T R   A G E   N E A
T O T E D   S T A E L
I M E T A   T E R M S
R A D O N   S A Y S O
```

4

```
S T R E P   M T I D A
P A O L I   A E S O P
A T A I L   R H I N O
S U N D A Y B E S T
    E F I L E
A M I D   P E D A L S
M F D       D O O
O R E I D A   N A P A
    S A M S A
  A N D R E W G O L D
O R L O N   I N O U R
T E E N A   N A N N Y
C A R E Y   E G A D S
```

5

```
S A H I B   I N T E R
E N O L A   S W A L E
P O T A T O S A C K S
S A S   T S E   T E T
    I L L I N I
S T E R E O   A C U P
M O N A D   F I A T S
A N D I   M O R L E Y
    E L V I R A
E D A   I N E   I A T
V I V I A N V A N C E
I N O I L   E N G E L
L O R I S   R E E S E
```

6

```
H E L D   S A B R A S
O M O O   O T O O L E
B A C O N P O W D E R
O G I V E   O S E S
    E L I H U
S T A R   S A T U R N
H I T   O L N   R E I
R O T I N I   A B B E
    S A P I D
U H O H   S L I C E
S A W T H E L I G H T
T H E A I R   B O A T
A N D R E A   S R T A
```

7

```
T O S S   O D E S S A
E N O L   R A N K E R
M A M A   I D E A T E
P I M P L E D
O R E   A N Y M O R E
    L E S T   A N A D
G U I L T   G R I M M
E S E S   A L T O
T E R E N C E   N A G
      U T E N S I L
S A L A M I   O K R A
A W A K E N   D I E S
P E N A N G   E N D S
```

8

```
M R E D   D C A R E A
D I N A   E L D E S T
S A V E   L I S T E N
E S E   I U M   D S O
    L Y N X E S
S L O A N E   L C D S
S O P H S   C I A O S
I P S O   B O N M O T
    O B L I G E
A M B   L O N   A S E
M O R R O W   O W N S
S E E Y O U   C A I N
O N R A M P   H Y P E
```

9

```
B I C S   A W A I T S
A L A E   L A N C E T
G E N X   K P D U T Y
    A U P A I R
  A D A Y   T E L L S
P S A L M   I S I A H
E S D       G R O
T E R N S   A R H A T
A S Y L A   N A T S
    E L B O W S
A T E A S E   B O T H
W I N S A T   A U R A
L A O T S E   R T E S
```

10

```
S E N A T   S M I L E
A L E R O   E A R E D
L O W I N T E R E S T
S I T Z   O T C
    O S S O   N I S
I R E N I C   D O S T
Y A K A M A T R I B E
A M E N   N E E D N T
R A D   V I E W
    D E N   A G R A
N A T A L I E W O O D
R E A D D   B A L S A
C R U S T   B Y F A R
```

11

```
A S W E   H O A R S E
C A E N   O L D M E N
M E N U   R E D S E A
E S T R A N G E
    U E L E   R S V P
K E N S I T   S A I L
T E D       L O I
E L E V   R A T T L E
L Y R E   A M B I
    R A T I O N A L
D O C I L E   N E E D
S C A L E D   E S O L
S A W Y E R   S S N S
```

12

```
F P A   F A R   I Q S
L A M   E R E   D U O
E S A   N C R   E A R
E T T A   T A M M I E
    L E O N I
C H U M P S   N E T S
S I N A I   K E Y I N
I P S A   S U R E T Y
    T E E N A
T A M A R A   L E G O
O D A   R M N   R A I
M E I   O A S   D T S
B E D   R N A   E O E
```

Solutions

13

```
D I N S   ■ S Y L A R
I S E E ■ S T O O G E
S L A T ■ T A G O U T
K A R A T E ■ U S E S
■ ■ B E A V E R ■ ■
R A E ■ H E P T A D S
A R E ■ I D O ■ M I A
W I R E T A P ■ A A R
■ ■ V I L E S T ■ ■
E D G E ■ L E P E R S
R U A N D A ■ A U E L
S M I L E S ■ C R A Y
T A N Y A ■ ■ E S M E
```

14

```
G R O S S ■ L A T T E
R I V A L ■ E P S O N
A G E N A ■ G R A I L
S H R E V E P O R T ■
■ T H R E E U P ■ ■
A J A ■ G L O S S Y
M A U D E ■ L S A T S
O B L I G E ■ U R L
■ T O T A S T E ■ .
■ M U T T O N H E A D
A S C I I ■ N O R M A
A R L E S ■ A R N E L
A P A S T ■ S E E D Y
```

15

```
F A B I O ■ D O I N ■
A L E R S ■ I N B E D
J A C K S O N F I V E
I N O ■ E X E ■ D A M
T O M B O Y S ■ E D O
A N E T ■ C A Y M A N
■ ■ ■ W R O T E ■ ■
O N L O A N ■ S P A D
L O I ■ I T E M I Z E
I B E ■ S I G ■ L A T
O L D K I N G C O L E
S E T I N ■ O A S E S
■ S O N G ■ S W E A T
```

16

```
H U S H ■ S L I G H T
A S I A ■ I A M T O O
H A R D A S N A I L S
A C E R B I C ■ ■ ■
■ ■ O B S E R V E D
P A T S Y ■ T E A S E
E L E A ■ ■ G M A N
L O T U S ■ N I P I T
F E R R A R I S ■ ■
■ ■ L A S T L A P
J E R E M Y I R O N S
A G O R A E ■ A M A S
L O W E N D ■ R A T T
```

17

```
E L I S A ■ V E T S
R A N O F F ■ I R O N
R A T I T E ■ E N Y O
■ ■ H E E L E D ■ ■
L G E ■ R T E ■ P I A
O O M P H ■ C O A T S
C L A R O ■ U N R E P
A E I O U ■ M E T R E
L M N ■ R P M ■ T S R
■ ■ I S A I A H ■ ■
O P U S ■ S N A R E S
B A N A ■ O G R E S S
E C H T ■ S P E L T
```

18

```
I N A C A B ■ J I N K
O R W E L L ■ E L E E
C A S S I U S C L A Y
■ A V E C ■ A R S ■
S K I R E S O R T ■
A Y N ■ B R I E F S
C A T T Y R E M A R K
S T E R E O ■ ■ S E E
■ R U N T O S E E D
T R L ■ T H R A ■
B E A L L E N D A L L
A N C E ■ R A I D E D
R E E K ■ S N E E R S
```

19

```
R O N C O ■ C U P I D
A H O O T ■ A N E R A
M E N L O ■ P I K E R
A D D L E P A T E D ■
■ A E S O P ■ ■ ■
P L I E ■ P I E R R E
E A R N S ■ E L A N D
S A Y S H I ■ S R A S
■ ■ E D D I E ■ ■
■ B A R G A I N F O R
M A T E O ■ N O I R E
P R I M A ■ A R E N T
G E T I T ■ R E D E S
```

20

```
B A H T ■ D A C C A
A D A Y S ■ I N R E M
G E I C O ■ R E E S E
■ L O F A T ■ M T S
B S E ■ A L I F E ■
O I S E ■ T E D D Y S
S T E L A ■ D I E G O
S E L E C T ■ C M O N
■ A C T A S ■ E R E
A B S ■ U H L A N ■
S A S H A ■ O C T E T
T R I T T ■ G A H A N
O B E S E ■ ■ T E N T
```

21

```
G A S P ■ O B E S E
A L O H A ■ H E X E S
F E L I X T H E C A T
F A D ■ E O E ■ I L O
E S E ■ S S N ■ S U P
S T R S ■ C R E E P S
■ ■ S T A Y S ■ ■
G O E S O N ■ G O V S
U L U ■ T I A ■ M E A
A D D ■ T N N ■ E I N
R H O D E I S L A N D
D A R E R ■ A I R E R
S T A C Y ■ D A D A
```

22

```
S O P O R S ■ L O B S
O S I R I S ■ A R L O
S O C C E R ■ M E A L
■ ■ A S L ■ I A M B I
P A Y ■ S A N Z ■ ■
S T U ■ D R E S S Y
A N N ■ G O I ■ C H A
T O E T A P ■ H A W
■ ■ U P T O ■ O W L
E V I L S ■ O R L ■
R E N I ■ S H E A R S
L E A P ■ H E D R E N
E R N S ■ A D D S T O
```

23

```
S U M ■ P A L ■ F E Z
U N I ■ L U I ■ R T E
D I R ■ O D O ■ E C U
S T A R W I T N E S S
■ N A E ■ T E T ■
U N D I D ■ A G H A S
R E A L ■ ■ A R C A
L O R I S ■ O T O E S
■ I N C ■ S E W ■
Z I G G Y M A R L E Y
W A H ■ L A G ■ I N A
E N T ■ L Y E ■ N U N
I S S ■ A S S ■ E F G
```

24

```
G U T S ■ D U M P O N
E M M A ■ E S H A R P
R O A N ■ C L O S E R
I K N O W I T ■ ■ ■
■ ■ ■ A D A P T E D
T S E T S E ■ S I L O
W I D T H ■ I S T L E
O R E O ■ U N T I E S
S E R P E N T ■ ■ ■
■ ■ ■ A E R O S O L
A U R I G A ■ O U Z O
T R A I L S ■ O R Z O
E L Y S E E ■ H E Y S
```

Solutions

25

```
A S H   A M T   F A Y
E T O   D I I   A L E
N E W   O N T   C T A
E F S   U N U   E H S
A F I   R E L   T E T
S I T N   S A S H A Y
    H O N O R E E
I N A R U T   G N U S
N I N   M A I   A P E
E N G   E F T   T E E
S E I   R A Y   I N S
S O N   A T O   O D A
E F G   L S U   N S W
```

26

```
H A Y E S   L E T T S
A S A L E   A R H A T
I K N O W   M I A T A
R F K   E R E C T E D
D O E   D E R   S R I
O R E G O N   A N S A
    C O N   T I O
A I L S   C O N T R A
B M I   E F S   R E P
A P P E A L S   I P O
C A P E S   E N G E L
A L E N E   R A H A L
B E R Y L   S E T T O
```

27

```
S O B I G   I B L E
P A L A U   A V A I L
A T O L L   N O S E D
D E W   A L I   I D E
E R O   G Y M   C T R
S S N S   R A D I O S
    E P S I L O N
R U S T I C   I S B N
E G S   N A G   T R U
O A T   F L Y   I O R
I R A B U   R I N G S
L T C O L   O N C U E
S E K O   S I T E S
```

28

```
P A M P A S   R T S
E T A L I I   F I A T
P A R A D E   R E L Y
    S E N T E N C E
A M A T   A A A
T U L I P   S K I F F
M M D C L   S Y R I A
O S A K A   O F O L D
    N N E   R C A S
B E R I B E R I
L O A F   L O D G E S
I N G E   E M A I L S
P S U   D A Y L I T
```

29

```
P U C K S   M E C C A
A P R I L   A L O U D
S H A D E   F L O R A
T I C   P H I   K E G
E L K   T O O   I R E
S L E D   A S S E S S
    R E C R O O M
G A B L E S   B O S S
L E A   N E T   N U T
O R R   T R Y   S P A
S A R G E   P E T E R
S T E E R   O V E R T
Y E L L S   S E R B S
```

30

```
P A S S   J C R E W
O C H O   B E H A V E
O R A L   U N I T E D
R E N A M E   N E S S
    G R I N G O
B A H   N O R   B O W
E R A   U S O   U N O
T M I   T A U   D E W
    G E I S H A
E C H O   R E A P E D
B L O U S E   H E R R
B U R R O S   A S I A
S E N D S   S T E W
```

31

```
C O R K S   P A C E R
O P E R A   A F O R E
M E D I C I N E M A N
E N D S   N E W E S T
R U E   B E L   T E E
S P R A I N   U S S R
    R O G E R
D I S K   L A N C E S
I M P   P I T   A N T
S P I C E S   K Y L E
M A R A T H O N M A N
A L I K E   R E A C T
L A T E R   B E N E S
```

32

```
C A P T   C O P S
O H I O   R O D E O
M A N N   W A G E R S
A S K S   O W N
    F I D O   A J A R
B A L L E D   C A P E
U N O   N Y C   K E N
O N Y X   B A R E S T
Y A D A   O P A L
    N A Y   B L T S
I S L A N D   B O O O
S E E D Y   L Y N N
M E N U   E D G Y
```

33

```
C U B A   L A S S I E
O P U S   A T T I R E
D O G S   M O R T A L
E N S E M B L E
    B R O   L E B O N
F L U T E   S T U D Y
I O N       G I N
F I N D S   C A S E Y
A S Y E T   H I M
    F R E E R E I N
A L L I E D   C A S E
J O I N E D   O N E S
S L E E P Y   N Y E T
```

34

```
P O D S   P E P P E R
I K E A   A R R I V E
E L A N   D R O N E D
R A N G E R O V E R
    T H E R E
E M B O S S   D A R N
L O Y       B I O
F O E S   M O S C O W
    I S A A C
    R O L L S R O Y C E
M A D E I T   T O R Y
E V I N C E   T R E E
T E E T E R   Y E W S
```

35

```
L A W   P R O
I D O   E A T   W A S
M R R I G H T   O R E
P I S A   M O T R I N
E V E N I   U S E S
D E F   S E A T T L E
    O P E N S U P
S C R E E D S   I S M
C A W S   T A C K Y
O N E T O N   S T A B
L O A   D I S P U T E
D E R   O N O   R E S
    R E X   E S T
```

36

```
C H I   A T M   S A P
L A W   S H E   E R R
A H A   P A N C A K E
W A S P   T U B
    W E B S   S T A B
W A R Z O N E   A B E
I M O   Y O U   K E N
F I N   S T R E E T S
E D G Y   R O M A
    U N I   O L D S
R U M M A G E   E A T
A G O   S H Y   F R Y
W H O   A T E   T E X
```

Solutions

37
```
T A C O S   W A T C H
A L O N E   A L O H A
P A R A D E F L O A T
E N D   A X E   L I E
      S T A R T S
S Y S T E M   W H I M
P O P E S   B E E N A
A U R A   F R E D D Y
    O M E L E T
S T U   T E N   R E I
K I T C H E N S I N K
I M E A N   A U D I E
P E D R O   N E E D S
```

38
```
C L E A R   S P R I G
H O U S E   W H I N E
E I G H T Y E I G H T
A T E   R E A   H E F
P E N   O S T   T R I
O R E O   T E A S E T
      U S E R S
S C O R E R   P R O P
P A X   A D D   E R R
A N Y   T A O   A C E
N I G H T Y N I G H T
K N E E L   T R A I T
S E N S E   S A N D Y
```

39
```
W A T T S   G E T T O
A R R O W   A K R O N
S T A T E   L E A N S
H I P   E L I   P I E
E S P   P A L   P E T
S T E M   S E W E R S
    R A M   O A R
R E J O I N   S K I T
O N O   D A B   E N E
A T H   B Y E   E T A
R I N G O   T A P E S
A R M E D   T H E R E
T E D D Y   Y A R N S
```

40
```
G L A D   M A I L E R
A I D E   A D M I R E
Z E A L   D U P L E X
A D M I R A L
        E S T E F A N
H O O P L A   L O D E
A N G R Y   B I R D S
M I L O   W I S E S T
S T E P P E D
      A T E I N T O
R A D I S H   C O A X
A V I A T E   E A S E
Y E S M A N   T H E N
```

41
```
T E N T S   T U D O R
I Q U I T   E M O T E
C U R S E   M A C O N
T A S   E A P   T O T
A T E   P B J   O L E
C E D E   R O A R E D
    A M I A B L E
O H G O S H   A D D S
N O R   L A W   P R E
E M U   A M Y   H O V
L A D E N   A B O V E
E G G E D   T A T E R
G E E K S   T H O S E
```

42
```
D E B T S   T A R A S
O M A H A   A R O M A
C I T E D   K E B A B
E L M   A W E   I Z E
N I A   T O O   N O R
T O N S   K N O W N S
    F A R   E L I
S H O W E R   E L S E
E A R   W E T   L U X
E V E   A D O   I M P
S A V E R   A L A M O
A N E N D   S E M I S
W A R E S   T A S T E
```

43
```
C H O P   S W O O S H
L I R A   I H A D T O
A F E W   N I T E R S
P I O N E E R
        B A R B A R A
I N A P O D   O V E N
C O N A N O B R I E N
E N D S   C A N D L E
D E S T R O Y
        A N S W E R S
M A R G I N   H A I L
E V E N S O   O S L O
T E M P E R   S T E W
```

44
```
B A R S   M I M I C
I M O K   O M E G A S
T O M A T O S A U C E
E R A   I D O   A T E
R A N T S   M A N U P
S L O W   H A R A S S
      E R O D E
S T R E E P   S I C K
T H E T A   M O C H A
E R N   C D S   I O N
P O T A T O S A C K S
S W A N E E   F L E A
  S L E D S   T E D S
```

45
```
O W L   A T E   L E G
N O I   T A R   I V E
C O S M O K R A M E R
E L A I N E   P O R E
      L E O N A
A W O L   N O R M A L
L E V I S   S T A R E
A B A C U S   F E E D
        E N T E R
S P I N   A L O H A S
C A T T Y R E M A R K
A P E   E T C   L E E
R A M   E S T   L A W
```

46
```
A B B A   F A C I A L
R O U T   E N A C T S
M A T H   A G R E E D
    T E S T E R
  D E N Y   L E F T S
R E R A N   A L L O T
O F F         U P A
S O L O S   T I T A N
E G Y P T   A N T Z
      A R R I V E
U N I Q U E   A R L O
R E B U T S   I B E T
L A M E S T   N Y E T
```

47
```
W A R S   C O I F S
A B E T   A R N I E
S A V A N N A H G A
      P A S T A
S C A L P   O L I V E
C A R E S   R E N A L
R I G         O L D
A R O M A   N A I V E
M O N E T   A B L E R
      L E O N A
H A V A N A C U B A
A R I S E   U S E R
M I N E S   S A N E
```

48
```
L O I N S   R A F T S
I N D I A   A L O H A
S T O P S   M E R R Y
B A N   S A P   G E S
O P T   I D S   E A T
N E R V E S   O T T O
    E E R   F R A
G A M E   G E R B I L
A V E   T E E   O N O
R E M   A L L   U F O
I N B O X   S A T A N
S U E D E   A L I C E
H E R D S   D I T T Y
```

Solutions

49

```
M A S S . P U S H U P
A N O N . E S T A T E
I N F O . L E A D E R
N E T . M O S T . . .
E X T R A S . S H E A
. A U D I T . A V A .
F A C E T . O P R A H
E G O . V O T E D . .
W E S T . P E N C I L
. I D E S . I R A . .
C O N M A N . I D O S
B R E E Z E . M E N S
S E E R E D . O R S O
```

50

```
. . U Z I . . .
T A Z . P A R . Z I P
A V I . A C E . S R I
E I G H T H . L A K E
. A G E . A T O Z . .
S T Y X . R O U S E D
P O M . B Y E . A V E
A R A R A T . T G I F
. R I T A . H A L . .
Y E L P . Y O U B E T
A R E . A L L . O Y L
K E Y . S O D . R E C
. . I R S . . .
```

51

```
E G G . B I T . . .
N O R . A M Y . B A G
C L E A N U P . E S E
A F A R . P E N S K E
M E T E S . . O T I S
P R E . I T S G O N E
. S U N R O O F . . .
J E T S K I S . A N A
A C H E . . A B L E R
P O I S O N . A B U T
A N T . N U R T U R E
N O S . U K E . M A R
. . S E T . S L Y
```

52

```
C L O W N S . . L A P
L A R I A T . W I F E
I M E L D A . O M E N
. . D A N B R O W N .
S P E W . S A L . . .
C U R I E . I D T A G
A M I L E . T W I N E
R A N D R . S I M O N
. W I G . D E N T . .
L A K E E R I E . . .
A X I S . O N W A R D
L E N T . S T E R E O
A D D . S O B E I T .
```

53

```
D E C A L . A G A P E
E R A S E . B A N A L
M I S S T H E M A R K
I N E . M O L E . . .
. . G E M . S O F A .
P H R A S E S . M E L
H O U S E . I D E A S
I L L . E A T I N T O
L E E K . R U G . . .
. I K E A . C O O . .
S H A N I A T W A I N
H E R D S . E A G L E
E X I S T . D R E S S
```

54

```
Z I P S . O T T A W A
E W A N . I R I S E S
N O R A . N I C H E S
. K I T K A T . . . .
A P P L E . D A B S .
S A L S A . S C O T T
I R A . . . A A H .
F I C U S . F A R G O
. S E G A . O R D E R
. A N D R E W . . .
A G E N D A . N A P A
B E N D E D . A L E C
C L E A R S . S K I T
```

55

```
B R E W S . A R M S .
R O Y A L . D E E P .
O N E S I E . D A L E
. E N D S . O P E N .
T E X T . S U N S E T
A V A . P A S S . . .
G E M . A Y E . P E W
. A N T S . O R E .
S A L U T E . S P E D
C L O T . S H A Q .
R O T H . T E N U R E
U N T O . A T I O N .
B E A R . D O Z E S .
```

56

```
H A L F W A Y . A S H
A M E R I C A . M O O
S C O O P U P . P U N
. O E R . A L S O .
P O R T . A P P E A R
A X E L . S I P . .
C O C O A . G L A S S
. O L D . E R I K .
S I M P L E . J E D I
O T I S . N B A . .
D A N . A V O C A D O
A L E . P E R K S U P
S Y S . T R E S S E S
```

57

```
M I L O . J A C K O
A T A D . O T H E R
M E M O R Y L A N E
A M E R I C A . . .
. . . B E S T M A N
G L A S S . T H E M E
R A C Y . E M I T
A M E N S . W E E D S
M A S C A R A . .
. W E I G H T S
E A S Y S T R E E T
S W E E T . O R E O
P E E R S . W A S P
```

58

```
H A H A . T E R E S A
E V I L . W R A P U P
R I G S . E N T I R E
A S H . A L I . C I X
. N E R V E S . .
A T O N C E . A M I N
W O O D S . S N I D E
N A N U . O U T D I D
. P A C M A N . .
U H S . F L O . I B E
P O T A T O . A G E S
O N E S E C . C H A P
N E W A R K . S T U N
```

59

```
B O L D . A S S E T
I D E A . C H I L I
T O N Y C U R T I S
E R A S U R E . . .
. . . R A W H I D E
D O W S E . D E V I L
A R I A . R A N K
T A N G O . S O N G S
A L D E N T E . .
. . . S E A T T L E
O S C A R M A Y E R
R E A L M . S P A R
R A T E S . K E N S
```

60

```
S M U G . C O U P .
H O M E S . O W N E D
R U B L E . P E D R O
A L I . R E P . E M U
N I L . B R O . R I G
K N I T . E L E C T S
. . C H I C A G O .
F L A U N T . O V A L
A O L . H O V . E V A
L U C . A R C . R I P
S N O B S . R E C A P
E G R E T . S M O T E
. E D G E . O P E D
```

Solutions

61

```
CHIC   PARIS
HERA  AWASH
AMERICANME
   OVER
MADLY  ENACT
ONE  YOOHOO
UNITEDFRONT
TIGERS  LEE
HENCE  CRESS
   CHOO
 DELTABLUES
UNION  ESAU
BEERS  SERB
```

62

```
ACTED  GOTHS
CARGO  RURAL
AMIGO  OTERI
REC  ROW  APP
ELK  DAN  TOP
 QUIT  FLOE
CAUSE  GRIND
AREA  COOK
RRS  TOO  ESP
LAT  ODD  DEA
ONION  OWING
AGONY  NORSE
DENTS  ENTER
```

63

```
LAG  OTT
AVE  IRA  FIT
RATTLER  ASA
ELSE  KAPLAN
DOTED  OLAY
ONO  AMERICA
 GETEVEN
ONELANE  GIT
RATE  READY
ADHERE  APOP
TIE  INGRATE
ERR  DYE  ROO
  SAM  TON
```

64

```
LIMBS  SCRAM
ACURA  CHILI
THROWTHINGS
HID  ERE  GOS
ARE  DIM  IRE
MORT  BEANED
  ROUST
LATENT  MOPS
ORE  EAT  VIA
ACE  SRI  ELF
THIRTYTHREE
HENNA  LULUS
EDGAR  EGYPT
```

65

```
EDEN  CHESS
LEGO  AUDIO
FLOWERGIRL
  ASSET
PRAYS  OPAL
LEG  AVERAGE
ALA  YAM  IRA
NAMASTE  RED
EXEC  ROSES
  TOUGH
RINGBEARER
ADORE  ROVE
POWER  AMEX
```

66

```
WASH  CADDIE
ANTE  ARRIVE
STAR  READER
PITT  MAC
 EZRA  UPTO
ELF  EXPLAIN
GOALS  EARLY
AVIATOR  TEX
DERN  RUBY
 CUD  AFAR
PAYOLA  ROSA
ALUMNI  QUIP
DEMEAN  SLAT
```

67

```
PAT  PAM  ABS
ARI  EGO  JOE
PUM  PIN  ART
AGE  LEARNS
YUL  HEYS
ALIKE  BAM
 ANNA  ELAN
 EEL  LEGAL
 ETAT  AMI
SAYSHI  ZEN
ADO  SKI  ITI
GAG  PEC  NAN
AMA  ANY  EGG
```

68

```
PEP  KFC  APP
ORE  ELLIPSE
TRACYAUSTIN
 ASTER
HAST  ASAP
ARI  HAVEAGO
STEVEDALLAS
PIGIRON  VIE
SEES  YENS
 ITSME
MATTHOUSTON
ERASERS  AWE
WEB  MET  DEW
```

69

```
BAWL  LOREN
ERIE  AFIRE
GERALDFORD
ONE  AYE
TASER  RIVAL
 BAG  RACE
AUTOMOBILES
SKIN  DRS
KENYA  OHARA
 DEN  LOM
CHEVYCHASE
OUTIE  OMEN
DEALS  TOSS
```

70

```
MACE  OTHER
OPALS  PAYME
CANIT  EXPEL
HID  RAN  ERA
ANYWAY  RAP
 WHINE  ALS
TAROT  ABCDE
ALA  STRUT
PUP  INNING
IMP  APE  VIE
ONEAL  SLICE
CURVE  TOTES
ASSES  PYRE
```

71

```
INK  ARK  ABS
RAN  BEN  FAT
AMERICA  ERA
 EAT  POWER
COPY  ASK
ANA  KRACKEL
LED  NBC  NAE
MISTOOK  IST
 VCR  ICES
FLASK  OAK
LAX  OATMEAL
ACE  UNI  RBI
WED  TYS  SET
```

72

```
SOLO  JOSHED
ERIN  UMPIRE
NETS  NEATEN
DOTH  END
 LOLA  EBAY
PEEROUT  IPA
EPEES  REGAL
CIV  STUMBLE
KCAR  WEBE
 USE  ARTS
DEARME  STEP
UMLAUT  SHEA
GUILTY  YAMS
```

Solutions

73

```
L O T   S U B   P U B
A M A   U S A   E P A
P A P T E S T   P A Y
U H O H   R H E T T
P A N E L   S T A R R
      M A P   C L E O
R A P   W I N   K E Y
A L O E   P E G
J A P A N   W R O T E
  S T R I P   I C O N
A K A   P U P T E N T
C A R   P R O   A T E
T N T   Y E T   N O R
```

74

```
P A G E D   T I G H T
A C E L A   E R R O R
C I T I Z E N K A N E
E D S   Z E N   N E E
    A L L I E D
A R G U E   S A S S Y
L O A D   T O K E
P E R I L   L E N I N
    G O O N I N
M A O   C O T   A S P
I F Y O U R E A B L E
T E L L S   R O B O T
T W E E T   S K Y P E
```

75

```
C O V E S   R O M P S
A R I A L   E M I L E
M E R R Y   M A N I C
E G G S   B A N N E R
R O I   T E X   E R E
A N N U A L   P S S T
  I N U T E R O
C I A O   W R E T C H
O T S   J A R   A R E
V A L L E Y   A F A R
E L I A N   S L A V E
T I M O N   I O T A S
S A S S Y   T E S T Y
```

76

```
A B E L   R I V A L S
P E L E   O N E S I E
E A S E   W A N T O N
S U E G R A F T O N
      R E N E
D E C A Y   W H A L E
I R O N   U H O H
S A N T A   E X A M S
      M E L T
  S I O U X F A L L S
R E S I S T   B E A T
H E L L E R   L I M A
O D E S S A   E S P N
```

77

```
M A Y A S   A G E S
A D O B E   P E R T
D O U B L E P L A Y
      E L S E
C L A Y   T A R G E T
R A T   R I N S E
I D E A   M O S S
S L U R P   M E T
S E P T I C   S E X Y
    G A G A
  T R I P L E J U M P
  H E R E   M A R I A
  E V E N   S K I L L
```

78

```
N A P E   E M B L E M
E S A U   M A L A W I
C H U G   E L A T E D
K Y L E   R I M
    A N T I   E B A Y
N O D E A L   S O L O
O R E   B L T   B A D
U S E S   A R A B I A
N O N O   G A R Y
    L E A   A F R O
B R I D E S   B L O W
R E V E L S   L A M E
A V E R S E   E Y E S
```

79

```
W I M P Y   A T S E A
A M O R E   C H A N G
N O N O S   M A T T E
E N D S   R E T U R N
D I A   H E S   R E D
  T Y P E S   I D E A
    M A R T I N A
S H O W   S W A Y S
C A R   M O O   N I P
R I N G I N   N I N A
A L I E N   D O G G Y
P E N N E   A S H E N
E D G E S   M E T R E
```

80

```
L I F E S   A S T O
A G E N T   S P A R
B E T T Y W H I T E
S T A R   H E N
    I S A   S A G A
A C C E P T S   B O X
W O R S E   A C U T E
E R A   D A K O T A S
D E M O   P E R
    L O P   O R E O
  C L I N T B L A C K
  H A V E   A L P H A
  I D E S   N A T T Y
```

81

```
L E O   F A B   R I P
E L F   I R E   O N E
A L F A L F A   L A W
P A Y N E   M E L D S
    O T T   E V E R
S E U S S   D A R E D
P A R   C A R
A R R O W   R O O M Y
  P O L E   E R A
R I C E S   M A S S E
E E K   S T I L T E D
A C E   O W N   E G G
P E R   N O D   R A Y
```

82

```
L E N A   S H E I L A
I M A C   C O R N E D
M A N E   A M E N D S
B I C Y C L E
S L Y   H E R S H E Y
    D E E D   C A K E
S T R A W   B A R E S
A R E S   M I N D
N E W Y O R K   Y R S
    S H E R B E T
T R I C K Y   H O P E
U N L O A D   E Y R E
G A L O R E   A S O N
```

83

```
S A W T O   H A S T A
T R A I N   O N I O N
D I S N E Y W O R L D
    H A N O I   S L Y
I B E   E D E N
M E D U S A   O P A L
A L U M S   D I R G E
C A P P   P A R E R S
    S P A N   S A T
A L E   O L I V E
M I D D L E E A R T H
E M A I L   L I V E R
N A M E S   S L E D S
```

84

```
M A G I C   C A M P S
I R E N E   O H A R A
S M O K E   W A R E S
F A R   L O B   T Y S
I N G   O N A   H O E
T I E S   E R R A N D
    C L I E N T S
C O L O N Y   S T E P
O R O   H E W   E M U
R I O   A D E   W E T
G E N U S   A P A R T
I N E R T   V E R G E
S T Y L E   E N T E R
```

Solutions

85

```
J A P A N   A M A Z E
A W A R E   L E M O N
M E L E E   A H A N D
    M A D A M   R E S
O W E   L O O S E
M A T T E L   A T O M
A N T E S   I N T R O
N E O N   U N D O E S
    S T A R T   S O S
P A T   A L E R O
O N A I R   G O U D A
R E T R O   R U R A L
T W E E N   A T S E A
```

86

```
M A G S   A G L O W
A N A T   G U I D E
I N G A   P E N C I L
D A G G E R S   E N D
    I S L A
O F F   I N N   J F K
W E T   S K I   O R E
E D S   E C O   K I N
      A B L E
P U N   F L E A B A G
A N I M A L   N O N O
S I N A I   D O T O
S T A R R   S K I N
```

87

```
R A G   T A B   C A R
O N O   E L I   O W E
A N I M A L S   M E D
M A N O R   T R I
    G N U   R A N T O
B E B O P   O H G O D
E V A   F E D
T A C O S   C R O S S
A N K L E   A I R
    W E D   N O W A Y
S P A   A G I T A T E
H E R   T A N   R O N
E N D   E Y E   D P S
```

88

```
A S H E   C A M E I N
C O A L   A T O N C E
A L P O   L O R D E D
T O P P L I N G
    Y E A   E A G L E
T E D D Y   S N O O P
E R A       O N E
E G Y P T   L O D G E
N O S I R   O F T
    G A S O L I N E
A C T O U T   A M E R
R E S U M E   T E A R
T O E T A P   E S T S
```

89

```
N T H   F R O   S P A
I R A   E E N   H A M
P E T E R C O Y O T E
S E S A M E   O P E N
    T I D Y U P
S E M I   E A S E L S
E C O N O   M A R I E
T O N G U E   I S L E
    G O T M A D
A S O F   P R I E S T
W O L F B L I T Z E R
E L I   E O S   R E O
S E A   D Y E   A M Y
```

90

```
P E P S   S W A Y Z E
A Q U A   H O M I E R
C U P S   A M E N D S
T I P S O V E R
S P Y   V E N I S O N
    L E A D   C E D E
A T O L L   W A X E D
C A V E   M I N K
E J E C T E D   I R A
    T A L E N T E D
T A O I S T   A T R A
O F N O T E   S E A M
S T O N E D   A N N S
```

91

```
B A H   D E A
A V A   O R R   A R I
R I T C H I E   X E R
B A C H   C A M E R A
E T H E R   A B U T
D E E   E A C H O N E
    T A B L O I D
P E P T A L K   Y D S
E L I M   E D S E L
T I E S U P   O P R Y
E T C   C A L O R I E
S E E   L I E   A D S
      A N D   Y E T
```

92

```
F I F E   P A J A M A
O R A L   E N A M E L
R O C K A N D R O L L
A N T   I T S   N B A
G O O   D U O   G A Y
E R R S   P O P
R E S E T   N E W T S
    E E K   T A R T
A S H   X E D   Y E A
A C E   T R I   T A R
R O L L I N G R O C K
O R I O L E   O G L E
N E X T E L   D O E R
```

93

```
U L N A   T O S S E D
T O O L   O R I O L E
A L S O   R A N D O M
H A T T R I C K
    R O B   L E N I N
S C I F I   E R O D E
C A N       S E W
A N G L E   G R E A T
R E S E T   I E R
    T H I N D I M E
G A E L I C   S N A G
M A L I C E   E G G O
S A F E S T   A S I S
```

94

```
M A T T   O S C A R S
O N U S   U T O P I A
M E N U   T O L E D O
S W A N   S P A
    A S I   S L A P
B E R M U D A   O L E
I N S I D E S C O O P
T O V   S C H E M E S
E S P N   H E N
    O N A   T A D A
D E M E A N   U S E R
I R O N I C   R I C E
N E E D L E   Y A K S
```

95

```
R O M A N O V   L O L
A B I L E N E   O S U
F E L I X T H E C A T
F R O N T   I M A G E
L O R E   S C A L E S
E N D   L I L I E S
    P I X E L
    C R A T E S   N A B
C H E S T S   M O R E
H A S T E   V I O L A
O S C A R W I N N E R
S T U   E A S T E N D
E E E   D R E S S E S
```

96

```
M O P   A P P E A L
E X E C   S I E R R A
N E A R   H E A R T Y
U N R E S T
    L E T O N   E Y E
N A B   O N A   L E D
A P U   O K S   M A G
S E C   L U C   E R E
A S K   S T A R R
      C R A F T S
M A T Z O H   C U R E
A D H E R E   E D E N
S O O N E R   D E T
```

Solutions

97

```
S T A N D   J A N E
C O L B Y   M A N E S
O U T A N D A B O U T
P S I   E R R   I R A
E L M   S U V   N A T
S E A M   G E N T L E
      A I S L E
A B S E N T   T A P S
R E T   T O M   R U T
M A O   A R I   G N U
I N L I K E F L Y N N
N I E C E   F I L E T
G E N E   S E E D S
```

98

```
F R A M E   C A S T S
R A M E N   H I T U P
O V E R T H E L I N E
Z I N   R E C   G E E
E N D   Y A K   M U D
N E S T   R E C A P S
      A S T R O
N O P R O B   P O R T
E P A   B E E   P E R
R E D   E A T   U S E
U N D E R T H E S E A
D E E R E   A R E N T
A D D E D   N A S T Y
```

99

```
S C A T S   B I E R S
W O V E N   I S L E T
O P E N I N G M O V E
R O N   F O G   P I E
D U G   F L A   E S P
S T E W   A M U S E S
      O W N E R
M A R K E R   N A S A
A P E   E Y E   D E T
D O C   P A D   R A T
C L O S I N G T I M E
A L I K E   E A V E S
P O L A R   S P E N T
```

100

```
H A Y E S   W A Y U P
A L O N E   H O U S E
M A G I C C A R P E T
S N A G   A L T
      M O V E A W A Y
G I J A N E   A L E
A R O S E   P I N T A
W O K   C O N D O R
K N E E P A D S
      V A N   P A R E
U N D E R T H E R U G
S H O R T   I C I N G
S L A Y S   S T A T S
```

101

```
M E M E S   S A M B A
A L A M E   T R A I T
X E R O X   A C I D S
I V Y   E R R   N E E
M A L   D I D   E T A
U T A H   P O L L
M E N U S   M O O R E
      D E U S   X B O X
O R C   G P A   S M U
P A R   G A B   T A L
E V A D E   A G E N T
R E B U S   C U R I E
A S S E T   I M S A D
```

102

```
P E A C E   A I D E S
A L L A N   C R O U P
S P A R E C H A N G E
T A S   M A E   K E N
A S K   I N D   E N D
S O A K E D   A Y E S
      A S Y E T
P S S T   C A L A I S
I O N   C A T   S N L
G O O   U N I   T H E
S T R I K E T H R E E
T H E R E   U B O A T
Y E S E S   P O S T S
```

103

```
W A D S   T E L L O N
H I R E   O R I O L E
O D I N   F I B B E D
M E E T   F E Y
      D O K E   A F R O
C O F F E E S   R A D
U N I F Y   O P I N E
B E G   S T R E E T S
A S S T   R E E D
      O W E   L E A H
W O N T O N   O G L E
A B O A R D   U G L I
R I D L E Y   T S A R
```

104

```
C O H A N   A B H O R
O R A T E   D I A N E
R I P E R   A G N E S
P O P   V I P   U S E
S L Y   E N T   K I N
      E H S   R E E K E D
      A L G E R I A
S O N O R A   N H L
I N U   A C T   H O S
E L K   S H E   A R C
N I K O S   A G R E E
N E A L E   R E R A N
A S H E S   S T Y L E
```

105

```
L I Z A   Z O O M I N
E R I C   I M P O S E
W E P T   P E S T L E
      W O M A N   T E D
P A I R E D   S T Y
E R R   D E B
W E E   I E R   Z A P
      A D A   I P A
T I C   O U T P U T
O N O   T O N I C
R A N C I D   M O N A
A N G O L A   E D E N
H E A L T H   D E W Y
```

106

```
S P A   O F F
P E P   H A L   I A N
E P I S O D E   T W O
E P E E   E A T S A T
D E C A F   H E R E
O R E   I N R O A D S
      O B V I O U S
I N F I E L D   Y A P
D U C T   S H A L L
E R A S E S   I S L A
A S K   S H O T P U T
L E E   P O P   I R E
      N E T   E E S
```

107

```
P A N D A   T I A R A
U S E U P   A D D E D
S L E E P E R S O F A
H A D   L A T   R I G
E N L   E V A   E N E
S T E P   E R A S E S
      O L S E N
T R A D E D   D I S S
R E D   A R T   S U P
A D J   T O O   R I O
C O U C H P O T A T O
E N S U E   T W E E N
D E T E R   H O L D S
```

108

```
H A W K S   S O N G S
A V A I L   T I A R A
T E N N I S E L B O W
E N D   P E P   B O Y
R U E   S T S   E V E
S E R F   S O L D E R
      B R A N D
B O D I E S   S C A T
O R E   S I D   R N A
W I N   I D O   A T M
W O U N D E D K N E E
O L D I E   G E N U S
W E E P S   E G Y P T
```

Solutions

109
ESC · AMI · · PTA
NIL · DEN · · YES
TEA · ADS · · REP
ASS · MIT · · APE
ITS · SCI · · MEN
LASS · ALLIES
CHILLED
ATHENS · OSLO
CHE · VCR · CON
TED · OHO · HOE
ICU · LON · END
VAL · VON · MEG
ENE · ELY · EYE

110
GORGE · NADAL
UHAUL · EWING
SNIPE · PANTS
HOSTCITIES
EATOUT
ADD · UNEVEN
NOUNS · EDITH
DEPOTS · RAL
TEABAG
LOSTCITIES
BEAUS · DONNA
RETRO · UNION
ASHEN · PEASE

111
BESET · ASPEN
ALERO · BERNE
SNARK · IGORS
SIR · YUL · BOT
ENCLOSE · ALL
SOHO · ENABLE
WENDELL
ARABIC · PEGS
TOR · CATSCAN
WAR · ERE · AGE
IDAHO · ROUGE
LINEN · MISER
LETME · SLEDS

112
WART · SASHAY
ALOE · ENTICE
NAYS · NOISES
DIRT · INN
ORSO · GRAF
MAGUIRE · AXE
ARENT · STYLE
PER · EMPIRES
SASS · ONTO
MAN · AMOK
REWARD · NATO
ITALIA · INTO
PARLAY · COOK

113
TACOS · SHAFT
ATARI · PALIN
CONAN · ARENT
KNICKKNACK
LEEKS
BAKERY · SEEK
ALI · ELF
TEXT · IRONIC
OSCAR
KNOCKKNOCK
PROBE · EAGLE
TITAN · ITRAN
ASIDE · NEEDS

114
DEFS · REMADE
ICET · EVENLY
SHEA · BIRDIE
HOLYMOLY
OAR · LIKE
SEQUINS · SAG
KLUTZ · PINTA
IMA · EVICTED
DODO · ACE
ROLYPOLY
KARATE · ASIA
IGETIT · CLAW
NOLESS · KORN

115
SAL · ERR · POD
USA · WOE · AHA
DISPELS · SIR
SAVE · LESSON
ELBOWS
EDGEOF · EGAD
LEA · ATM · OWE
MESA · HEROES
CHEWED
JOLTED · SLAM
APE · MIXTURE
KEN · ICY · CIA
END · NEZ · KAT

116
FORKS · GIBBS
ADIEU · OHARA
NOTES · TOKEN
GRAPHPAPER
AIRS
AFEW · YELLOW
SITAR · COACH
STAYED · OTTO
DESK
CROSSWORDS
CLANK · AVERT
HAITI · MEDIA
ADDON · PROPS

117
IMPS · COOPS
RARE · LADDER
IRON · ORDERS
SCHEDULE
OCT · OSCAR
LUCAS · STOLI
ASK · NAB
SEEDS · SCANS
TRYIT · ERR
PRICETAG
PUPPET · DILL
ASSESS · OSLO
LAIRS · STAB

118
DOHS · IRISH
SARAH · MEDIA
ALAMO · ICONS
PILLOWTALK
ETHAN
NEWT · ATTEND
OWE · ATE · MOO
REBORN · NUDE
BROKE
SHEETMUSIC
JOEYS · ATONE
IMSET · RESIN
BEADS · TROT

119
JUMP · ASPIRE
ONES · DEADON
ETNA · DALLAS
SOULSISTER
MINOR
JOUST · NYLON
OAK · EWE
GREET · WHOLE
NACHO
BIGBROTHER
DOCILE · DIVE
DRONES · ODES
TENETS · GENT

120
CAPS · MEADS
ACURE · AGREE
SHRIMPTOAST
III · EAT · BIT
NES · RRS · IRE
ORTEGA · ACER
TECHS
ZOLA · HAHAHA
ERA · GUT · NED
AIM · ATE · GAD
LOBSTERROLL
OLDIE · SPREE
TEARS · MARS

Solutions

121
LOSE · CAROB / IVAN · BANANA / MELD · UNITED / BRAE · TIM / DART · ASPS / GOFREE · LOEW / OHO · MRS · USA / BIRD · KEEPON / YOKO · NEWS / TMI · IPAD / BESTOF · NONE / INHERE · GONE / CLYDE · SNAP

122
BUFFS · DDAY / UNLIT · TORTE / SMITE · OMAHA / TOP · AID · WAR / LOP · DNA · INN / ERIK · STANDS / NESTEGG / GIGGLY · ESPN / RNA · ALG · TOE / ABC · TEA · ROW / MOOSE · READE / PRIED · BOWLS / ANNA · ONSET

123
ORDERS · ASTI / NARROW · BOAR / EQUATE · ABBA / SUN · ODE · ELI / EEK · REVERES / CLAM · NEGATE / SIS · NOS / THATOK · SASS / ROSEHIP · JAN / AOK · ONO · UVA / UPUP · SPIDER / MEND · KINGME / ARKS · INNEED

124
SCAMPI · ERMA / POPART · GOON / YOULOOKGOOD / EBON · MRS / PASSE · IBM / ASP · AFLAME / THATSBETTER / HEROIC · EMO / KEG · ASSES / PEP · NASA / ILLDOMYBEST / BLUE · PEEWEE / BAGS · STREAM

125
JAPAN · BIKES / ARENA · ITALY / WITCHDOCTOR / SASH · ASH / OWW · YMCA / CONVENT · AOL / OBEYS · ASIDE / BOA · TACKLES / BETS · MOI / LAB · TOME / MEDICINEMAN / EVADE · BANJO / NAMES · AMISS

126
RUSTS · ABBOT / ALLAH · PREGO / SNAKE · PEALE / PAPERPLATE / PEEKS / REDHAT · FOUR / OREOS · COUPE / NEAT · SURTAX / DWEEB / PLASTICCUP / FEATS · CHASE / ATSEA · LEVER / RETRY · EXERT

127
WITS · APPEAL / HAHA · TOOTLE / OMAR · DULCET / MATAHARI / SLAW · OWNS / INTERNS · HIP / OOHED · QUAKE / USA · COUNTED / SETS · PALS / HOTTOWEL / SALAMI · CHAI / IRONIC · KATE / BEGETS · STAN

128
AHA · GAB · ASK / COD · OLE · PTA / TWOANDA · NAY / NEAT · ERA / GABOR · SPARK / UNIT · GMA / MYTHREESONS / EEL · SAIL / ACURA · HOTLY / RAN · CHEF / SID · HALFMEN / ORE · EVE · AYE / NOR · DEN · YEW

129
INERT · YMCA / NEVER · PEARL / HEAVYHANDED / ADD · MET · APE / LEE · EAT · MER / EDDY · DOZES / ARENA / DAZED · PARS / TED · BOB · VEE / ANA · UFO · ACE / LIGHTFOOTED / OREOS · TRADE / NOSE · HIRED

130
PCS · MSG / AHA · ALL · POD / JOHNDOE · ANA / ARAB · BEACON / MURAL · LIFT / ASA · OKEEFFE / DAVINCI / PRETEND · CBS / LOST · SPORE / AMENDS · ECON / TAR · UPTREND / ANT · MAR · ACE / PRY · NOR

131
STEP · MASCOT / ORAL · ARCADE / LISA · NEATEN / DOTS · CAN / ETCH · SCAM / VARIOUS · ALA / ERECT · CANON / RIG · SPANDEX / BAGS · ARTY / HIS · ECHO / ASSESS · DAUB / NEEDLE · UNTO / TEASED · PETE

132
EYES · EDISON / ROVE · DANUBE / IDEA · INFLOW / CARROTCAKE / COHEN / IDAHO · STAKE / FEW · REV / SWEAT · SCENE / RISKY / PUMPKINPIE / DENOTE · IOWA / ESCROW · CLOT / LOSSES · SONS

Solutions

133

```
HAHA  CASINO
OMAR  ABATED
LENT  REUSED
ENDSWELL
  SIRE  THEA
ATHEART  ELS
SHARP  ROAMS
AOK  STANDON
PRES  ACES
  WORKSHOP
EATING  TADA
GLANCE  AKIN
GADGET  RENT
```

134

```
BISON  LAVER
ONCUE  IRENE
THATSAFIRST
TAR  TNT  SUI
OLE  SOS  ERE
MESS  NURSES
  SKYPE
ESTEEM  VATS
LEO  NOS  SEW
IDS  YUM  LEE
JUSTASECOND
ACEIN  LAPSE
HEROS  TREYS
```

135

```
MINIS  HATCH
INANE  ATEAM
STRAW  REALM
SOCCERBALL
  ADIOS
TURN  BREEZE
ERA  LID
ANGELA  DIPS
  MAYBE
HOCKEYPUCK
MELEE  TALON
ORDER  ERNIE
DRESS  STALE
```

136

```
SPARS  SHORT
HASAT  HAVEN
ALICE  ARENT
MOTHERLAND
  EPEES
SMALLF  SLOW
LEX  YUM  AWE
CLEO  GASPED
  NIECE
  SISTERCITY
COSTA  ARNIE
TOTAL  MECCA
STORY  ETHER
```

137

```
DISCO  UNFIT
OTHER  ZORBA
WARNS  IFOLD
  LETON  ASEA
BIDS  UNIT
LAD  ADORERS
ONE  MID  DOO
GODDESS  FAD
  WEST  ALDA
HAHA  SOLAR
EXERT  DAKAR
LLAMA  OMEGA
PETER  ROSES
```

138

```
REBUS  DOPER
ALEPH  ERODE
SALSA  SETIN
CIG  MGS  ATE
ANI  SUE  TOW
LEAD  ERRORS
  NONSTOP
DOWSES  WAFT
INA  ASP  NEO
REF  TOE  CAN
GAFFE  SHARE
ELLEN  TAKER
SLEDS  SHEDS
```

139

```
  SIGMA  ABA
ADIEU  URN
CANADADRY
  ALIBI
HALS  OTERI
IGO  HADOVER
MISSAMERICA
OLEARYS  TOT
MERYL  PANE
  SEWER
NEWMEXICO
AAH  DECAF
PRO  SCENT
```

140

```
OAKS  KARATS
DREW  ITALIA
DINE  METALS
SAKE  KISSES
  ETHAN
YESSIR  KEA
ARE  PDA  INK
PRY  AMANDA
  OSING
IMPISH  EKES
MAITAI  MOLE
ORTEGA  INST
NETMEN  AGES
```

141

```
GOTOFF  CASA
ITALIA  ANON
ROBERTFROST
DOL  SEA  MOO
ELECT  SCION
REDO  ATHENS
  PEPSI
GREENE  RAMS
READD  SPLAT
ENG  OOH  UNO
WALTWHITMAN
OMEN  ORANGE
NEST  SEXIER
```

142

```
INCASE  MAAM
MARROW  IFSO
PSYCHO  SEWN
EDS  OKS  WET
LAOS  STABLE
SQUAT  ATALL
  RBI  ROD
ANGEL  SMART
MARRED  SPEW
EVA  SEA  PSI
NAPA  UNCLES
DJED  COGENT
SOSO  EXISTS
```

143

```
JAB  AGO  HAD
USA  LAB  ALI
SIR  PROGRAM
TART  REARS
ANYWAY  TYKE
  LOCK  ERAS
ACE  TAP  ENT
LOVE  SAGA
ACID  PLASMA
  ANITA  POOR
DISTURB  NOM
UNO  BOY  ERE
DEN  AVE  RED
```

144

```
MAJOR  RANUP
ALONE  ATONE
KAYOS  TERMS
ESC  ERA  MAT
IKE  TET  ADE
TABS  MANNER
  ROBOTIC
STONER  POOH
ART  ASP  UNO
LAH  GEL  SEN
IDEAL  ASIDE
VERGE  ZINGS
ASSES  ASSET
```

Solutions

145

```
. H E A T H . R E P .
. M A G G I E . E X A
N E W Y E A R S D A Y
C L A P S . . I S L E
A T I T . M I N U T E
A S I . I O W A N S .
. . M M X I I . . . .
. S N A P I N . S P A
S P A R S E . T H E M
C H U G . I R O N Y .
R E S O L U T I O N S
A R E . O F L A T E .
P E A . P O L L S .
```

146

```
S C A L P . B E A C H
P O L I O . E A G L E
E L L E R Y Q U E E N
C O Y . T A U . N A N
K R I S . W I N T R Y
L E N T . N E O . . .
E D G E S . T O R T S
. A M T . K E E L . .
C L A M O R . S A R I
A I R . T E A . D E N
S T E P H E N K I N G
E R N I E . N I E C E
D E T E R . A D D E R
```

147

```
S A J A K . S I M P S
E L A T E . A L E R T
D I C E Y . U S A I R
A S K . N O C A N D O
N O S . O N E . J E B
S N O U T S . J O S E
. N N E . P O E . .
C U B A . D A N G L E
O R R . D O L . R E X
A G O N I Z E . E S P
S E W I N . T H E T A
T O N K A . T E N E T
S N E E R . E W E R S
```

148

```
P I Z Z A . R A Z O R
I D E A S . O L I V E
N A R C S . L E P E W
O H O . U K E . P R O
N O T I M E . O U R .
. O K I N G . L S D
A L L E N . A R I E S
L E E . G U L A G .
B A R . F A T H O M
A N A . L O X . T R I
N I N J A . I M E A N
I N C A S . E A R L E
A G E N T . S I S S Y
```

149

```
A S H E S . A S I S
F L A M E . A N E R A
R O N I N . R A D O N
I O N . D A M . O N E
C P A . S N O . N O S
A S H E . T R U A N T
. M E L I S S A .
B R O K A W . A R T S
L O N . B A A . I R E
O N T . O R B . Z E N
O N A I R . B L O B S
M I N T S . R E N E E
S E A S . S O A K S
```

150

```
C A R E S . B E E F Y
A T O L L . I G L O O
L O O K I N G G O O D
A N T . C O D . I T E
I C E . E R E . S E L
S E R F . W A T E R S
. Y I E L D .
D O S I N G . S I T S
O R E . S I P . N O T
O W N . P A Y . T I E
F E E L I N G W E L L
U L C E R . M O R E L
S L A T E . Y E N T A
```

151

```
S C H W A B . R U B S
C L E E S E . E S A U
E A R T H M O V E R S
N I B . E E L . D R S
T R A P S . L O U I E
S E L L . S I P P E D
. E T H E R .
S U G A R Y . A P E S
A N O T E . S H A M E
L E A . S C H . T E N
S A L T S H A K E R S
A S I A . A V E N G E
S E E D . D E N T E D
```

152

```
B R I B E S . W I N
O B O I S T . L A D Y
S I N G T O . I R O N
. B E N I G N L Y
. S C R E E C H .
B L U E . S E T T E R
S A J A K . S L O M O
S M O K E R . U N I T
. F E A R N O T .
A T L A N T I C .
T H I S . S C H M O S
M O O T . O C E A N S
S U N . N I S S A N
```

153

```
I M S . A M P . W H O
G E T . C O L . R A M
O N A . E V A . I B E
R U N I T I N . T I L
. D I O N S . I T E
S K I I N G . N U T
A N N . E F G . G A T
V I G . O R A C L E
E G G . F R A M E .
T H U . A W N I N G S
I T A . T A G . T A T
M E R . A R E . E Y E
E D D . L D S . R E M
```

154

```
E L I N . S C A L E S
X E N A . T Y R A N T
C A S S I U S C L A Y
I S A A C . H A M M
T E N . Y A M . L E I
E D E N . F E M A L E
. I W I L L .
P A T T E R . K F C S
A L A . D E W . I R A
W K R P . I S L E Y
P A S S I O N P L A Y
A L A S K A . C U T E
W I L T E R . A P E S
```

155

```
M A S C . F R I E Z E
A S T O . R O L L E D
S H E L L E Y L O N G
S O V I E T S . P I E
E R I C A . S E T S
S E E . R A D I S H
. A N G E R .
R A I S E R . O C T
B A D D . M E T O O
A D O . W A I T O U T
M A R T I N S H O R T
B R E A S T . E L S E
I S S U E S . L E E R
```

156

```
S L A B S . S T A R
L I B E L . S T O I C
A M B L E . Q A N D A
M A R I E C U R I E
. E T H I C .
A S O F . I N H E R E
S E W . A C T . G A Y
H E L E N A . S O M E
. A N G S T .
M A R I O C U O M O
P E N N E . A D I E U
T O T E S . M I L E R
A W E D . P O S T S
```

Solutions

157

```
EVES . . DUSTS
PINT . MANTRA
IDEA . INDEED
CARBONCOPY .
. GLUTEN . . .
SKIER . DEMON
PEZ . . . ONO
ARENA . DANES
. . EDGING .
. GOLDENGOAL
WORSEN . ELMO
ENCORE . LIEN
BEANS . . SANE
```

158

```
TONE . MAKEIT
OPUS . ATONCE
TEMP . GORGED
ERE . PILE . .
MARCH . LACED
. OOO . SNAKE
POUT . . WREN
AUNTS . WAD .
CROON . ORGAN
. . NOOK . APE
OREGON . AMPS
BELIZE . PELT
SPINES . USES
```

159

```
THUMBS . DAD
VERILY . MILE
SENSOR . ASOF
. SCIENCES .
ARCS . ADO . .
VIRUS . GNAWS
ICANT . ETHEL
DENSE . SHORE
. . HAS . EYED
OPTIMISM . .
PAWN . NOODLE
ERIE . GROVER
NET . SENDER
```

160

```
TAGGED . CBS
EVERSO . GLUT
DENOTE . RATE
IRIS . SIESTA
USES . TYPED
MESA . MESSRS
. NORMA . .
SAVANT . NEAR
WRITE . ALTO
ACROSS . TUTU
MAIM . ABODES
IDLY . LAMEST
SEE . TRYSTS
```

161

```
BEERS . CODED
ADDUP . AWAKE
SIGMA . SEVEN
ITA . CPA . IOU
NOR . IRS . DUD
GRANNY . GATE
. LOGICAL .
SALT . NOBLES
ALA . ITS . AME
DUN . DOT . NBC
IMPEL . ULCER
SNORE . MOORE
TIERS . EGEST
```

162

```
CAN . ODE . . .
ALI . BEN . BBC
FATCITY . ALA
ESTA . RANDOM
. ALSO . ANN .
PANINI . WEDS
AMY . LTD . WII
DOLE . TENSES
. RIB . IROB .
TOOBIG . PESO
BUN . BENEATH
ASS . ERA . REM
. . TSP . SPY
```

163

```
STUDS . ANGST
ERNIE . FORTE
QUEENOFMEAN
USA . DNA . EGO
EST . STINKER
LEEK . ORE . .
. SNIP . SWAB .
. . TON . SCAM
MOBSTER . ALE
APE . IRA . CAR
KINGOFSWING
ENDON . PEACE
RESTS . YESES
```

164

```
GUPPY . IDOLS
ATARI . RADII
BACONPOWDER
SHOT . INN . .
. . EINS . BLT
FRISCO . SOSO
LETTUCEPRAY
IDES . CLINTS
TOM . PHIL . .
. . LEI . LAVA
TOMATOHONOR
AWAIT . RUNTO
NERDY . STEED
```

165

```
PERFUME . LIT
ELEANOR . ACE
RIMMING . PAX
. ITD . SENT
ORAL . ADULTS
OILY . YER . .
HOFFA . EVADE
. EMI . EXES
SEQUIN . YELP
CRUD . TAS .
ROE . TOBACCO
ADS . ONEYEAR
PET . NELSONS
```

166

```
BOOM . KUWAIT
ALIT . ORELSE
SILVERBELLS
IVE . LEA . SAT
SERBIAN . TMI
. RAN . WAIF
DENIS . PERCY
ELEM . SEA . .
MET . ATTRACT
INF . DOE . PIE
GOLDENRINGS
ORIOLE . NEAT
DEXTER . CARS
```

167

```
OSCAR . FROZE
RALPH . LAPEL
IHOPE . OPERA
GAS . TAP . NOP
IRE . TIP . YES
NAYS . DEPOSE
. OUR . DRU
STUPOR . ORSO
PAR . NEC . HIP
ICE . ADO . EMU
ROYAL . SLAPS
AMEND . MERLE
LASTS . OATES
```

168

```
TOGS . BEHAVE
IHOP . AVATAR
DIOR . SENECA
YODELING .
. FAINT . BED
ABODE . SCARE
CORE . ODIE
MOMMA . INFER
EKE . PLATO .
. LEONARDO
MONAMI . CYAN
INACAN . TONE
RAVENS . SUES
```

Solutions

169
```
B O L T S . . . D A M
U T A H A N . O O Z E
S O W E T O . C Z A R
T O Y S . S T E E L E
U L E E . . W A N E S
P E R V . W I N S A T
. . E V A N S . . . .
D A B N E Y . E R A S
A M U S T . . L O V E
R A R E S T . E D E N
E Z R A . S A V E R S
M O O S . E V E N S O
E N S . . E N T E R
```

170
```
N A B S . S O A K E D
O V U M . U M P I R E
V E R A . D E N T A L
A C T S . O N E .
. S H A K . A U T O
S O B E R U P . L A P
E B E R T . E R E C T
P O E . S T R E E T S
T E S H . H U B S .
. E Y E . E G G S
B U R E A U . C O R E
A T O L L S . C L A W
R E D S E A . A D D S
```

171
```
S W I P E D . P I G
T E R E S A . I O W A
S T E N C H . A L O T
. G O L D M I N E
I N O U R . E T C .
C A N I T . S H E D S
E D E N . E C R U
S A A B S . T W A I N
. C O T . H A R P S
C A R O U S E L .
A M O K . A R R I V E
M I S S . N E U T E R
E D S . E S S A Y S
```

172
```
F A K E . S A B R E
A G E D . P R E E N
B A N S . P A E L L A
R S T . A R I . M A C
I S U . C E N . O T T
C I C A D A . O N E S
. K I C K O U T .
B O Y D . N U R S E S
E N D . M E S . T N T
A T E . O S T . A G O
V I R G O S . O K R A
E M B E R . B E A T
R E Y E S . I S M S
```

173
```
D A V I D . W A V E D
O L I V E . A G I L E
R A R E R . L O R A X
M S G . B L T . G I T
S K I . Y A Z . I N E
. A N T . T E N N E R
. I N S I D E R .
F A S T E N . W E D
A W L . R O D . C I G
C H A . P S I . O V A
T I N G E . S T R E P
O L D E N . C A D R E
R E S E T . O U S T S
```

174
```
T O S S . B L O W U P
N E W T . L O U I S E
T R E Y . U N T R U E
. E L S E . W E A R
P A N E L S . I S L S
O L E . A B E T .
P L Y . S R I . S E A
. S H O E . I M P
P A R T . T I S S U E
O M A R . H O O T .
N O J O K E . R E D S
D R I V E R . T R I O
S E V E N S . A S P S
```

175
```
S A A B S . S E T I N
O C T E T . I V O R Y
A T O N E . L I L A C
P I Z Z A R O L L S .
. M I S T .
W O L F E D . W H A T
A W A R D . M I A T A
S E G A . B I N D E R
. Z O O S .
. M O Z Z A R E L L A
C A R L O . E M A I L
O L S E N . A M I T E
G E O D E . D A R E S
```

176
```
H A D . C U P . S P A
O N E . U S A . T A N
O K T O B E R F E S T
P L O W E D . O A T H
S E X E S . F E M U R
. S T A R . E R A
P O S . E S E . R E X
A N T . A H E M .
C A U L K . P A C K S
E D N A . A R A R A T
C I N C O D E M A Y O
A M E . H A S . V A N
R E D . O M S . E K E
```

177
```
S A G A . B U F F E R
P R O B . E N A B L E
O I L S . A D R I F T
T A F T . D O G .
. C A S E . O G R E
M E L I N D A . L A D
I V A N A . S M O K E
K I P . G E T E V E N
E L S E . L O N E .
. J A M . A S P S
I N H E R E . C L U E
S A U C E R . E A R N
T H E T A S . S P E D
```

178
```
P A S T . F A R O F F
E X P O . I B E R I A
C L A Y . D E T E R S
S E C O N D L Y .
. E T A L . P S S T
S C R A P E . E P E E
A H A . . I R E
M A C S . T U S C A N
S P E W . A N T E .
. E U P H O R I A
H E A R S E . G A S P
O L I V E R . I C E E
E L D E R S . E K E S
```

179
```
C O S . G A B .
A R T . A R E . S A T
S A R A L E E . T W O
U N I T . A R A R A T
A G N E W . L O R E
L E G . I S L A N D S
. C A L L I N G .
J O H N D O E . B B C
O P E N . N O R A H
W R E A T H . H E R A
L A S . R U S S E T S
S H E . A L A . Z O E
. P A Y . E N D
```

180
```
N A T U R E . S U D S
A M A Z O N . A S I A
D A R I N G . J E E P
A N T . A L B A .
L A S T . I R K I N G
. E A S E . D O O
F R E N C H T O A S T
G O D . E M T S .
H E Y Y O U . U R G E
. O F F S . O E R
J U R Y . F O S T E R
O R E O . I M P O S E
E N D S . N E A R E D
```

Solutions

181

```
E B B . P A D . . .
S E A . B R A . S K I
C A B A R E T . H A T
O N Y X . S E N O R A
R I C E S . . O P A L
T E A . A C C E P T S
. R A V I O L I . .
S U R R E A L . N B A
U N I T . A N G E L
A G A S S I . U C L A
V E G . M O R T A L S
E R E . O W E . R O K
. G A P . T W A
```

182

```
L I L . A B E
O N A . B O N . F A B
S T U . B A D C A L L
T O N E R S . I S L E
I N D Y . T A H O E
T E R R I F Y . I T D
. Y E S O R N O
M C C . T R O U N C E
Y A H O O . I S L A
G R U B . G O T H O T
O N T O P O F . O S E
D E E . E L F . O E R
. A D S . T R Y
```

183

```
C U T . A S P
A S I . G O O . F A T
R E G R O U P . I C Y
A S H E . R E S T U P
T U T T I . P A T E
S P A . S I N U S E S
. S A N T A N A
R E A L T O R . F A B
A L D A . C H I L L
D O R S A L . I D L E
A P U . F R E D D I E
R E M . R O Y . L E D
. O N E . E D S
```

184

```
A B H O R . H O P S
C O U P E . E M I T
M I N T J U L E P S
E L K . E S P N
. A C E . S U M O
M A E S T R O . N A W
A M U S E . N A D A L
P E R . D O T C O M S
S N O B . S H H
. Y A L E . V I C
M A N G O J U I C E
A L O E . O F T E N
N E W S . B O O S T
```

185

```
. S H O O . S H E E N
S T E I N . C A N D O
T A B L E F O R T W O
E R R . L O P . R A N
A V E . A R E . E R E
M E W I N G . T E D S
. B E E P S .
S P A M . T A P S O N
N A P . A S S . O L E
I N E . S T S . L I V
P A R T Y O F F I V E
E M C E E . O L D E R
D A U N T . R O S S
```

186

```
S W A M P . B A B A R
A R B O R . A M O L E
S I L V E R S P O O N
S T Y E . H A L T E D
. S L Y L Y .
G O B O O M . Y U P
O R A N G E C R U S H
B E G . T H E M E D
. C H I P S .
S A L A A M . P L E A
P U R P L E H E A R T
A D O R E . A C T I I
M I N I S . S T E N T
```

187

```
J A P A N . B A C K S
O R A T E . A G L O W
H A N E S . D E E R E
N B C . T W O . A B E
N I A . S A M . N U T
Y A K S . R E B U T S
. E A R . N I P
T A B L E S . T H A T
E R A . T E N . I R A
A M T . A X E . T O P
P A T T I . A C T U P
O D E O N . T H E S E
T A R T S . H I R E D
```

188

```
M E T . B U S
A N A . E T A . T I C
N A M E T A G . E D U
I M P S . H A M M E R
L E A P S . I P A D
A L F . A M S T E L S
. L O R E T T A
S P O K A N E . R I M
E U R O . P R I C E
T R I K E S . I Z O D
T E D . T H E P O N D
O R A . C O W . N I L
. H E E . A C E
```

189

```
C L A S S . K R A F T
H A D T O . L E M O N
A M M A N . E B E R T
D A I L Y B E A S T
. R E S E N T .
C H A R . N E E D E D
A O L . T E X . E V E
B E S T O F . S C A M
. A N I M A L .
V A N I T Y F A I R
R I D G E . B A R R E
O V A L S . A R E A S
M A M E T . D I D N T
```

190

```
N A S T Y . P A S T A
E X T R A . A S T O R
T E E U P . R H I N O
. P E P S I . L E D
G O P . E A S E L
A V I A R Y . A S K S
G E N T S . A R T I E
A R G O . O N S A L E
. S M A R T . N O M
J U T . B R A N D
A T O N E . C O I L S
M A N E T . I N N E R
S H E D S . D E G A S
```

191

```
A N G E R . S T E E L
V E R N E . H E L L O
A V E D A . A L V I N
T A G . D A M . I C E
A D O . I M S . S I R
R A R E L Y . A C T S
. Y A Y . H B O .
S W A T . K I S S M E
C O B . S O B . T A X
R O B . C I A . E R E
A L O H A . C O L O R
P E T E R . H E L O T
E N T R Y . I R O N S
```

192

```
W I D E . F R I D A Y
I T E M . D E N O T E
R O B B E R B A R O N
E N T E R . J A N S
. D R A M A .
A C T S . T O M A T O
B O O . P A W . L A W
C O P C A R . M I N E
. O N I C E .
E D A M . A D I E U
R U B B E R B A N D S
O N B A S E . L I N E
S K A T E D . S T A R
```

Solutions

193

```
A L E . R P M . . . .
V A L . A A A . T H U
A D E P T L Y . W E T
T I V O . M O D E L T
A D E L E . . E L L E
R A N . L O N G F O R
. T H E R E S T . . .
S C H E M E R . H B O
H A H A . O W N E R .
A M O R A L . H I Y A
N E U . P O L Y G O N
K O R . O W E . H U G
. . . P E T . T R E .
```

194

```
M T V . F B I . J A B
I R E . A Y N . A C E
S E E . R E D . C H E
O K R A . B I C K E R
. . R O Y A L . . . .
S E E T H E . A S I A
H E L L O . K I T T Y
E L S E . B E M U S E
. . S P I N E . . . .
T E A S E R . D A W N
R U M . A D D . F E Y
A R E . C I A . R E P
P O X . H E Y . O D D
```

195

```
C A M U S . C A C T I
A C O R N . O C E A N
B I B L E . H E L P S
I D I . A D E . L E I
N I L . K I N . M R S
S C E N E S . J E S T
. A B R A H A M . . .
L I L A . V E R B A L
A N A . P O L . R D A
R E B . O W L . A R S
E V A N S . C A N I T
D E M O S . A L E V E
O R A T E . T A S E D
```

196

```
R E N A L . P E P S I
A R E N A . A R R I D
Z I G G Y . R I O T S
Z E A L . R I C O . .
. T E X A S . F O G .
P A I R E D . P H O .
L I V . S I P . O N E
O D E . C E N S O R .
Y E N . H A N O I . .
. A W O L . U T A H .
L I N E R . A G I L E
I N C A S . S A V O R
P A Y N E . S T E E R
```

197

```
S O L . P O E . . . .
T H O . A L L . B A T
E D W A R D S . E D U
L E E S . S E N D I N
L A S S O . A R E A .
A R T . F U R I O U S
. B U F F A L O . . .
G R I S S O M . M A H
R O D E . P A S T A .
A D D S U P . B U R T
D D E . G L A C I E R
S Y R . L E I . T S E
. . Y A M . E T D . .
```

198

```
B I B . P O R . J F K
A M I L A T E . A R I
B A K E R S D O Z E N
E X E R T . O O Z E D
. . O N A S P I T . .
A R M I E S . S T I R
B E A . R P I . U M A
C A N E . I N A P E N
. L Y R I C A L . . .
A D M I T . T I E G S
T E A C H E R S P E T
M A N . A C E T O N E
S L Y . D O E . S E W
```

199

```
P R O P E R . N O D .
R E S E D A . P A N E
S P U R N S . U S E S
. . F A C E M A S K .
R O D E . A M P . . .
E X E C . L I K I N G
D E L T S . T I G E R
S N I P E R . N O R A
. I M O . P R O M . .
T O R T I L L A . . .
E P I C . L I T T E R
L A S H . E N C O R E
E L K . R E H E A T .
```

200

```
A L B U M . . B A H .
L A U N C H . O L E .
A T T I M E S . U M A
R E T . A L I . V A T
M R S . H E R O I N E
. . W O N . M E A D .
. J O A N O F A R C .
T O R N . F A R . . .
W E I G H T S . S I P
I C E . A R T . O N O
N O N . S O C I A L S
G O T . Y A N K E E .
E L S . R E S T S . .
```

201

```
E H S . H A D . T B A
L A W . U N O . A R T
B R I D G E T . P A C
O S P R E Y . R I C O
W H E Y . E B O O K S
. . . . F A U C E T .
. T I T F O R T A T .
J U N I O R . . . . .
O R T E G A . P U M P
S T A R . N A S S A U
E L K . L E N I E N T
P E E . B Y E . R I O
H S S . J E W . S A N
```

202

```
T O D A D . P A P A L
E L I D E . I T A L Y
D E N I M . N E W E R
. G O I N G . S E E .
G O D S . O P T . . .
A D O . K N O W S A .
S I N A I . N A I L S
. E G G N O G . N I P
. . E G O . I G G Y .
B I G . K O O L S . .
I D A H O . N I O B E
D O Z E N . C A N O E
S L A N G . E D G A R
```

203

```
M A P . A B C . A D S
O F A . L E O . V I E
W I L L I A M T E L L
E R I E . B A N A L .
D E N A D A . C U T E
. . V E R A . E E R .
. S T E V E J O B S .
M I A . O N A N . . .
E Z R A . A R L I S S
D E B T S . O N T O .
I S A A C N E W T O N
C U B . A B E . O R G
S P Y . M A L . W E S
```

204

```
L I F E . P I N U P
O K R A . I S O N E
B E E R . T E A R U P
. E N G R . A T M .
H U T . L A R C H .
A S H . A V A . C A T
H E R . R E V . A N Y
A D O . E L I . R E P
. W A S I N . O W E .
. E L K . N E I L . .
S K I I N G . V I A L
C E N S E . A N T I
I D E S T . N A A N
```

Solutions

205

```
HOSED ERASE
ANKLE MARES
STUMP INCAS
PAL OWL ALA
SPLASHY DAY
   RIO TINS
WHATSWHAT
CRAB WOO
HES THRUSTS
ASH AOK CAP
STOOP SCARE
ELUDE UPBOW
DETER PASTS
```

206

```
CABS DEFUSE
OBIT ERASER
PETE LOCATE
STOP USE
 HOAX TRIP
SPOUSES ICE
TENTH TACOS
ARE ELEMENT
BUYS EMMA
  HIS ORAL
APRONS NOTE
GHETTO INON
ODDSON AIMS
```

207

```
SENTUP THUD
EVENSO WISE
MAITAI OPEN
INNS NFS
   TOTAL
ACES ARENAS
HUNTANDPECK
ABOARD SWAY
 ASPIC
  LDL POEM
JIBE ICEAXE
OVER CHAFES
EYES KITSCH
```

208

```
HAS ARE
OTT POX BRO
WROTEUP RAP
LIPO NOJOKE
SAPPED AKIN
 ESTA WENT
ADD CNN NGO
RICK DEAR
MALE RESENT
ALONZO ICEE
DEC OURTOWN
ARK ONE RED
  TDS DRS
```

209

```
FILAS TUSKS
ERASE AFOOT
MOTHERGOOSE
UNI NET THE
RIN ACE HER
SCAR LAKERS
  PRIMO
BUSMAN SAFE
ENT DIG COX
AMA INN ARE
TAKEAGANDER
IDEAL WAIST
TESTS SWATS
```

210

```
JONI BERTHA
ABET LAYOUT
IOWA AVENGE
LES ACES
 WORKS ARM
SCORCH BLUE
COMESACROSS
ONES WHINES
TEN SKATE
  KIDD TAT
ALBINO WITH
SEESAW EMMA
SETSIN BEST
```

211

```
MISSM METAL
UNITE ELOPE
FORES RAISE
FREESAMPLE
  LISAS
EBAY SIESTA
LOL BID KEG
SPACES CIAO
  RETRO
REALSIMPLE
MULTI SPEAK
OLSEN EERIE
DEERE SLURS
```

212

```
MIT BAD
ORR ALE BBC
POI BIPOLAR
ENEMY PLATO
DIDA ECHO
SCALENE KEN
 NIGERIA
RID GARDNER
ARTS EDNA
CARPS HABIT
EQUALTO LGE
DIE AAA UMD
  POX EAR
```

213

```
FTS SUB GPA
YAK ASA REC
IRISMURDOCH
  KOA RAKE
LILYALLEN
ADO SEA
PILAF SMEAR
 MBA ART
 DAISYDUKE
PREZ PAO
ROSEKENNEDY
OAK INK YOU
MRS ASS ESP
```

214

```
RIB OLD MOM
ELO KID AHA
FORLOVE YIN
 SNAKE XBOX
STYX SOLE
AYE FASTED
NOS WOK ORE
GUTTER MAC
 EAST SOSO
MARX OPERA
AID ADVERBS
ADA BAT OLE
MAY SYS WET
```

215

```
TASES HABIT
AGILE IRISH
JOLIE GETTY
 EARTHS
HANS ATODDS
OUT ASI ERE
ODE FTD TIX
FIR TIE EVE
STAMEN ARES
 URGING
OPERA SNEAD
LOYAL LENIN
DWELL EXTRA
```

216

```
AMP AHS
CAR LEO TMS
ONESELF HIP
RUTH MAKEME
NATES ALIA
SLY HATRACK
 ICECOLD
PENALTY YEW
UMPS SHINE
RAISES INCA
SIN GUMDROP
ELK ARE ERO
  DEX DEN
```

Solutions

217

```
E B B . L E D . .
M A R . S P A . P A M
I N E E D I T . U N I
N A A N . C A R T O N
E N D O W . O T T O
M A P . E A R L I E R
. U M P T E E N .
U N D A T E D . G P S
N O D S . S A T A N
H O I S T S . D O J O
I N N . W I N E B A R
P E G . I D A . E M T
. N E W . D A S
```

218

```
A C R E S . C O L A S
C H I L E . S H E B A
E A G L E . A W F U L
. H I N T . E T T E
C A T S . W O L F .
H U H . S I R L O I N
E R A . A S S . O D E
R A N O N T O . T E E
. D U K E . E G A D
D E B T . R O A R .
A T L A W . A R E N A
R O U G E . F L E E S
K N E E S . S Y N T H
```

219

```
T E X T S . J C R E W
A A R O N . L A U R A
D R A N O . O T T E R
. Y E W S . C H I P
P A S S . A S H .
U M P . U P T O P A R
M E E T S . A N I M A
A N X I E T Y . X Y Z
. E D U . N Y S E
S Y N C . B I A S .
W O U L D . V I T A L
A U D I O . E V I T A
P R E P S . S E X E S
```

220

```
S C U M . I M S U R E
N A P A . N E U T E R
U M P S . S L E E V E
G E E K . I S M .
. R E A D . E G G S
F I D D L E S . R A P
I K E . A T T . A P U
R E C . S H A T N E R
M A K E . E Y E D .
. V I P . A S K S
A R M A D A . S L A T
L O A D E R . E A T A
S T R E A K . S M O G
```

221

```
J A I M E . E B A Y
A S P E N S . B I L E
W H O S T H E B O S S
. A R A B .
N E W S Y . O D O R
A T E . I N A R O W
W H A T S M Y N A M E
S E R I E S . L E S
. L Y N N . R O B O T
. S P A R .
W H E R E S W A L D O
E U R O . S E T O U T
S T A Y . R E A D S
```

222

```
H O R A . S K A T E
A R U T . C E D A R
N A M E . B A N A N A
G L O S S A R Y .
. R O T C . A G E D
J A M . O K S . R U E
A L I . O F T . A R E
D E L . P E R . P O P
A X L E . N O S E .
. A R C H I V E S
B M O V I E . T I D E
O O H E D . U N I T
G O O S E . P E T S
```

223

```
C I D E R . R E B U S
A D U L T . E R U P T
N E C K S . S I C K O
Y A K S . B E C K E R
O L D . P E T . B E E
U S U R E R . P U P S
. C E R A M I C .
I C K Y . T A C K L E
N O G . B E D . M A X
L O O T E D . F O R T
A L O H A . C L O S E
W I S E R . B I S O N
S T E M S . S P E N D
```

224

```
C L A Y S . D E F E R
N O R A H . A L L A Y
N A C H O C H E E S E
. O O H . C A T S
A L T O . A P T .
N E O . S T A R T I T
T A R T A R S A U C E
I F O R G O T . B O X
. U S O . P A N T
S K I S . M A A .
E A R T H S C R U S T
A L A M O . U T T E R
R E N E W . P I Z Z A
```

225

```
B A S I C . E L I A S
A M I S H . N O R M A
G E T T I N G G O O D
E L S . N E A . N U I
L I I . A F R . I N E
S A N D . E D I C T
. E R R E D .
. D U V E T . S H A G
R E P . M I D . O V A
A B S . A T E . B I N
B R E A K I N G B A D
B I L G E . S U I T E
I S L E S . E N T E R
```

226

```
. M I S C . A L F A
P I N T O . C A R L
O N E A R M . S N A G
E N E . D O B . D N A
M O D . O N A . A C E
. W A S N T T R U E
. A B B O T .
. D R O L L N E S S
L E O . E A R . H A D
A L L . U N O . A L A
M U L E . C U R S O R
A X E D . G O T O N
R E D S . E W A N .
```

227

```
S O F A R . S M A R T
E X I L E . E R R O R
T O N E D . A S I D E
. E X I T . C A S K
F E W . D I L L .
A X I S . L O A N E R
D A N C E . S U E D E
E M E R G E . S A G E
. A G E S . R E D
T O M B . K N O B .
A R A B S . A R E A S
P A U L A . R E E V E
E L L E N . L O R A X
```

228

```
U T O P I A . C A T
P A N I C S . H O H O
S T A G E S . O M A N
. O D E . G O B Y
M E N U . S A T .
E X I T . S P H E R E
G E N O A . T E N O R
S C E N I C . C I A O
. F R O . O D D S
T A C O . M T V .
O U Z O . P R E P A Y
B R A D . E U R O P E
E A R . L E S S E N
```

Solutions

229

J	I	L	L	S		S	I	N	G	S
A	V	I	A	N		I	N	A	L	L
M	O	M	M	A		E	S	S	A	Y
B	R	E	A	K	B	R	E	A	D	
		Z	E	B	R	A				
B	A	B	E		C	A	M	E	B	Y
I	D	O					R	O	E	
G	O	B	U	S	T		B	R	A	N
		S	H	E	B	A				
	B	R	O	A	D	B	R	U	S	H
H	O	O	P	S		A	L	P	H	A
U	N	M	E	T		L	E	T	I	N
H	Y	E	N	A		L	Y	O	N	S

230

I	C	E		O	A	T		T	O	P
N	A	P		F	O	R	S	A	L	E
F	L	E	A	F	L	I	C	K	E	R
O	M	E	N		P	O	E			
		N	O	R		T	R	E	Y	
	I	N	A	C	A	B		O	N	E
F	L	A	S	H	F	L	O	O	D	S
B	L	T		S	T	U	N	T	S	
I	S	I	T		S	E	T			
		V	I	A		A	S	H	E	
F	L	I	P	F	L	O	P	P	E	D
R	E	T	I	R	E	D		O	R	G
Y	A	Y		O	W	E		T	O	Y

231

M	C	A	N		H	I	T	S	A	T
O	H	N	O		A	R	O	U	S	E
J	A	N	I	S	J	O	P	L	I	N
O	R	A	T	E		N	O	U	N	S
			I	A	N	S				
P	R	E	S	T	O		M	A	L	I
J	E	A	N	S	J	A	C	K	E	T
S	O	R	T		O	R	G	A	N	S
			E	B	R	O				
A	R	S	O	N		O	V	O	I	D
J	U	N	K	J	E	W	E	L	R	Y
A	N	A	L	O	G		R	A	I	N
R	E	P	A	Y	S		N	Y	S	E

232

B	L	U	E	S		C	I	V	I	L
E	A	G	L	E		A	R	E	N	A
T	R	A	I	N	T	R	A	C	K	S
T	E	N		O	I	L		T	I	S
O	D	D		R	T	S		O	N	E
R	O	A	M		F	J	O	R	D	S
		S	W	O	R	E				
B	A	N	N	E	R		R	A	N	D
I	R	E		A	T	E		P	E	R
R	A	W		T	A	Z		A	C	E
T	R	A	S	H	T	R	U	C	K	S
H	A	G	U	E		A	S	H	E	S
S	T	E	E	R		S	E	E	D	Y

233

S	C	A	N	S		R	A	C	E	S
T	A	R	O	T		E	N	A	C	T
E	M	E	R	A	L	D	I	S	L	E
V	A	N		B	I	B		T	A	R
E	R	A		S	V	U		L	I	N
N	O	S	E		E	L	D	E	R	S
		W	O	R	L	D				
G	R	E	W	U	P		E	A	T	S
R	E	M		T	O	T		L	A	P
A	P	E		W	O	W		A	L	E
C	E	R	E	A	L	A	I	S	L	E
E	A	G	E	R		I	R	K	E	D
S	T	E	E	D		N	E	A	R	S

234

S	E	T		G	A	P				
A	S	H		P	R	O		P	C	S
I	C	E	P	A	C	K		R	A	T
L	A	M	E		H	E	L	E	N	A
O	P	A	R	T		A	T	O	N	
R	E	G		H	A	U	N	T	E	D
		I	C	E	T	R	A	Y		
I	N	C	O	M	E	S		P	S	I
D	O	W	N		A	P	L	U	S	
A	T	O	N	C	E		H	E	L	L
H	E	R		R	A	W	D	A	T	A
O	D	D		U	S	A		S	A	N
			D	E	Y		E	N	D	

235

G	E	L	D		S	T	J	O	H	N
L	A	I	R		U	R	A	N	I	A
I	S	L	E		N	I	N	E	T	Y
B	E	T	A		S	O	I			
		M	E	H		S	L	O	P	
A	U	S	T	R	I	A		E	A	U
M	R	M	O	O	N	L	I	G	H	T
A	G	O		S	E	T	S	O	U	T
P	E	G	S		S	O	S			
		A	P	T		U	S	E	S	
A	R	A	B	I	A		I	T	L	L
S	U	B	L	E	T		N	A	S	A
S	E	C	E	D	E		G	R	E	W

236

T	E	N		E	D	S		L	O	L
O	L	E		T	U	T		E	L	I
A	N	I		E	K	E		W	I	N
M	I	L		R	E	A		I	V	E
A	N	A		N	E	D		S	E	N
N	O	R	M	A	L		M	A	R	S
		M	I	L	L	I	O	N		
M	E	S	A		I	D	I	D	S	O
A	L	T		R	N	S		C	E	L
D	A	R		A	G	A		L	A	S
R	I	O		S	T	Y		A	L	E
I	N	N		T	O	S		R	I	N
D	E	G		A	N	O		K	T	S

237

A	C	R	E	S		I	N	D	I	A
S	H	E	E	N		N	O	U	N	S
T	O	U	R	I	S	T	T	R	A	P
R	I	B		D	U	E		E	W	E
A	C	E		E	G	G		S	A	N
Y	E	N	S		A	R	T	S	Y	
			O	P	R	A	H			
	P	E	N	A	L		Y	E	A	H
R	A	M		R	O	M		F	R	O
O	R	E		A	A	A		F	O	R
W	O	R	L	D	F	A	M	O	U	S
A	L	G	A	E		M	O	R	S	E
N	E	E	D	S		S	I	T	E	S

238

P	I	P		H	E	S				
O	N	E		E	V	E		B	O	O
E	S	T	O	N	I	A		R	O	W
		E	A	R	L		S	I	Z	E
J	E	R	R	Y		J	A	D	E	D
E	L	S		C	H	A	N	G		
T	I	E		L	I	N		E	R	A
		L	E	A	S	E		T	I	P
S	U	L	L	Y		B	I	J	O	U
I	T	E	M		C	A	M	O		
P	A	R		B	O	N	A	N	Z	A
S	H	S		A	R	K		E	O	N
			Y	E	S		S	O	Y	

239

N	I	L		C	O	M		I	A	M
E	G	O		U	N	A		T	R	U
P	U	T		P	E	R		C	T	S
H	A	T		P	I	T		O	U	I
E	N	E		A	N	I		U	R	N
W	A	R	S		A	N	A	L	O	G
		Y	O	U	M	I	N	D		
W	A	T	U	S	I		T	H	U	G
O	B	I		S	L	R		A	P	E
R	O	C		O	L	E		P	T	A
D	A	K		H	I	M		P	A	R
E	R	E		I	O	U		E	K	E
D	D	T		O	N	S		N	E	D

240

A	D	D	E	R		O	B	I	T	
L	E	A	S	E		N	O	N	O	S
B	A	K	E	D	A	L	A	S	K	A
U	F	O		O	N	E		P	E	G
M	E	T		S	T	A		A	N	A
S	N	A	G		I	V	A	N	S	
			A	S	P	E	N			
	A	T	S	E	A		T	O	P	S
D	E	W		A	S	H		L	A	C
O	R	O		S	T	U		I	T	O
H	A	W	A	I	I	F	I	V	E	O
S	T	A	I	D		F	L	I	N	T
	E	Y	R	E		S	L	A	T	S

Solutions

241

```
TAB FAD
ARI USE CAL
MALARIA RDA
ARLO ANDYET
LAYLA ISLE
ETC BLISTER
REBECCA
PAYRATE LOB
ALSO DUBYA
GETSIN VAST
EVA LOYALTO
DEL LOA LEN
SKY SRS
```

242

```
SOB POP BOT
PRO DIA ARE
AIRBALL CIA
CONE SMOKES
ELIAS VINE
KEN TALENTS
TWOPART
LSHAPED HER
ACED SCENE
ROUSES BUTS
DRS CLASSIC
SEA HAY STU
OWE RYE
```

243

```
YARDS RANUP
EBOOK OPERA
WILLIAMPENN
STOP SAL
HEINEKEN
RESIST ENO
EVENT TRAIL
DIN AMANDA
OLDHABIT
ASA TALE
TRUTHTELLER
LEVEE LETGO
CLASS FROGS
```

244

```
YEAST APES
ACTOR CORE
WHOLEWHEAT
NOP BEETS
SLED UNO
LOCKED BROW
ASHES GEESE
SLOW LOSSES
TOO KITS
CHINA PIN
WHITEWHALE
SORT AUDIT
JOEY YESES
```

245

```
ORCA SCALE
SOOT AARON
LOBE ASSESS
OKRA SHH
ASAP EBBS
PANERA WOOL
OLD FRO ADO
USER ANDREW
RODE GOOD
TAU OWNS
TYSONS FAIL
DEPOT ULNA
SNAKE SKEW
```

246

```
SCAMP SPATS
COCOA HASUP
ALERT IRONY
BARNEYFIFE
NETS
DEPOTS IRAN
OVENS CAIRO
HERB GENDER
USER
KETTLEDRUM
MALTA ARENA
ARMOR LINTS
CLONE SPOOK
```

247

```
MAP AWE SKI
TREASON PIN
VERMONT ODD
INTO ODE
HORDE MRFOX
MUD EBB
MISSISSIPPI
OKS REC
CLOWN ALONE
RON OMNI
INK WYOMING
SEE ITSABOY
PRY THE MMM
```

248

```
SLUM DABBED
PASA ERRATA
EVER ARARAT
CARYGRANT
LILY EPA
ALBANY GREW
NOUNS GEESE
KIDD CONDOS
AND CONE
HARPERLEE
WAITUP AURA
INSIDE LAIR
NATTER SUES
```

249

```
RIGA VEGAN
ODES ECONO
WORKAROUND
SLEEPING
REF EMAJ
PRISSY DATA
AIM LIZ
STAB SPRITZ
SEMI PEA
GREENTEA
PLAYAROUND
TAMER UNDO
ABYSS TESS
```

250

```
MADAM PAPAS
ASIDE ULTRA
THESTAMPACT
SET RUMS
TIRE THY
LOCALAREA
ALAN RINK
SIMIAMIGO
PEP LENO
BLAM KEA
FLORIDACITY
EERIE TASTE
WIRES ELSES
```

251

```
MASC RELAY
ECHO MODELO
ATOM ONEMAN
LIVE WINO
EATIN NOT
MOLTEN ADO
AMI EGG DON
KEN LONERS
ENG GATES
SHOW STAG
ATNOON SAGE
NOOSES INON
DEWEY EDGE
```

252

```
DADS MECCA
ILEUM TROOP
VIVIANVANCE
ITRY GOD
VICEVERSA
IDE TOE
AISLE EXPEL
OMM RAY
VOICEVOTE
IDE CLOT
VIRALVIDEOS
AMBLE SKILL
NESTS ANDY
```

Solutions

253
```
C A I R O   █ G H A N A
A L D E R   █ O U T E R
H A L F A N D H A L F
N N E █ L O S █ D L S
    █ A B L E D █
I R I S █ A N E M I A
N E C K A N D N E C K
A C H I E R █ I D E A
    █ T R Y A S █
L I Z █ I A N █ A F T
O V E R A N D O V E R
C A R O L █ E R O D E
K N O W S █ S E N S E
```

254
```
S O F A R █ B L E S S
P L U T O █ Y E M E N
I D L E S █ C A P R I
D A L █ E R O █ T I P
E G O █ S A L █ Y A P
R E F S █ C O M P L Y
    █ H O V E R E R █
T A I L E D █ G O D S
A R M █ S T Y █ M E N
B A S █ P O E █ I C E
O B E S E █ A T S E A
O I L E R █ S H E I K
S A F E S █ T E S T Y
```

255
```
B Y E █ S I T █ P E A
B O T █ P G A █ E G G
C U C K O O K A Z O O
    █ O T T E R █
B A M B O O I G L O O
A L I E N █ T H O R N
R E X █     █ P O E
A X I A L █ S P E N T
K A N G A R O O Z O O
    █ R H I N E █
Y A H O O T A T T O O
E W E █ O A R █ O U R
S E X █ D S S █ P I G
```

256
```
A L A S █ D E C A F S
F O N T █ A M O R A L
E D G E █ N I N E T Y
W E E P █ I T D █
    █ L O S E █ O D E S
B U F F A L O █ E D U
U N I F Y █ M A V E N
S T S █ S P I T I N G
H O H O █ I T L L
    █ N A G █ A R M S
B E F A L L █ N A I L
B R U I S E █ T Y R A
C A R R O T █ A S A P
```

257
```
S O F A R █ L O W E R
A L I C E █ A D E L E
F I N E S █ C E D A R
E V A █ T S O █ D I E
S I N █ S T S █ I N A
T A C O █ A T O N E D
    █ I C E B E R G █
T H A T L L █ A S K S
H A L █ A E R █ H O T
E B B █ P R E █ O R E
L E A R S █ F E W E R
M A T T E █ I M E A N
A S H E S █ T U R N S
```

258
```
G A G █ S A M █
O R O █ E R A █ B A R
D I R E C T S █ E R E
I S I T █ S H A L O M
V E G A S █ S E M I
A S H █ H A L I F A X
    █ T R I D E N T █
T R A I N E E █ B B C
H O H O █ S T E A L
I G E T I T █ O H I O
N E A █ T H E P I T S
E N D █ E R G █ N E E
    █ M U G █ D D S
```

259
```
A B E T S █ B E E C H
P Y L O N █ A G R E E
P L A Y I N G G O L F
L I T █ P I G █ T I N
E N E █ I C Y █ I N E
S E D O N A █ A C E R
    █ O G R E S █
G R I P █ A N I M A L
R E B █ U G G █ A M O
A T E █ N U I █ N E A
P E R S I A N G U L F
E L I O T █ E E R I E
S L A V E █ S T E E R
```

260
```
T I F F S █ E B B E D
A T A R I █ A R R A Y
B A C O N G R E A S E
    █ E G G O █ A G E D
B I B █ S T A T █
E R O S █ A T H E N S
L O O P S █ M E D I A
A N K A R A █ S I L K
    █ R I N G █ F E E
E L B E █ D A L I
T U R K E Y B A C O N
A L I E N █ O T E R I
L L O Y D █ R E S E T
```

261
```
B R O O D █ M I C R O
R E V U E █ E N R O N
E T E R N A L C I T Y
E A R █ C S I █ M A X
D I D █ H T S █ E R E
S L O P █ E S S A Y S
    █ S A R A H █
C A S I N O █ E T C H
A T A █ C I A █ O R O
R O D █ I D S █ Y A M
E N D L E S S L O V E
S A L O N █ E A T E R
S L E P T █ S W A N S
```

262
```
M A J █ D M V █
E M U █ D U I █ A A A
S O N N E T S █ U S S
H U E Y █ T A N G O S
E N A C T █ A U N T
S T U █ A M A S S E S
    █ A C R O B A T █
R E L E A S E █ A S K
O M A N █ L E M O N
B I S T R O █ R A C E
E L K █ A M E R I C A
S E A █ G A Y █ N E D
    █ E R E █ E R S
```

263
```
B O L T S █ B A L E D
O M A H A █ E R O D E
R A M E N █ A I K E N
G R A V Y T R A I N
    █ O O O H █
D A L I █ P U M P E D
A L E C K █ G A R B O
M A D E I T █ G O B S
    █ T O A N █
S A U C E B O A T S
M A R C H █ O L D I E
A G I L E █ V I O L A
S E D A N █ E A S E L
```

264
```
C O P S E █ F O L I O
T R A N Q █ I R O N S
R E D A U E R B A C H
    █ P I L E █ M A A
S P Y █ P S S T █
A R E A █ E U R O P E
Y E L L O W P A G E S
S P L A S H █ P L O T
    █ N M E X █ E N D
A A H █ O R E M █
G R E E N E N E R G Y
O I L E D █ O N E A D
G A L L S █ N U M B S
```

Solutions

265

```
O M A H A █ L O O P S
F A V O R █ E E R I E
F R E N C H F R I E S
S I R █ H A T █ O C T
E N T █ I N S █ L E E
T O S S E D █ B E S T
█ █ E S S A Y █ █
S L A W █ D I S P E L
T A N █ R O M █ A L E
A U G █ E W S █ R I A
F R O Z E N F O O D S
F E R A L █ O W L E T
S L A P S █ R E E D S
```

266

```
N O R A H █ I R A N █
A P O L O █ O A H U █
P A U L N E W M A N █
A L T █ G R A B █ █
█ S K I █ O L A F █
M R S P O C K █ A B U
R O M A N █ N A M E S
E D U █ G R U M B L E
D E G S █ I C Y █ █
█ P A C K █ A L A █
█ G A R Y O L D M A N
█ I S E E █ E R E C T
█ S H E S █ S E X E S
```

267

```
L A R K S █ F A C T S
I Q U I T █ L A U R A
F U N N Y █ O H B O Y
T A S █ L A Y █ A D S
█ H A I R D O █ █
A R O U S E █ T W I N
N O R T H █ S T A K E
D O T O █ P E E L E D
█ █ S T M A R K █ █
B R O █ A S S █ T A G
R E L A X █ I R A T E
A D D L E █ C O L O N
D O S E S █ K E L P S
```

268

```
P E S O █ C A L L O N
I V A N █ E L A I N E
C A F E █ N O T N O W
A N T I █ T E E █ █
█ E L L E █ S T A S
T A Y L O R █ T A R P
A S P █ U F O █ C I A
S T I R █ I M O K A Y
K O N A █ E A R L █
█ T E L █ N E T S
A G E O L D █ A B I T
P E R U S E █ T O N E
T E E T E R █ E X A M
```

269

```
G A I L Y █ F L A S H
A T S E A █ L E V E E
G O O D B Y E G I R L
G N P █ B O X █ A I L
L E O █ A M I █ T A O
E D D Y █ K N E E L S
█ █ A M I G O █ █
C L A M U P █ S I T S
R E V █ S P A █ C O P
A T E █ T U T █ E W E
W O N D E R W O M A N
L U G E R █ A W A R D
S T E W S █ R E N D S
```

270

```
D A N E █ A L I C E
O P E N █ N O N O S
G R E E K G I F T S
M O D █ A L S O █
A N Y O N E █ R A C E
█ U S E S █ R U E
I N D I A █ H O T E L
D A Y █ S W I T █
O W E D █ A N T L E R
█ A C R E █ A R E
R O M A N R U I N S
A R O S E █ S N I T
T O N E D █ S E E S
```

271

```
A C R E S █ I N L E T
B L U S H █ N I O B E
B O S T O N G L O B E
O T T █ O E R █ K I N
T H E █ T W A █ I N S
T E D S █ S T I N G Y
█ █ U R G E D █ █
S I P P E R █ S U N S
E G O █ S O D █ R I M
N U S █ T U E █ A N I
D A I L Y P L A N E T
U N T I L █ T R I T E
P A S T E █ S T A Y S
```

272

```
S A Y T O █ E G Y P T
A L O H A █ P R O S E
L A U E R █ C A U S E
T I R E █ R O B B █
█ E G R E T █ L A W
S T A G E D █ E C O
W A D █ C B S █ W H O
A R M █ L O O M E D
P A Y █ F U N N Y █
█ M O L E █ E M I T
C A I R O █ A M I G O
A G N E S █ T A N G Y
D O D O S █ A N D Y S
```

273

```
A P T █ C A B █
P O R █ A L A █ G A S
P L A I N L Y █ A T E
L I S T S █ S P R E E
E C H O █ █ E B A Y
S E T █ D I O R A M A
█ A R E A R U G █
L A L A N N E █ E Y E
O A K S █ █ I M A X
T R I P S █ S T O M P
T O N █ C O N S U M E
A N G █ A D O █ T E L
█ M E W █ H R S
```

274

```
A P P S █ M E G A N
P A R T █ A N N I E
P R I S O N Y A R D
L I N █ S T A T █
E S C A P E █ S P R Y
█ E A R L S █ R U E
B A T H E █ A R A B S
E C O █ Y E M E N █
D E N S █ N I C K E D
█ A L T A █ S L O
W A T E R M E T E R
A L O N E █ P E C K
R I N S E █ A R T Y
```

275

```
O R C S █ H E A V E D
G O U T █ A P P E A R
R U B Y █ W I N T R Y
E T A L █ A C E █
█ L E V I █ A F E W
C S I █ A I D █ I D O
R U B █ T A O █ J E N
E R R █ S N L █ I N K
D E E M █ P L O W █
█ E M U █ B A R S
F A L C O N █ A T O P
I P E C A C █ M E S A
B R E A T H █ A R E S
```

276

```
T R Y S T █ A L A R M
S A U N A █ M A N I A
O S K A R █ O U T D O
█ O K A Y E D █
L A N E █ O B E Y S
E G G S █ K A R A T E
G R O █ S O S █ K E N
G E L A T O █ I B I D
█ E D W I N █ G U N S
█ A N O I N T █
S H A R K █ N I T R O
H O N D A █ S T E A K
Y E A S T █ T E R M S
```

Solutions

277

```
P A S T E | N O R T H
A T L A S | A W A R E
M O U N T A I N M E N
E N D | E R R | A B C
L E G | E G O | P E E
A S E C | E B O O K |
| A R N I E |
| C A B O T | R U B S
S A T | T I S | T A C
O P T | A N T | O R E
F O U N T A I N P E N
A N N I E | N O I S E
R E E L S | G N A T S
```

278

```
O F F | L I B | W E B
O U R | A V O C A D O
P R E T T Y P E N N Y
S L E E T | D E A D
| C A E S A R |
M A E | A R I S T A
A P L U M N I C K E L
Y E L P E D | I D S
| S T Y L E D |
C A K E | U N D I D
O N E T H I N D I M E
P O P S O N G | N I P
A N T | E N E | G N P
```

279

```
P A R T S | T I R E S
A W A I T | A R E N T
R H I N O P L A S T Y
K I D | P A L | T I L
A L E | S T Y | E R E
S E R F | R H O D E |
| A E I O U |
| C A N D O | T A R P
P H D | I T S | V A L
S A O | T I T | A V A
H I P P O C R A T I C
A S T O R | I N A N E
W E S T S | P A R E S
```

280

```
A T T I C | S C R A M
L E A S H | Q U O T E
P R I M E N U M B E R
I M P | S E A | B A G
N E E | T A R | E S E
E D I T | R E A R E D
| W E L S H |
B O T A N Y | A S P S
E N E | T A B | P A T
E T H | I L L | O R O
F I R S T L E T T E R
E M A I L | N O O N E
D E N S E | D E N T S
```

281

```
F A C T | I N T R O
A Q U A | G A B O R
T U R P E N T I N E
S I D E D O O R
| S I R | D O P E
S A L U T E D | D O A
I H O P E | I R O N S
L O W | D I V E R G E
L Y E S | M E A
| C U B I C L E S
S E R P E N T I N E
A N I T A | O M I T
D E P O T | R E D S
```

282

```
A P P L E | S L E P T
L O R A X | T O W E R
P R I D E | E V E R Y
S E C | R A R E |
| E L T O N | P H O
L A C Y | K U D R O W
A D U L T | M A I N E
V O T E R S | T M E N
A S S | A L G A E |
| H I Y A | C U E
D O N O T | M O U N D
A L A M O | M A T T E
D E T E R | A R S O N
```

283

```
A R E N A | C A R D S
T O N E R | O P E R A
B O S T O N L E G A L
E M U | M I L | A K A
S I R | A C E | L E D
T E E S | E G R E S S
| T I G E R |
S T E R N O | S C A R
T O N | D I S | O D E
O P T | I N K | R E T
C H I C A G O H O P E
K A R A N | A U N T S
S T E P S | L E A S T
```

284

```
M A R I S | T O G A
O Z O N E | H U R L S
W A L K T H E T A L K
I L L | T E A | P I E
N E O | O A T | P E W
G A N G | D R E A D S
| E M C E E |
T A T T O O | L O B E
U V A | J A W | L O X
F I B | I C E | D O C
T A K E T H E C A K E
S T E N O | D O G I E
| E Y E S | S P E E D
```

285

```
Y O Y O | Y A P P E D
A H O Y | O V E R L Y
R I G S | G E N O M E
D O I T | U R N |
| B E A R | E Y E S
T H E R A T | D O V E
H E R | A P U | G E T
O A R S | A S I A N S
U T A H | R O T C |
| A L F | A L S O
A M E L I A | L A I D
D O R E M I | I S L E
D O R S E T | A S K S
```

286

```
E S Q U E | T O Q U E
H O U S E | E R U P T
S P I E L | S O O T S
| C R Y P T | T O Y
A R K S | E T N A |
H I Q | S T U B B E D
A C U R A | B A L L Y
B E E H I V E | E S E
| S O L O | D Q E D
E P T | B A Y O U |
G E I C O | A V O I D
A R O M A | R E T R O
D U N S T | D R E A M
```

287

```
C A L | B A T |
A N I | E L I | T A D
E G G H E A D | H B O
S O H O | S E Q U I N
A L T E R | U N D O
R A N | I N S I D E R
| I N G R A T E |
D I N E S A T | R B I
E D G E | E A R L S
C A R D I O | C O A L
O R O | P A R T A K E
R E D | O H O | D E S
| D U B |
```

288

```
I M P | E S P |
D I L E M M A | H D S
I T A L I A N | O R O
| Y E L L | I G O R
A C D C | L A M A Z E
D U O | S P O O N |
D E M | C O N | S P Y
| I R A T E | H O E
P A N A M A | N E X T
I R O N | T H O R |
L E E | B O O T O U T
L A S | R E L I E V E
| I S M | S A X
```

Solutions

289

```
S W F . E B B . .
O E R . D E E . F L A
L E E R S A T . R O N
E N E R . T A L E N T
M I D S T . I A G O
N E O . A L A S K A N
. M A D E W A Y .
O F F B A S E . F I R
V E R B . D I R G E
A V I A T E . R I N G
L E E . E C U A D O R
S R S . A H S . A R E
. L O A . Y E T
```

290

```
S W A N S . G O F O R
P I N U P . A L O N E
E L I T E . B E R T H
E L M . E B B . T I E
C I A . D R I . U M A
H E L D . I N A N E T
. C O L O G N E .
T A R M A C . S C A M
E R A . C H A . O L A
A R C . O E R . O L D
P I K E S . A S K E D
O V E R T . B E I G E
T E R R E . S T E E R
```

291

```
H A W K E D . C L O D
E X H A L E . A I D E
R E E L I N . J O I N
. N E T . S U N N Y
A P P . E S P N .
M A I . P A S S B Y
E G G . F L Y . W O O
N E S T E A . I R K
. O A T H . N E E
S H O O T . O W E .
H O N K . S T I F L E
U P T O . K E L L E R
N E O N . A L L U D E
```

292

```
R O S S . S A L A D
A L I K E . C L O N E
D I X I E C H I C K S
I V E . L O O . A L P
S I R . Y U L . L E O
H A S P . R A R E S T
. I N T R O .
S H I N E D . B E T A
A E S . W A G . N A M
S R S . S T A . A M A
S O U T H E R N M A N
E I E I O . Y I E L D
S C R E W . P L E A
```

293

```
H O W D Y . M A T T
O P E R A . U S H E R
T H E I R . T H E M E
D E P . N B A . C P A
A L I . S O N . R O M
T I N Y . A T T Y .
E A G E R . S W I S H
. W E E K . A N N E
M A I . L A B . G E L
A L L . A Y E . G E M
R O L E X . A M A Z E
T H O S E . C O M E T
A W E S . H E E D S
```

294

```
T A R P S . S E A T S
A R O S E . M E D I A
K A T I E H O L M E S
E R A . H O T . I D S
R A T . E R E . R Y E
S T E E R S . N E E D
. T E E T H .
H I N D . S E L D O M
E M U . S H E . I P O
R P M . T O N . S P A
B U B B A W A T S O N
A T E I T . G E E S E
L E D G E . E N D E D
```

295

```
Y A C H T . B A S K S
E T H E R . A N N I E
S H A R O N S T O N E
M O M . W O E . O K S
A M P . E N D . P O T
N E S T L E . B Y S O
. A S O N E .
A M O S . T O T E M S
R A N . P H D . D O T
A D S . R E O . I R E
B E T T Y R U B B L E
I D A H O . B A L E D
C O R E R . T R E Y S
```

296

```
N A Z I S . B U M P S
I T Y O U . A S L I P
B O X U P . T A K E I
B M W . R A H . J R R
L I V . A R T . I R E
E C U S . R U S H E S
. T O T E B A G .
B U S S E S . O F F S
E R R . M T S . E R E
E S Q . P S I . D E N
P U P I L . L A C E S
A L O N E . A M B L E
T A N K S . S P A Y S
```

297

```
C A P R I . Q T I P S
A L L E N . U R B A N
S P A D E . A A M C O
H O T H E A D S .
. A D E . H A Z Y
M A R T Y R S . L E E
A L E . O O P . E T A
Z E N . U S E D C A R
E X E S . O N E .
. C O L D F E E T
J A M I N . S A W T O
A L O F T . O C E A N
R A D I O . N E S T S
```

298

```
H I M O M . B A J A
E R I N S . E X A M
R E S U M E . D E N Y
. S P A S M S .
C A M . G E R . M G M
L L A M A . S P R E E
O V I T Z . M I M E D
S I N A I . I N U S E
E N E . N U N . S E A
. R E S I S T .
J O K E . A V I A T E
A R I D . E R R E D
W E D S . R E D D Y
```

299

```
B A C K . P A C T S
E T H E R . E T H A N
A R E N A . S L O M O
R I D . I R K . C A R
D A D . L E I . O L E
S L A W . S E A L E D
. R O B E R T A .
P A C K E R . A T O P
A S H . A V E . E R A
U S E . C E N . C I D
L U E G O . O T H E R
A R S O N . S W I N E
S E E D S . O P T S
```

300

```
D I S C U S S . T E L
O N T A R I O . A L A
C A E S A R S A L A D
K N E E L S . R E I D
E E L S . P E N N E
D T S . P R I N T E R
. S A U N A .
D A S H I N G . D O M
O T T E R . G O R E
N E R D . B E L L E S
K A I S E R R O L L S
E S P . A I R B A S E
Y E S . R O S E R E D
```

Solutions

301

```
CAKES SEAMS
OPERA AWAIT
MOLAR VERNE
ELS ANA ONE
ALE HOG NIL
TOYS TENSES
  GIVESUP
HARDUP BEST
EVA LAM LIE
RIM CDE LEE
MAMMA ALIST
ATEIN DANTE
NERDS EDGAR
```

302

```
HALFBAD
ALABAMA LAW
VISITOR ALI
ICE SEASON
NERDS SCENE
SPAIN CRED
  RISENUP
SPIN WASOF
PINTS HEIRS
RETYPE NEO
ACE ATWATER
YER TRAPEZE
  SENORES
```

303

```
AZTEC INKS
LOATHE DINE
ENTAIL ANEW
SEE ECHOES
  RANCHO
CUTRATE SAP
CHOMP APPLE
CST POPQUIZ
  RECORD
DIVIDE WED
ICON ARTERY
SKIS NEWBIE
HYDE TOBED
```

304

```
LAG PET
ORR AAH CAR
CEO PRIMATE
UNCLE SUSHI
STEERS THEN
ROOT TONI
SPY REP RAN
HUSH ALEC
ALTA MARROW
SLOWS SEESA
TURNOUT DAD
APE SRI IKE
  ABC TAD
```

305

```
PROS IDIDIT
LUNA RESALE
ALEXPKEATON
TEN RIP AVA
ORDAIN BEN
PEGS LIT
SORTS ABETS
ANA TAMA
LAC GUNNED
AWE ERE ORE
MICHAELJFOX
IRAISE LADY
SERVES ONES
```

306

```
MUSCLE MAR
ANCHOR FORE
TERESA ARIS
HAAS SECEDE
ISPS ATSEA
SEER ESCORT
  EARTH
ORACLE ERGS
BIGOT CURE
TERROR KNOT
USED ATEOUT
SEES PERUSE
END TASTER
```

307

```
SAJAK BASKS
UTURN AGENT
ARNIE GENIE
RAIDER RIGA
ECO SEA OHM
ZERO ALERTS
  SARCASM
PROFIT POPS
LAP POD MIA
ACRE REJECT
SHALL FUNKY
MENSA ENTER
ALOAD RESTS
```

308

```
TOTEM KICKS
ORAMA ABOAT
REBUT NEURO
SIL TRY CEO
ODE HOE HEP
ATSEA ATMS
  HOWMUCH
SPEX OPTED
LEI MFA IED
IRS AFT SRI
MUSIC RESIN
USURY EXUDE
PEEKS EPEES
```

309

```
UPPER ALPHA
MARIA POLAR
PLANT PLATE
SLY RALLY
ITALY INN
TUNICS KNEE
ANGLE SIGHS
MIME PULPIT
ETA TONTO
NEVER STS
ACTAS ISSUE
POISE SAUNA
UPSET ELMER
```

310

```
BIKE PANAMA
IDOL ITALIC
LEAP NOSALE
LALALAND
ASA CAGES
ELBOW EQUAL
TIE ISA
CZARS RENEW
HAREM AXE
LASTPAGE
SUBARU OPAL
YVETTE SINK
SANEST EGGS
```

311

```
DOC CHI CAN
APU REC UTE
SIR EYEBROW
HERBS CARPS
YET ALI
RAFTS PLEAD
ILL DNA
PLACE FIFTY
VAL ERA
ABOVE REVUP
FOREVER ONE
ERE EVE ROW
WED NAT
```

312

```
ATHENS ATAD
THECIA DATE
EXACTS IRON
TOT ADAMS
PAW YMCA
ETA RESCUE
NOV IFS OHS
SPEEDO LOO
NEXT DHL
NINJA WDS
OHIO PIANOS
TONY OCTANE
SPAS PEAPOD
```